CONCISE
DICTIONARY
OF
MUSIC

CONCISE
DICTIONARY
OF
MUSIC

PETER BROOKE-BALL

Tiger Books International PLC, London

TIGER BOOKS INTERNATIONAL
LONDON

© Geddes & Grosset Ltd 1993

This edition published in 1993 by
Tiger Books International PLC, London

ISBN 1-85501-365-7

Printed and bound in Slovenia

A

A the sixth NOTE of the SCALE of C; it is the note to which instruments of an orchestra are usually tuned (*see* TUNING).

Aaron *or* **Aron, Pietro** (*c.*1490–1545) Italian music scholar who was born in Florence, became a canon of Rimini, and in 1516 established a music school in Rome under the patronage of Pope Leo X. He was the first to abandon Latin for the vernacular in writing on counterpoint and musical history. His works, the most notable being *Thoscanello de la musica* (1523) are listed in *Musik Literatur*, Becker, Leipzig, 1836.

a ballàta (*Italian*) "in ballad style."

a battuta (*Italian*) "with the beat," indicating a return to strict TIME.

abbacchiota (*Italian*) "with melancholy expression."

Abbado, Claudio (1933–) Italian conductor who studied in Milan and Vienna and at the age of twenty-five won the KOUSSEVITSKY Award. He became musical director of La SCALA in 1971, principal conductor of the London Symphony Orchestra in 1979 and of the Berlin Philharmonic Orchestra in 1989. His speciality is nineteenth- and twentieth-century music.

abbandonarsi (*Italian*) "with fury," "violently."

abbandono (*Italian*) "passionately."

abbreviations are employed in music for terms of expression, as *dim.* for DIMINUENDO, *f.* for FORTE; as arbitrary signs, such as two DOTS on either side of an oblique line for repetition of a group of NOTES; or as numerals, which serve as shorthand symbols for various CHORDS in FIGURED BASS.

Abel, Carl Friedrich (1723–87) German composer and noted player of the VIOLA DA GAMBA. In London in 1758 he became Master of Chamber Music to Queen Charlotte, and then from 1763, in conjunction with Johann Christian BACH, organized, conducted and performed in a series of annual concerts. He wrote pieces specifically for the viola da gamba in addition to other types of chamber music, as well as symphonies.

Abendlied (*German*) an "evening song," often of religious significance.

Abendmusik (*German*) an "evening performance of music," particularly those performances of mainly religious music given at the Protestant church of Lübeck in Germany between 1673 and 1810.

Abendstänchen (*German*) "serenade."

a bene placito (*Italian*) "at pleasure."

absolute music *or* **abstract music** instrumental music that exists purely as music and does not attempt to relate to a story or image. It is the opposite of PROGRAMME MUSIC.

absolute pitch *or* **perfect pitch** the sense by which some people can exactly identify, or sing without an accompanying instrument, any NOTE they hear.

abstract music *see* **absolute music**

Academic Festival Overture the name given to an orchestral piece (Op. 80) by BRAHMS. It was written after Brahms had received an honorary degree from the University of Breslau, and was first performed in 1881.

Académie de Musique the French ACADEMY OF MUSIC, which has exercised a profound influence upon French music from its establishment in 1669 by letters patent from King Louis XIV, its purpose being "to present in public opera and drama with music, and in French verse." Abbé Perrin, Robert Cambert, and the Marquis de Sourden were the founders. From the days of LULLY, RAMEAU, and GLUCK, the institution has fostered the growth of lyric drama. It has always received a subsidy from the French government.

Academy of Music means, properly speaking, an organization of music teachers and performers, such as the ROYAL ACADEMY OF MUSIC, instituted in London, 1824.

a cappella *or* **alla capella** (*Italian*) literally "in the chapel style"; it is a term that has come to mean unaccompanied choral singing.

accel. the abbreviation for ACCELERANDO.

accelerando (*Italian*) "quickening"; a term used to indicate a gradual speeding up of pace (abbreviation ACCEL.).

accent the emphasis given to specific notes to indicate the RHYTHM of a piece of music.

acciaccatura (*Italian*) an ornamental or auxiliary NOTE, normally the SEMITONE below, played just before, or at the same time as, a regular note. An *acciaccatura* is written in small type before the regular note and has a stroke through its tail. From the Italian *acciacciare*, to crush.

accidental a NOTE in a piece of music that departs by one or two SEMITONES from the KEY SIGNATURE. It is indicated by a SHARP, FLAT or NATURAL sign before it. An accidental holds good throughout a BAR unless contradicted.

accompaniment music supporting a soloist or CHOIR (2). An accompaniment may be provided by an orchestra, organ or, most usually, a piano.

accordion a portable REED ORGAN, which was invented in Germany in the early nineteenth century. Air is forced through the reeds by means of bellows that are operated by the player's arms, and notes and chords are played by pressing buttons. The *piano accordion* has a keyboard (operated by the right hand) for playing MELODY NOTES, and buttons (operated by the left hand) for simple chords. The accordion is associated with informal or FOLK music, but it has been used by serious composers such as TCHAIKOVSKY, SHOSTAKOVICH, and the American Roy HARRIS.

Acis and Galatea a MASQUE by HANDEL, which was first performed in about 1718. The libretto was by John GAY (from Ovid and with additions by Alexander Pope, John Dryden and Hughes) and tells the story of two lovers and Polyphemus, a jealous, one-eyed giant who kills Acis by crushing him under a rock.

Acis et Galatée an opera by LULLY with a libretto

by Jean Galbert de Campistron, which was first performed in 1686. HAYDN, too, wrote an opera or masque on the same subject. *See also* ACIS AND GALATEA.

acoustic guitar *see* **guitar**.

acoustics (1) a branch of physics that is concerned with SOUND. The main characteristics of a sound are its PITCH, intensity, RESONANCE and quality. (2) the characteristics of a hall or auditorium that enable speech and music to be heard without the sounds being distorted. In a concert hall with good acoustics, sounds from the stage can be heard clearly in all quarters.

act tune *or* **curtain music** an instrumental piece of music that is played between the acts of a play while the curtain is down. It is usually associated with seventeenth- and eighteenth-century music. *See also* ENTR'ACTE; INTERLUDE; INTERMEZZO.

action (1) the mechanism of a keyboard instrument that links the keyboard to the strings or, in the case of an ORGAN, to the PIPES and STOPS. (2) the gap between the strings and FINGERBOARD of a stringed instrument as dictated by the height of the BRIDGE.

Adam de la Hale *see* **la Hale, Adam de**.

Adler, Larry (1914–) American-born harmonica player, a virtuoso performer whose unique talent is acclaimed worldwide by classical and popular musicians alike. He has had concert works composed for him by VAUGHAN WILLIAMS, MILHAUD, JACOB and ARNOLD. He himself has written film scores, the best known being the music for *Genevieve* in 1953.

ad lib. abbreviation for AD LIBITUM.

ad libitum (*Latin*) literally "at pleasure" and usually abbreviated to AD LIB. In music, the term is used to indicate that, when playing a piece, a performer can: (a) alter the TEMPO or RHYTHM; (b) choose an alternative PASSAGE by the composer; (c) improvise a CADENZA; and (d) include or omit a passage if he or she so chooses.

adagietto (*Italian*) (1) "slow" but not as slow as ADAGIO. (2) a short composition in an adagio TEMPO.

adagio (*Italian*) (1) literally "at ease," i.e. at a slow TEMPO. (2) a slow movement.

adagissimo (*Italian*) "very slow."

added sixth a frequently used CHORD created by adding the sixth note from the ROOT to a MAJOR or MINOR TRIAD; for example, in the KEY of C major, A is added above the triad of C-E-G.

additional accompaniments new or revised PARTS for extra instruments written by later composers and added to seventeenth- and eighteenth-century works in order to increase fullness. In many cases, the additions did not match the quality of the original music, but MOZART once wrote additional music for HANDEL'S *MESSIAH* when an organ was not available.

à deux cordes (*French*) *see* **a due corde**.

a due corde (*Italian*) "on two strings"; when applied to music for stringed instruments, the term means that a piece should be played on two strings, not just on one.

Aeolian harp a type of ZITHER which has strings of similar length but of different thickness. The instrument is not actually played but left outside

10

to catch the wind; different CHORDS are sounded according to the speed of the wind, which makes the strings vibrate faster or slower (*see* VIBRATION). The name is derived from Aeolus, who was the Greek god of the wind.

Aeolian mode a MODE that, on the PIANO, uses the white NOTES (3) from A to A.

aeolina a type of HARMONICA.

aeoline a soft ORGAN STOP that imitates the sound of the AEOLIAN HARP.

aerophone any instrument in which movement of air causes sound; for example, ORGAN, OBOE, TRUMPET, FLUTE, etc.

affannatol (*Italian*) "distressingly."

affannosamente (*Italian*) "restlessness."

affannoso (*Italian*) "sadly."

Affektenlehre (*German*) a musical theory formulated in Germany during the eighteenth century, which held that music should be judged by the way in which it arouses certain emotions, such as sorrow, happiness, etc.

affettuoso (*Italian*) literally "tender" or "affectionate," i.e. an indication that a piece of music should be played with tender feeling.

afflizione, con (*Italian*) "with affliction."

affrettando (*Italian*) "hurrying with excitement."

Afranio, Canon (*fl.* sixteenth century) a priest who, according to some authorities, invented the bassoon. Born in Pavia, he became canon of Ferrara.

Africaine, L' MEYERBEER's last opera and, like all his other operas, very popular when first performed. In the composer's opinion it was his masterpiece, but today "O Paradiso" is its one memorable aria. The libretto, by SCRIBE, tells of how the navigator Vasco da Gama is torn between two loves—Inez, daughter of a Portuguese nobleman, and Selika, a captive slave and a queen in her own land. Freed from prison by Inez and twice rescued from death by Selika (l'Africaine), da Gama's final choice brings about Selika's tragic suicide.

agevole (*Italian*) "with agility."

agevolezza (*Italian*) "lightly."

agiatamente (*Italian*) literally "comfortably," i.e. an indication that a piece should be played with a certain amount of liberty. Not to be confused with AGITATAMENTE.

agilità, con (*Italian*) "with agility."

agilmente (*Italian*) "in lively style."

agitato, agitatamente (*Italian*) literally "agitated", "agitatedly", i.e. an indication that a piece should be played restlessly or wildly.

Agnus Dei (*Latin*) "O Lamb of God"; the concluding part of the Latin MASS. Numerous musical settings have been written for the Agnus Dei.

agogic a note that is made to stand out by being lingered on rather than by being played more loudly. It may be the first note of a phrase, or an important high or discordant note.

à grand choeur (*French*) "for grand chorus."

à grand orchestre (*French*) "for grand orchestra."

Aguado, Dionisio (1784–1849) Spanish composer, born in Madrid, who wrote an excellent method for the guitar and also composed much music for that instrument, on which he was a virtuoso.

Aida a tragic opera by VERDI to a four-act libretto by Antonio Ghislanzoni. First performed in the Italian Theatre, Cairo, in 1871, the opera was commissioned by Ismail Pasha (Khedive of Egypt). The story is set in ancient Egypt and concerns a warrior, Ramades, and an Ethiopian slave, Aida, who loves him. Ultimately, through treachery and the consuming jealousy of the princess Amneris, who also loves Ramades, the two lovers are entombed together alive.

air (1) a simple TUNE or SONG. (2) a melodious BAROQUE composition.

Air on the G String the name given to August Wilhemj's arrangement for violin and accompaniment of the second movement of BACH's Suite No. 3 in D. The transposed violin part is played on the lowest (G) string.

al segno (*Italian*) literally "to the sign" (i.e. to a standard symbol used in musical NOTATION, *see* Appendix). The term is used in two ways: it can instruct the player either to go b*ack* to the sign and start again, or to *continue* until the sign is reached.

Albéniz, Isaac (1860–1909) Spanish pianist and composer who was a child prodigy and went on to write operas, orchestral pieces and songs. He is best known for his piano suite *Iberia,* comprising twelve technically demanding pieces, redolent of the unmistakable rhythms of Spanish folk music. He has had a lasting influence on Spanish music.

Albert, Prince (1819–61) German-born prince consort of Queen Victoria (1819–1901), whom he married in 1840. He used his influence as consort to advance the cause of music in every way. He composed songs, church music, and an opera; he directed the Antient Concerts, and introduced many great works into England, among them SCHUBERT's symphony in C, and WAGNER's LOHENGRIN.

Albert Hall *see* **Royal Albert Hall**.

Albert Herring a comic chamber opera by BRITTEN (Op. 39) to a three-act libretto by Eric Crozier. It was first performed at GLYNDEBOURNE in 1947. The story concerns Albert, a shopkeeper with a domineering mother, who is elected King of the May. He subsequently gets drunk and, thus encouraged, manages to escape from the clutches of his mother.

Alberti bass a simple accompaniment to a MELODY consisting of "broken" or spread CHORDS arranged in a rhythmic pattern. It is so called because Domenico ALBERTI used it in his keyboard SONATAS.

Alberti, Domenico (1710–40) an Italian singer, composer and harpsichordist who wrote many unremarkable works and is largely remembered for his use of "broken" chords in his pieces for harpsichord.

Albinoni, Tomaso (1671–1750) prolific Italian composer, he was among the earliest to write concertos for solo violin. He wrote more than forty operas. BACH composed fugues on themes by Albinoni.

alborada (*Spanish*) literally "morning song"; a form of popular Spanish music for BAGPIPES and

14

SIDE DRUM.

Albumblatt (*German*) literally "album leaf"; a popular title given by nineteenth-century composers to short, instrumental compositions (often for the PIANO) and of a personal nature.

Alceste a three-act opera by GLUCK with a libretto by Ranieri Calzabigi; the original, Italian version (1767) was revised by GLUCK into a French version (1776) to a libretto by François du Roullet. The story is based on a tale by Euripides: Alcestis gives up her life to save her husband, Admetus, and is rewarded by being restored to life. Other operas by the same name were composed by LULLY (1674) and HANDEL (1734), among others.

Aldeburgh Festival an annual music FESTIVAL held in June, which was founded by Benjamin BRITTEN and the tenor Peter PEARS at Aldeburgh, Suffolk, in 1948. It maintains its strong association with Britten, many of whose works were first performed there.

aleatory music music which contains unpredictable or chance elements so that no two performances of a piece are ever similar. It is a form explored since 1945 by composers such as CAGE in his *Music of Changes*, and STOCKHAUSEN and Morton FELDMAN.

Ali Baba Luigi CHERUBINI's opera, first produced July 22, 1933, at the Grand Opéra, Paris (*see* PARIS OPÉRA). It was built up in part from his *Faniska* and *Achille*, with a new overture to a libretto adapted from his *Koukourgi*.

Alkan, Charles Henri Valentin (the pseudonym of **Morhange, Charles Henri Valentin**) (1813–

88) French composer and pianist who was a close friend of LISZT and CHOPIN One of the foremost piano teachers of his day, he wrote many piano pieces of great complexity, often using ideas ahead of their time.

alla breve (*Italian*) (1) an instruction that a piece of music should be performed twice as fast as the NOTATION would suggest. (2) 2/2 TIME.

alla camera (*Italian*) "like chamber music."

alla diritta (*Italian*) "with direct intervals."

alla marcia (*Italian*) "in march style."

alla mente (*Italian*) an obsolete harmonic system of thirds and FIFTHS, based on PLAINSONG.

alla militare (*Italian*) "in military style."

all' antico (*Italian*) "in ancient style."

allargando (*Italian*) literally "getting broader," i.e. an indication that a piece should be played grandly whilst at the same time getting slower.

alla russa (*Italian*) "in Russian style."

alla scozzese (*Italian*) "in Scottish style."

alla siciliana (*Italian*) "in Sicilian style."

alla tedesca (*Italian*) an abbreviation of *alla danza tedesca,* meaning "in the style of a German dance." *See* ALLEMANDE.

alla turca (*Italian*) literally "in the Turkish style."

alla zingarese (*Italian*) literally "in the style of gypsy music."

alla zoppa (*Italian*) literally "in a limping way," i.e. in a syncopated (*see* SYNCOPATION) rhythm.

allegretto (*Italian*) a term indicating light and moderately quick movement, but not as fast as ALLEGRO.

allegro (*Italian*) literally "lively", i.e. in a quick

TEMPO. The term is often used as the title of a
bright composition or MOVEMENT.

allemande (*French*) an abbreviation of *danse
allemande* or "German dance," of which there are
two forms. (1) a moderately slow dance used by
seventeenth- and eighteenth-century composers
as the first MOVEMENT of a SUITE of four contrasting
dances. (2) a brisk dance of the eighteenth and
nineteenth centuries, similar to the WALTZ.

allentando (*Italian*) "slowing down," i.e. a term
used to indicate that the TEMPO of a piece of music
should be slowed down.

all' ongarese (*Italian*) literally "in the style of
Hungarian [gypsy] music."

alphabet the letters used in music as they occur in
the natural SCALE are C, D, E, F, G, A, B. The
oldest HARPS and shepherd PIPES are believed to
have had seven TONES, to which the Greeks gave
the names of letters, A being the lowest. Greek
NOTATION became highly complicated with the
development of the MODES, and Pope Gregory the
Great (540–604) changed church notation, again
employing the first seven letters, indicating the
lower OCTAVE by capitals, and the upper by small
letters. NOTES were gradually added to the lower
A, and when the modern scale was adopted in the
sixteenth century, the lowest tone had become C
instead of A. In addition, Germans use H for B
natural, B for B flat.

Alphorn (*German*) a primitive type of HORN with
no valves, traditionally played by Swiss herdsmen to call in their cattle in the evening. Made
from wood and bark, alphorns usually have an

upturned bell which rests on the ground, and they can be up to 3 metres (10 feet) long. Various composers, including MAHLER, have used the alphorn in their compositions.

Also sprach Zarathustra (Thus spake Zarathrustra or Zoroaster) a tone poem by Richard STRAUSS (Op.30) which was inspired by NIETZSCHE's poem of the same name. It was first performed in Frankfurt in 1896, but found a new and appreciative audience when it was used as incidental music in the Stanley Kubrick's film (1968) *2001: A Space Odyssey*.

alt an abbreviation of the Latin phrase *in alto,* which means "high". It is used for the NOTES in the OCTAVE rising from G above the TREBLE CLEF; the notes in the octave above that are said to be *in altissimo.*

alto (*Italian*) "high" (1) the highest adult male VOICE, which is now used only in male-voice CHOIRS (2). (2) an addition to the name of an instrument to indicate that it is one size larger than the SOPRANO member of the family; for example alto CLARINET. (3) a low female voice that has a greater compass than the male alto voice (usually, and more properly, called CONTRALTO).

alto basso (*Italian*) an obsolete Venetian stringed instrument, the tambourin du Béarn.

alzando (*Italian*) "raising, elevating."

amabile (*Italian*) "lovingly."

amabilità, con (*Italian*) "gently, tenderly."

amarevole (*Italian*) "sadly."

amarezza, con (*Italian*) "with sadness."

amarissimamente (*Italian*) "very bitterly."

amarissimo (*Italian*) "in mournful style.

Amati the name of a famous family of violin-makers who worked in Cremona, Italy, in the sixteenth and seventeenth centuries. The most famous member of the family was **Nicolo Amati** (1596–1684), who taught Antonio STRADIVARI and Andrea GUARNERI.

ambo a platform from which the CHOIR (2) sang in early Greek churches.

ambria an African cylindrical DRUM with wood or iron vibrating tongues.

Ambrosian chants a collection of CHANTS or PLAIN-SONG, used in Milan Cathedral, which are named after St Ambrose (*c.* 340–97), Bishop of Milan, who greatly influenced church singing and may have introduced the antiphonal singing of the Syrian church. Despite bearing his name, the earliest surviving chants were composed long after his death.

amen (*Hebrew*) "So be it."

America the Beautiful the poem which has become the national song of the USA. The first version of the poem was written in 1893 by Katharine Lee Bates (1859–1929) but she simplified it some ten years later. More than sixty tunes have been written for the poem, but those by Will C. Macfarlane (1870–1945) and S.A Ward are the most famous.

American in Paris, An a descriptive piece for orchestra by GERSHWIN (1928) in which, amongst other unusual instruments, four taxi horns are played. The incidental music for a film (1951) of the same name was based on Gershwin's original composition.

American organ *or* **cabinet organ** a REED ORGAN, similar to a HARMONIUM except that air is sucked through the reeds instead of being blown through them.

American Quartet the String Quartet in F (Op. 96) by DVORÁK, which he wrote in 1893 and which was largely inspired by Black American melodies. For a time it was known as the Nigger Quartet but this title has been abandoned as insulting.

Amor brujo, El (Love, the Magician) a ballet in one act with music by FALLA and a scenario by Martinez (based on an Andalusian gypsy tale of a girl haunted by her dead lover's spirit). It was first performed in Madrid in 1915 and is unusual in that the ballerina has to sing as well as dance.

amore, con (*Italian*) "lovingly, tenderly."

a moresco (*Italian*) "in the Moorish style."

amorevole (*Italian*) "affectionately."

amoroso (*Italian*) literally "lovingly", indicating that a piece should be played with warm affection.

amplifier any device, particularly an electric one, which renders a sound louder.

ampolloso (*Italian*) "inflated style."

ampoulé (*French*) "bombastic."

anabasis (*Greek*) a succession of ascending tones.

anacrusis (*Greek anakrousis*, literally "a prelude") an unstressed NOTE or grouping of notes at the beginning of a musical PHRASE; it can also mean an unstressed syllable at the beginning of a SONG.

anche (*French*) a REED used in the MOUTHPIECES of WOODWIND instruments.

ancora (*Italian*) literally "again," "yet" or "still," as in *ancora forte* meaning "still loud," and *ancora più forte* meaning "yet louder."

andante (*Italian*) literally "going" or "moving," it is usually used to indicate a moderate TEMPO or a walking pace. *Più andante* means "moving more" or slightly faster. Andante is sometimes used as a title for a moderately slow piece of music.

andantino (*Italian*) "less slow" (i.e. slightly faster) than ANDANTE.

Anderson, Lucy (née **Philpot**) (1790–1878) English pianist, born in Bath, who introduced into England many great works by BEETHOVEN, HUMMEL and others. She was the first woman to play at the Philharmonic Concerts in London and was also a sought-after teacher, her pupils including Queen Victoria and other members of the Royal Family.

Anderson, Marian (1902–) American contralto who from 1935, when she appeared at the Town Hall, New York, became famous throughout the world as a concert-hall singer of great dramatic power. In 1955 she sang Ulrica in Verdi's *Un Ballo in Maschera*, her operatic début and a specially memorable event as she was the first black singer to appear on the stage of the METROPOLITAN OPERA, New York.

anelanza (*Italian*) "shortness of breath."

anesis (*Greek*) from high to low PITCH; lowering pitch of strings.

Anfang (*German*) literally the "beginning"; *Anfangs* means "from the beginning."

21

Angeles, Victoria de Los (1923–) Spanish soprano born in Barcelona, where she studied at the Conservatorio and first appeared in opera as the Countess in *The* MARRIAGE OF FIGARO in 1945. In 1950 she sang Mimi in LA BOHÈME. A year later came her début at the METROPOLITAN OPERA, New York, followed by appearances throughout the world in operas that include CARMEN, *The* BARBER OF SEVILLE, *The* MAGIC FLUTE, *La* TRAVIATA, LOHENGRIN, TANNHÄUSER, and MADAM BUTTERFLY. Her concert-hall recitals too, some of which have featured the songs of her native land, have delighted her audiences.

anglaise (*French*) short for *danse anglaise* or "English dance," i.e. a lively dance in quick time, such as a HORNPIPE.

Anglican chant a characteristically English way of setting to music prose, psalms and canticles, in which the number of syllables per line can vary. To accommodate this irregularity, the first NOTE of each musical PHRASE is a RECITING NOTE which is timeless and is used to sing as many syllables as necessary before moving on to notes which are sung in time and which normally carry one syllable each. In many respects, it is a simple form of GREGORIAN CHANT.

anima (*Italian*) literally "soul" or "spirit," as in *con anima,* which means that a piece should be played "with soul" or "with emotion."

animato (*Italian*) literally "animated."

animo (*Italian*) literally "spirit," so *con animo* indicates that a piece should be performed "with spirit."

animoso (*Italian*) "spirited."

Animuccia, Giovanni (*c.*1500–71) Italian composer, he is called the "Father of the Oratorio." A friend of St Filippo Neri, he composed the *Laudi* (*see* LAUDA)—of which ORATORIO was the development—to be sung at the Oratory of St Filippo.

Anrevi, Francesco (1786–1853) Spanish composer, born in Barcelona, who wrote on theory, composed church music, and directed in Barcelona, Valencia, Seville, and Bordeaux

Ansermet, Ernest (1883–1969) Swiss conductor who was appointed conductor of Sergei Diaghilev's Ballet Russe in 1915. In Geneva in 1918 he founded L'Orchestre de la Suisse-Romande. His interpretations of twentieth-century music, notably the works of STRAVINSKY, brought him fame. In 1946 at GLYNDEBOURNE, he conducted the first performance of BRITTEN's opera THE RAPE OF LUCRETIA.

answer the second entry of the main SUBJECT (theme) of a FUGUE which is played a FIFTH higher or lower than the first entry. In a *real answer,* the subject and answer are identical; in a *tonal answer,* the intervals in the answer are changed.

Antheil, George (1900–59) American composer and pianist of Polish descent who gained notoriety by incorporating the sounds of motor horns, door bells and aeroplane engines in some of his compositions, most notably his *Ballet mécanique,* which was first performed in front of an amazed audience in Paris in 1926. He also composed operas, including *Transatlantic* (1930), *Helen Retires* (1934), and *Volpone,* as well as piano sonatas, symphonies and film scores.

anthem the Anglican equivalent to the Roman Catholic MOTET. An anthem is usually an elaborate musical setting of non-liturgical words sung by a church CHOIR (2) without the congregation; SOLO parts are common and accompaniment by an ORGAN is usual. Notable among early composers of anthems were BYRD and GIBBONS. PURCELL and WESLEY composed popular anthems.

anticipation the sounding of a NOTE (or notes) of a CHORD before the rest of the chord is played.

Antigone Felix MENDELSSOHN's music to Sophocles's tragedy, consisting of an introduction and seven numbers, was first performed at Potsdam, Germany in 1841.

antiphon the sacred words, sung in PLAINSONG by two CHOIRS (2), before and after a PSALM or CANTICLE in a Roman Catholic service. *Antiphonal* is an adjective applied to the musical effect achieved by two choirs (or groups of instruments) which are positioned in different parts of a hall and sing (or play) alternately, one "answering" the other.

anvil a PERCUSSION INSTRUMENT consisting of steel bars that are struck with a wooden or metal mallet. It is meant to sound like a blacksmith's anvil being struck with a hammer and was used by both VERDI (in *Il Trovatore*) and WAGNER (in *Das Rheingold*).

aperto (*Italian*) "use damper pedal."

a piacere (*Italian*) literally "at pleasure," meaning that the performer of a piece of music is permitted to take a certain amount of liberty, particularly with TEMPO, while playing it. *See also* AD LIBITUM.

Appalachian Spring a ballet by COPLAND which was written for the ballerina and choreographer Martha Graham, and was inspired by Hart Crane's (1899–1932) poem about country marriage. It was first performed in New York in 1945, and, often also played as a concert piece, has been popular ever since.

appassionato, appassionata (*Italian*) literally "impassioned" or "with passion or feeling," hence the title *Sonata appassionata* which was given to BEETHOVEN's Piano Sonata in F Minor (Op. 57).

appenato (*Italian*) "with suffering or grief."

appoggiando (*Italian*) literally "leaning"; when applied to musical NOTES, this implies that they should pass very smoothly from one to the next.

appoggiatura (*Italian*) a term for a "leaning" NOTE (*see also* APPOGGIANDO), indicated in the SCORE. (1) a *long appoggiatura* is a note of varying length that is different from the HARMONY note. (2) a *short appoggiatura* is a very short note of indefinite length, sometimes accented, sometimes not. (3) a *passing appoggiatura,* as used in the eighteenth century, normally occurs when the principal notes of a MELODY form a sequence of thirds and it is played before the beat.

à quatre mains (*French*) "for four hands."

à quatre seuls (*French*) "for four soloists."

à quatre voix (*French*) "for four voices."

a quattro mani (*Italian*) "for four hands."

a quattro soli (*Italian*) "for four soloists."

a quattro voci (*Italian*) "for four voices."

après-midi d'un faune, Prélude à 1' (Prelude to the Afternoon of a Faun) an orchestral TONE

POEM by DEBUSSY, written in 1892–94 and first performed in Paris in 1894. Debussy originally intended to write a set of three pieces to illustrate the poem by Stéphane Mallarmé (1842–98) (*Prélude, Interlude,* and *Paraphrase finale*), but only finished the first part. In 1912 the Russian dancer Vaslav Nijinsky (1890–1950) based a ballet on the music.

Arabeske (*German*) *see* **arabesque**.

arabesque (1) a florid treatment of thematic music. (2) a lyrical piece of music that employs an exaggerated and elaborate style, as used by SCHUMANN and DEBUSSY.

Archduke Trio the nickname given to the Piano Trio in B Flat (Op. 97) by BEETHOVEN, composed in 1811 and dedicated to Archduke Rudolph of Austria.

Archer, Frederick (1838–1901) English organist, born in Oxford. He went to the USA in 1881, where he composed *King Witlaf's Drinking Horn* and other cantatas; wrote *The Organ, The College Organist* and conducted the Pittsburgh Orchestra (1895–98) and the Boston Oratorio Society (1887), and was organist of the Plymouth Church, Brooklyn.

archet (*French*) a BOW, such as is used to play a stringed instrument.

archi (*Italian*) literally "bows"; a term that refers to all stringed instruments played with a BOW.

archlute a large double-necked LUTE or theorbo, popular in the seventeenth century having eight single or double strings on the keyboard and eight open DIAPASON strings, used for the lowest part of ACCOMPANIMENT.

arco (*Italian*) the singular of ARCHI. It is the usual instruction to play with the BOW after playing PIZZICATO.

ardito (*Italian*) "bold," "energetic."

Arensky, Anton Stepanovich (1861–1906) Russian composer, born in Novgorod, who studied under RIMSKY-KORSAKOV at the St Petersburg Conservatory. He wrote three operas as well as symphonies, a violin concerto, cantatas, church and chamber music, and incidental music to Shakespeare's *The Tempest*. However, his best-known works are his piano pieces, especially his Piano Trio in D Minor (Op. 32).

Aretinian Syllables UT, RE, MI, FA, SOL, LA, by which Guido Aretinus or d'Arezzo, a tenth-century French Benedictine monk and teacher of music designated the HEXACHORD TONES.

Argyll Rooms a concert venue famous as the scene of the best London concerts from about 1800 to 1829. The Philharmonic Society, later to become the Royal Philharmonic Society, performed there, first at their location in Argyll Street, and then in Regent Street.

aria (*Italian*) a SONG or AIR. Originally the term was used for any song for one or more voices but it has come to be used exclusively for a long, SOLO song as found in ORATORIO and OPERA.

Ariadne auf Naxos (Ariadne on Naxos) an opera in two acts with music by Richard STRAUSS and a libretto by Hugo von Hofmannsthal (1874–1929). Two versions were written. The first version (first performed in Stuttgart, 1912) was designed to follow Molière's (originally Jean-Baptiste

27

Poquelin; 1622–73) play, *Le Bourgeois Gentilhomme,* but was not successful. In the second version (first performed in Vienna, 1916), an operatic prologue was substituted for the play, and proved more successful. The story is the mythological tale of Ariadne being abandoned by her lover Theseus on the island of Naxos, where she is consoled by Bacchus. From time to time there are comic interruptions from a *commedia dell'arte* troupe whose actions form the sub-plot of the opera.

arioso (*Italian*) literally "like an ARIA." (1) a melodious and song-like RECITATIVE. (2) a short AIR in an OPERA or ORATORIO. (3) an instrumental piece that follows the style of a vocal arioso.

Armida the name of operas by several composers including LULLY, GLUCK, HADYN, ROSSINI, DVORÁK. The inspiration for these operas was the poem *La Gerusalemme liberata* (*Jerusalem Delivered*) by Torquato Tasso (1544–95), which is about the Crusades.

Armstrong, Louis (1900–71) Black American jazz trumpeter and singer who remains one of the greatest figures in jazz history. He was born into poverty in New Orleans but started playing the trumpet at the age of 12. In 1922 he migrated to Chicago and later to New York. With his bands he made numerous recordings of such tunes as "Willie the Weeper" and "West End Blues." After 1946 he concentrated on being an all-round entertainer but he never lost his worldwide popularity. He delighted in his nickname "Satchmo," meaning "satchel mouth."

28

Arne, Michael (1740–86) English singer and composer who was the illegitimate son of Thomas ARNE. His best works were for the stage and he worked with the great impresario, David Garrick.

Arne, Thomas Augustine (1710–78) a prolific English composer of operas, oratorios and instrumental pieces. His operas include *Artaxerxes* and *Thomas and Sally*, but his best-known work is his masque *Alfred*, which contains the famous song RULE, BRITANNIA!

Arnold, Malcolm (1921–) English composer, trumpeter and conductor. His innovative compositions include seven symphonies, ballet music, numerous concertos for various instruments, as well as chamber and choral and orchestral pieces such as the *Tam o'Shanter* Overture. To the public at large, he is best known for his film score for the film (1957) *The Bridge on the River Kwai*.

arpa (*Italian*) the HARP.

arpa doppia (*Italian*) a double HARP.

arpanella (*Italian*) a little HARP.

arpeggiare (*Italian*) literally "to play the HARP," i.e. to play CHORDS "spread out" as they are on the harp. *See also* ARPEGGIO.

arpeggio (*Italian*) "HARP-wise," i.e. an indication that the NOTES of a CHORD should be played in rapid succession, as they are on a harp, and not simultaneously.

arpeggione an obsolete instrument invented in 1823, which is a cross between a VIOLONCELLO (cello) and a GUITAR, with six strings played with a BOW, and a fretted keyboard. SCHUBERT wrote a sonata for arpeggione.

arpicordo (*Italian*) HARPSICHORD.

arrangement an adaptation of a piece of music for
a medium different from that for which it was
originally composed.

Arrau, Claudio (1903–91) influential Chilean
pianist who opened his own piano school in San-
tiago, Chile, and taught in Berlin from 1925–40.
He was recognized as one of the greatest interpreters of works by BEETHOVEN, and was also
admired for his playing of CHOPIN, LISZT, BRAHMS
and SCHUMANN.

ars antiqua (*Latin*) the "old art," i.e. music of the
twelfth and thrirteenth centuries as opposed to
ars nova, the new style of music that evolved in
the fourteenth century

ars nova (*Latin*) *see* **ars antiqua**.

Art of Fugue, The (**Die Kunst der Fugue**) a
keyboard work by Johann Sebastian BACH, comprising thirteen fugues and four canons, that
demonstrates virtually all possible contrapuntal
treatments of a solitary theme. It was written in
1749 and published a year later.

Ashkenazy, Vladimir (1937–) Russian-born pianist and conductor, who studied at the Moscow Conservatory. He won jointly with John OGDON the
Tchaikovsky Competition in Moscow in 1962. In
1963 he came to Britain, then settled in Iceland with
his Icelandic wife in 1968. He is famed for his
interpretations of, in particular, MOZART, BEETHOVEN,
and CHOPIN. In 1987 he was appointed musical
director of the Royal Philharmonic Orchestra.

Asioli, Bonifacio (1769–1832) Italian composer
who also wrote valuable books on theory. He

composed masses and a concerto while still under the age of eight. He composed, too, for the theatre, and wrote orchestral pieces. For a time he was censor at the Milan Conservatory.

assai (*Italian*) "very," as in *allegro assai,* "very fast."

assez (*French*) "moderately," as in *assez vite,* "moderately quick."

atabal a Moorish DRUM.

a tempo (*Italian*) "in time"; a term that indicates that a piece should revert to its normal TEMPO after a change of speed.

Athalie incidental music, consisting of an overture, a march, and six vocal numbers, composed by Felix MENDELSSOHN for the tragedy by Jean Racine (1639–99). It was first performed completely in Berlin in 1845.

athematic music music that does not have any THEMES or TUNES as such; it is concerned with exploring the unconventional possibilities of sounds.

atonal music music that is not in any KEY. Atonal music is particularly associated with the works of SCHOENBERG, although he preferred to use the word *pantonality,* meaning a synthesis of all the keys.

attacca (*Italian*) "attack," i.e. start the next MOVEMENT without a pause.

Attwood, Thomas (1765–1838) English composer who was organist at St Paul's Cathedral, London. He was a pupil of MOZART in Vienna and became a close friend to MENDELSSOHN. He wrote ANTHEMS for the coronations of George IV and William IV.

aubade (*French*) "morning music," as opposed to a SERENADE, or evening music.

Auber, Daniel François Esprit (1782–1871) a French composer who wrote some forty-five operas, including *La Muette de Portici* (1828) and *Fra Diavolo* (1830). In 1842 he followed CHERUBINI as director of the Paris Conservatoire.

Augarten a public garden in a Viennese suburb, which was opened to the people by Emperor Joseph II in 1775. Here MOZART gave a series of early morning concerts, and BEETHOVEN and the violinist George Bridgetower played the KREUTZER SONATA from manuscript.

augmentation the lengthening of the time values of NOTES in melodic parts with the result that they sound more impressive and grand. The opposite of augmentation is DIMINUTION.

augmented interval the INTERVAL formed by increasing any perfect or MAJOR interval by a SEMITONE.

augmented sixth a CHORD based on the flattened SUBMEDIANT that contains the augmented sixth INTERVAL.

augmented triad a TRIAD of which the FIFTH is augmented.

a una corda (*Italian*) "on one string" (*compare* A DUE CORDE). In the context of a PIANO, it means left-hand PEDAL, i.e. reducing the volume.

Auric, Georges (1899–1983) French composer and the youngest member of *Les* SIX. His compositions include operas, piano and chamber pieces, as well as music for films (particularly those of René Clair [1898–1981] and Jean Cocteau[1899–

1963]) and ballets, the most notable of which is *Les Matelots*.

autoharp a type of ZITHER in which CHORDS are produced by pressing down KEYS (1) that dampen some of the strings but let others vibrate freely. The instrument was invented in the late nineteenth century and was popular with American folk musicians.

avant-garde (*French*) literally "vanguard," a term applied to music (or any other art) that is considered to break new ground in style, structure, or technique.

Ave Maria (*Latin*) "Hail Mary," a prayer to the Virgin Mary used in the Roman Catholic Church. It has been set to music by numerous composers including SCHUBERT, and LISZT, and GOUNOD in particular.

Avison, Charles (1709–70) English organist and composer, and the author of the controversial treatise *An Essay on Musical Expression*, which was first published in 1752 and which provides valuable evidence of the musical tastes and opinions of the time.

Ave Maris Stella (*Latin*) "Hail, Star of the Sea," a Latin HYMN.

B

B (1) the seventh note of the scale of C major. (2) abbreviation for bass or for Bachelor (as in B. Mus., Bachelor of Music).

Babbitt, Milton [Byron] (1916–) American composer and mathematician whose early works were influenced by WEBERN and SCHOENBERG and who later turned to ELECTRONIC devices such as SYNTHESIZERS and tape recorders. His compositions include several orchestral and choral pieces as well as *Composition for Synthesizer* and *Vision and Prayer,* which had words by Dylan Thomas to a tape accompaniment.

baby grand the smallest size of grand PIANO.

Baccalaureus Musicae (*Latin*) Bachelor of Music (B.Mus.).

Bacchanalian songs are those sung in worship of Bacchus, the god of wine, and hence drinking songs.

Bach, Carl Philipp Emanuel (1714–88) German composer who was the second son and pupil of Johann Sebastian BACH. He was a famous harpsichordist and was particularly well known for his skill at improvising. His compositions include two oratorios, 50 keyboard concertos and many

34

songs, but his great claim to fame is that he is credited with developing the SONATA FORM. His treatise *An Essay on the proper method of playing keyboard instruments* provides an invaluable insight into the techniques and playing styles of his era.

Bach, Johann (John) Christian (1735–82) German composer and the eleventh and youngest son of JOHANN SEBASTIAN BACH by his second wife. He studied under his father but moved to Italy in 1756 and then to London in 1762, where he settled (which is why he is sometimes referred to as the "English" Bach). He became music tutor to Queen Charlotte in 1763, the year when his first opera, *Orione*, was performed. He befriended MOZART when the eight-year-old prodigy visited London and was an early influence on the young Austrian's style, especially with regard to piano concertos. His compositions include thirteen operas (such as *Amadis de Gaule*), an oratorio, and many piano concertos and symphonic pieces. As well as leaving a lasting impression on Mozart, his subtle way with melody also influenced HAYDN and BEETHOVEN.

Bach, Johann Christoph (1642–1703) German organist and composer who was the cousin of JOHANN SEBASTIAN BACH's father. He composed several choral and instrumental pieces of which *Ich lasse dich nicht* is the best known.

Bach, Johann Christoph Friedrich (1732–95) German composer who was the eldest surviving son of JOHANN SEBASTIAN BACH's marriage to his second wife. He was taught by his father and subsequently wrote a broad variety of music, including oratorios, concertos, sonatas and chamber music.

Bach, Johann Michael (1648–94) German organist and composer who was the son of JOHANN SEBASTIAN BACH's great-uncle and the father of the great composer's first wife, Maria Barbara. His output includes motets and some organ music.

Bach, Johann Sebastian (1685–1750) German composer who was one of the most influential in history. He was orphaned at the age of ten, and consequently went to live with his elder brother, JOHANN CHRISTOPH, who was his first keyboard teacher. In 1700 he became a chorister and he may have learned from the resident organist at St Michael's Church, Lüneburg. In 1703 he became a violinist in the Weimar court orchestra and then the organist at Arnstadt. In 1707 he was organist at Muhlhausen and married his cousin, Maria Barbara. He went back to Weimar in 1708 to become court organist, and it is during this period that he composed most of his organ music. In 1717 he became director of music (KAPELLMEISTER) to Prince Leopold at the court of Anhalt-Kothen and concentrated on composing secular works, including the BRANDENBURG CONCERTOS. His wife died in 1720, and the following year he married Anna Magdalena Wilcken. He was appointed cantor of St Thomas's in Leipzig in 1723, and that is where he spent the rest of his years. During this phase of his life he composed religious pieces such as his ST MATTHEW PASSION. In 1740 he began to have trouble with his eyesight, and by the time he died he was completely blind. He had twenty children, but only ten survived infancy.

During his lifetime, Bach had an unparalleled reputation as an organist, but his compositions were considered old-fashioned and were only accepted by a minority. He had little time for opera, but his most powerful works express an unsurpassed dramatic and emotional force. Bach's profundity enriched every type of music that he was required to produce, and his music has influenced succeeding generations of composers. WAGNER said of Bach's work that it was "the most stupendous miracle in all music".

Bach's principal works include: the ST JOHN PASSION, the ST MATTHEW PASSION, the CHRISTMAS ORATORIO, the Mass in B minor (*see* B MINOR MASS), and the six Brandenburg Concertos. He also wrote numerous cantatas and pieces for the harpsichord and organ, two violin concertos, as well as many pieces of chamber music, and of his keyboard music, the *Well-Tempered Clavier* and the *Goldberg Variations* are supreme.

Bach, Wilhelm Friedemann (1710–84) German composer and organist who was the eldest of JOHANN SEBASTIAN BACH's sons. He was taught by his father (who may have written *The Well-Tempered Clavier* for him) and became a reputable freelance organist. However, he struggled to make a living and ultimately died in poverty; at one time he passed off some of his father's works as his own. Ironically, many of his organ compositions proved popular after his death and are frequently played today.

Bach trumpet a nineteenth-century valved TRUM-
PET which was designed to make it easier to play
the high-pitched parts that were originally composed by BACH and his contemporaries for a natural (unvalved) trumpet.

back the lower part of the sounding box of string
instruments, connected in VIOLS to the sounding
board or belly by a sound post set beneath the
bridge. Its construction and material vitally af-
fect the quality of the TONE (3) produced.

badinage *or* **badinerie** (*French*) literally "frolic,"
a term for fast, frivolous music.

badinerie (*French*) *see* **badinage**.

Baez, Joan (1941–) American folksinger, renowned for her "protest songs" on civil rights and
the Vietnam War in the 1960s. She was closely
associated with Bob DYLAN in the peace movement.

bagatelle (*French*) "trifle," a short, light piece of
music, usually for piano, for example, BEETHOVEN'S
FÜR ELISE.

bagpipes a reed instrument in which air is supplied to the PIPE or pipes from an inflated bag.
Bagpipes are known to have existed for 3000
years or more and hundreds of different types are
found today. The best known form of bagpipe is
played in Scotland and consists of a *bag* which is
inflated through a pipe and is held under the arm;
a CHANTER (a REED pipe with finger holes) on which
the MELODY is played; and several DRONE pipes,
each of which is tuned to a different note. Air is
rhythmically squeezed from the bag by the arm
(and is then replenished with more breath) and is

forced out through the chanter and drone pipes.

Bailey, Norman (1933–) English baritone who above all is famed for his singing of WAGNER. His Hans Sachs in DIE MEISTERSINGER, his first Wagnerian role, was a triumph at SADLER'S WELLS in 1968, a triumph that was to be repeated in many opera houses, most notably at BAYREUTH. He was later to repeat his success as Wotan in the *Ring Cycle* (*see* RING DES NIBELUNGEN, DER)and Amfortas in PARSIFAL. Besides Wagner, he has excelled particularly as MOZART's Figaro, and as Balstrode in BRITTEN's PETER GRIMES.

Baillie, Dame Isabel (1895–1983) Scottish soprano who gave her first public concert with the HALLÉ Orchestra in 1921. She was first heard in London in 1923, and from then until the 1950s she sang with all the leading conductors of the day. Her high-quality voice excelled in ORATORIO, especially in HANDEL's MESSIAH. According to many, her recording of "I know that my Redeemer liveth"from that work has rarely been surpassed.

Baker, Dame Janet (1933–) English mezzo-soprano (formerly a contralto) of international repute. She was famed for her dramatic roles (for example, Dido in PURCELL's DIDO AND AENEAS) but was equally capable of singing comic parts, such as Dorabella in MOZART's COSÌ FAN TUTTE. As a concert hall singer, she is especially remembered for her renditions of some of MAHLER's works. She was appointed a DBE in 1976.

balafo an African XYLOPHONE.

Balakirev, Mily Alexeyevich (1837–1910) Russian composer, famed for his leadership of a group of nationalistic composers known as The FIVE, or "The Mighty Handful," for whom he set up a free music school. After a turbulent life in which he had numerous jobs, not all linked to music, he became the director of the Court Chapel in 1883. He was a fine pianist and his virtuoso piano piece *Islamey*, an oriental fantasy, proves his talent as a composer as well. His other works include two symphonies, two symphonic poems (*Russia* and *Tamara*), an overture (*King Lear*), a piano sonata, and songs.

balalaika (*Russian*) a FOLK instrument of the GUITAR family, with a triangular body. It is of Tartar origin and usually has just three strings and a fretted FINGERBOARD. Balalaikas are made in several sizes and are often played in concert with one another.

Baldwin Piano Co. an American company that manufactured the Baldwin, Ellington, Hamilton, Howard and Modello PIANOS, and player and reproducing pianos, with factories at Cincinnati and Chicago.

Balfe, Michael William (1808–70) Irish composer, baritone singer and violinist. Amongst his most noted roles as a singer were Figaro in *The* BARBER OF SEVILLE and Papageno in *The* MAGIC FLUTE. He wrote twenty-nine operas, of which *The Bohemian Girl* (1843) is the best known, a ballet, choral works, and songs.

ballabile (*Italian*) "in a dancing style."

ballad (1) a simple, easy-to-sing SONG for SOLO voice; such songs, which frequently dealt with contemporary events, were printed on broadsheets and sold at public functions and fairs between the sixteenth and nineteenth centuries. (2) a sentimental "drawing-room" song of the late nineteenth century, sometimes referred to as a "Shop BALLAD" to differentiate it from the type of songs that were sold by street vendors. (3) a narrative song or operatic ARIA.

ballade (*French*) (1) a type of medieval French poetry, often set to music by TROUBADOURS. (2) a nineteenth-century term, coined by CHOPIN, for a long, romantic instrumental piece. Chopin wrote four outstanding ballades.

ballad opera popular OPERA composed of dialogue and SONGS with tunes borrowed from FOLK music, popular songs, and sometimes opera. They first appeared in the eighteenth century in England, probably the best-known being *The* BEGGAR'S OPERA.

ballata (*Italian*) a SONG-tune form of the fourteenth century, which may be danced.

ballatetta (*Italian*) a little BALLATA.

ballet a dramatic entertainment in which dancers in costume perform to a musical ACCOMPANIMENT. Mime is often used in ballet to express emotions or to tell a story. Ballet has a long history that dates back to before the Middle Ages. In the sixteenth and seventeenth centuries, ballets often included singing and consequently were closely linked to OPERA. By the end of the eighteenth century, however, ballet had evolved more gymnastic qualities and, although it was still included as an integral part in many operas, it also kept a separate existence. In the nineteenth century, ballet achieved new heights of popularity in France and spread to Italy and Russia where several schools of ballet were established that incorporated traditional dancing into their teaching. TCHAIKOVSKY'S ballet scores (for example, SWAN LAKE and *The* SLEEPING BEAUTY) had a massive influence on Russian ballet and greatly added to its international appeal. The Russian choreographer and entrepreneur, Sergei Diaghilev (1872–1929), encouraged young composers such as STRAVINSKY and RAVEL to write ballet scores. At the start of the twentieth century, ballet became immensely popular in England. VAUGHAN WILLIAMS, BLISS and BRITTEN all composed notable pieces for ballet, and the outstanding British choreographers Sir Frederick Ashton (1904–88) and Sir Kenneth Macmillan (1929–92) helped to maintain the interest. In the USA, the choreographer George Balanchine (1904–83) had an equally powerful influence, and many American composers, such as COPLAND and BERNSTEIN, have since written ballet music. Meanwhile, PROKOFIEV'S masterpieces (for example, *Romeo and Juliet* performed by the Bolshoi) maintained Russia's great tradition in dancing. Today, ballet is witnessing a new revival, with SCORES being produced by young composers and with energetic companies establishing new dancing techniques on both sides of the Atlantic.

Balling, Michael (1866–1925) German-born conductor best known for his connection with the BAYREUTH Festival (1906–14) and as conductor of the HALLÉ Orchestra (1912–14).

Ballo in Maschera, Un *see* **Masked Ball, A**.

ballonzare (*Italian*) "wild, reckless dancing."

Baltazarini, Baltagerini (*fl.* sixteenth century) Italian violinist who introduced Italian dances into Paris, from which opera and ballet were developed. In 1577 he became intendant of music to Catherine de Medici (1519-89), who changed his name to Beaujoyeulx.

Baltzar, Thomas (1630–63) German-born violinist, who served at the court of Queen Christina of Sweden. He was the first great violinist to visit England, and such was his skill and virtuosity that he was rewarded by being appointed a member of the private music of the king, Charles II, in 1661.

band a term used to describe virtually any group of instrumentalists except a concert ORCHESTRA, for example dance band, JAZZ band, POP band, MILITARY BAND.

banjo a GUITAR-like, stringed instrument of Black American origin. It comprises a shallow metal (sometimes wood) drum with parchment stretched over the top while the bottom is (usually) left open. Banjos can have between four and nine strings, which are played by plucking either with the fingers or a PLECTRUM.

Banks, Donald (1923–80) Australian-born composer who studied with Mátyás György Seiber (1905–60) and DALLAPICCOLA. He came to London in 1950, where he wrote music for orchestra, a horn concerto, a violin concerto, and chamber music. He also composed for the theatre, films, and television. Devoted to New Music and ELEC-

TRONIC music, his work was also greatly influenced by JAZZ and the ideas and example of Milton BABBITT.

Bantock, Granville (1868–1946) influential English composer and conductor who actively encouraged young composers (SIBELIUS dedicated his 3rd symphony to him). His works, which included symphonic poems, operas and choral pieces, followed the ROMANTIC tradition. Perhaps his best known work is his tone poem *Fifine at the Fair*. He was knighted in 1930.

bar (1) a vertical line (bar line) drawn down one or more STAVES of music. (2) the space between two bar lines.

Barber of Seville, The (Il Barbiere di Siviglia) the title of a comic opera by ROSSINI with a libretto by Cesare Sterbini (based on Beaumarchais's Pierre Augustin Caron de [1732–99] play of the same name). The story tells how Count Almaviva succeeds, with the help of Figaro (the barber of Seville), in wooing Rosina, the ward of the protective Dr Bartolo. MOZART's *The* MARRIAGE OF FIGARO is a sequel to the story. Rossini's opera, not to be confused with PAISIELLO's earlier version of the tale, was first performed in Rome in 1816 and was an utter failure due in part to a series of comic accidents and in part to the presence in the audience of a Paisiello claque.

Barber, Samuel (1910–81) American composer and singer whose works include two operas (*Vanessa* and *Antony and Cleopatra*), ballets, symphonies, concertos, choral works and piano compositions. In 1931 he composed *Dover Beach*, a setting of Matthew Arnold's poem for string quartet and his own voice. His best-known work is *Adagio for Strings* (1936), which is taken from a string quartet.

barber-shop quartet a quartet of amateur male singers who perform CLOSE-HARMONY arrangements. The tradition originated in barber shops in New York in the late nineteenth century.

Barbiere di Siviglia, Il *see* **Barber of Seville, The**.

Barbirolli, Sir John (Giovanni Battista) (1899–1970) outstanding English conductor, of Italian origin. He began his musical career as a cellist, and appeared first as conductor with his own string orchestra in 1924. In the twenties and thirties he conducted the British National Opera Company, the Scottish Orchestra, and the New York Philharmonic Orchestra. In 1943 he became conductor of Manchester's HALLÉ Orchestra, which he stayed with for the rest of his life and transformed into one of the world's leading orchestras. He was also the conductor of the Houston Symphony Orchestra (1961–67). He was knighted in 1949.

barbiton the seven-stringed LYRE of Anacreon; an obsolete variety of VIOLIN.

barcarolle (*French*) a boating song with a rhythm imitating that of songs sung by gondoliers.

bard a Celtic minstrel, part of whose job it was to compose SONGS for his master. Bards traditionally held annual meetings (*Eisteddfods*) in Wales and these have been revived in recent times as competition FESTIVALS.

Bardi, Count Vernio (Giovanni) (1534–1612) Italian composer who wrote an early form of opera which was performed in his home in Florence by a group of his friends. He was attached to the court of Pope Clement VIII.

Barenboim, Daniel (1942–) Argentine-born Israeli pianist and conductor who is famed for his interpretation of late nineteenth- and early twentieth-century music. His first appointment as a conductor was in 1966 with the English Chamber Orchestra. Since then he has conducted with the Berlin Philharmonic, the New York Philharmonic, and L'Orchestre de Paris. In 1989 he became director of the Chicago Symphony Orchestra.

Bargaglia, Scipione (*fl.* sixteenth century) Italian composer and theorist who, according to Dr Charles Burney, the music historian, was the first to use the word "CONCERTO."

barginet *or* **bergeret** a shepherd SONG.

baribasso (*Italian*) "deep BASS."

baritenor a low TENOR.

baritone (1) a male voice, midway between BASS and TENOR with a range of approximately two OCTAVES. (2) a BRASS INSTRUMENT of the SAXHORN family.

Barley, William (*fl.* sixteenth and early seventeenth centuries) English music publisher who succeeded to a music printing business conferred by Queen Elizabeth's patent upon Thomas MORLEY. Publications are dated London, 1595 to 1609.

Barnby, Sir Joseph (1838–96) English composer, especially of church music. He composed 246 hymns and the oratorio *Rebekah*. He conducted

Royal Academy of Music concerts and held posts as organist and choirmaster. He is notable for introducing to English audiences the Passions of J. S. Bach. He was knighted in 1892.

Barnett, John (1802–90) English composer and singer who wrote about 4,000 songs. He directed at the Royal Opera House, and he himself wrote romantic operas with supernatural or fairytale themes, the most famous of which was *The Mountain Sylph.*

Baroque (*French*) literally "grotesque," but it has become a term used to describe the lush style of music typical of the seventeenth and early eighteenth centuries also applied to other arts.

Barraqué, Jean (1928–73) French experimental composer who explored the possibilities of voice and percussion instruments, as in his piece entitled *Le Temps restitué.*

barrel organ a mechanical ORGAN of the eighteenth and nineteenth centuries in which air was admitted into PIPES by means of pins on a hand-rotated barrel. It was restricted to playing a limited number of tunes but was nonetheless frequently used in church services. *See also* MECHANICAL INSTRUMENTS.

barroco (*Italian*) "whimsical, eccentric."

Barstow, Josephine (1940–) English soprano who since her appearance as Cherubino in *The* MARRIAGE OF FIGARO in 1967 has literally gone from strength to strength—for she excels both as singer and actress in the dramatic roles created by VERDI, JANÁCEK, and Richard STRAUSS. In 1986 she appeared at Salzburg in the first production of *Die Schwarze Maske* by the twentieth-century Polish composer Krzysztof PENDERECKI.

Bartered Bride, The a comic opera by SMETANA to a three-act libretto by Karel Sabini. The story tells of a love intrigue abounding in many misunderstandings and lighthearted liaisons set in a Bohemian village. The opera was first performed in Prague in 1866.

Bartholomew, William (1793–1867) English music scholar who adapted most of MENDELSSOHN's vocal pieces to English, and translated libretti.

Bartók, Béla (1881–1945) Hungarian composer and pianist who was initially influenced by the works of LISZT and Richard STRAUSS, but who later turned to the study of the traditional folk music of his homeland. He earned an enviable reputation in Europe as a virtuoso pianist but many of his compositions were not well received in Hungary until the staging of his ballet *The Wooden Prince* in Budapest in 1917. During the 1920s he resumed his career as a pianist and was given a salaried post at the Hungarian Academy of Sciences in 1934; his position at the Academy was ostensibly offered to him so that he could continue to compile a collection of Hungarian folk songs. In 1940 he emigrated to the USA and taught at Columbia and Harvard Universities.

Bartók's music has a highly individual quality, not always instantly accessible, that combines traditional folk elements with the contemporary. His intensely creative mind forced him into many problems with composition but his works remain powerful and contain a melodic and rhythmic quality that are unique to him. Although he died in poverty, he is now revered as one of the great forces of twentieth-century music.

Bartok's principal works include: *Duke* BLUEBEARD'S CASTLE (opera); *The Miraculous Mandarin* (ballet); *Cantata profana* (a choral piece); and six influential string quartets. In addition he wrote many orchestral works, including his concerto for orchestra, two violin concertos and an unfinished viola concerto; chamber pieces, piano sonatas, and numerous arrangements of folk songs.

baryton (*German*) an eighteenth-century German stringed instrument, played with a BOW.

Basie, "Count" (William) (1904–84) Black American jazz pianist, band leader and composer. He started his career as a variety show pianist but on "discovering" jazz he formed his own band in 1935. His group made several recordings and became famous for its driving rhythms as well as its virtuoso soloists.

bass (1) the lowest adult male VOICE. (2) an abbreviation for DOUBLE BASS. (3) an addition to the instrument name to indicate the largest member of a family of instruments (except where CONTRABASS instruments are built).

bassa (*Italian*) "low."

Bassani, Giovanni Battista (1657–1716) Italian composer and violinist born in Padua. He composed six operas and thirty-one vocal and instrumental works and three oratorios, and directed music at Bologna and Ferrara Cathedrals.

bass-bar a strip of wood glued as reinforcement under the BRIDGE (1) inside the BELLY of instruments of the VIOLIN family.

bass clarinet a single-REED instrument built an OCTAVE lower than the CLARINET, with a crook and upturned bell.

bass clef *see* **clef**.

bass *or* **base dance** a slow dance resembling the MINUET.

bass drum a large PERCUSSION INSTRUMENT consisting of a cylindrical wooden hoop which is usually covered on both sides with vellum. It is common in MILITARY BANDS in which it is suspended vertically from the shoulders and beaten with two sticks.

basse danse (*French*) literally "low dance," i.e. a dance in which the feet are kept low to the ground.

basset horn an ALTO CLARINET.

bass flute an ALTO FLUTE with a PITCH a FOURTH lower than a "concert" or normal flute.

bass horn a deep B flat HORN, doubled like a BASSOON, which succeeded the SERPENT but was in its turn succeeded by the OPHICLEIDE.

basso continuo *see* **figured bass**.

basso ostinato (*Italian*) "obstinate bass," a GROUND BASS, i.e. a bass FIGURE that is repeated many times throughout a composition (or part of a composition) while the upper parts vary.

bassoon a double-reed instrument dating back to the sixteenth century that consists of a wooden tube doubled back on itself. It has a compass from B flat below BASS CLEF to E on the fourth line of the TREBLE CLEF.

Bastien and Bastienne Mozart's operetta written in his twelfth year, to a libretto by F. W.

Weiskern, was performed in Vienna in 1768 in the garden theatre of the "discoverer" of mesmerism, Anton Mesmer (1734–1815).

baton the stick used by a CONDUCTOR to give his commands to performers.

batterie (*French*) (*also* **battery**) (1) a seventeenth- and eighteenth-century term for ARPEGGIO. (2) the PERCUSSION section of an ORCHESTRA.

Battle Sympony the English name of Beethoven's *Wellingtons Sieg, oder Die Schlacht bei Vittoria*, also known as *Wellington's Victory*.

battub (*Italian*) *see* **beat**.

battuta *see* **al battuta**.

Bauernleyer (*German*) HURDY-GURDY.

Baumgarten, C.F. (*fl.* late eighteenth century) composer of operas and pantomimes, including *Robin Hood* (1786) and *Blue Beard* (1792), while leader of the English Opera at COVENT GARDEN, London (1780–1794).

Bax, Sir Arnold Edward Trevor (1883–1953) English composer and pianist who was greatly influenced by Irish folklore and by the poetry of W. B. Yeats (1865–1939). He adopted a richly romantic style in his compositions, the most notable of which are his symphonic poems (for example, *The Garden of Fand, Overture to a Picaresque Comedy* and *Tintagel*). He also wrote 7 symphonies, concertos for violin and arranged many folk songs. He was knighted in 1937, and was appointed MASTER OF THE KING'S MUSICK in 1942.

bayles (*Spanish*) gypsy dance songs.

Bayreuth a town in Germany where WAGNER arranged for the building of a festival theatre which has subsequently become internationally famous for staging his operas. Built to resemble a Greek amphitheatre, the theatre holds 1,800 people, and the special feature of a herod surrounding the orchestra pit gives the auditorium an acoustical excellence ideal for Wagern's music. The first performance of the entire *Ring Cycle* (*see* RING DES NIBELUNGEN, DER) was given in 1876 in the new theatre.

beat (1) a unit of rhythmic measure in music, indicated to a CHOIR (2) or ORCHESTRA by the movement of a conductor's BATON. The number of beats in a BAR depends on the TIME-SIGNATURE. (2) a form of twentieth-century POPULAR MUSIC with a steady and powerful RHYTHM.

bebop a JAZZ development of the 1940s in which complex RHYTHMS and harmonic sequences were carried out against rapidly played melodic IMPROVISATION. It is particularly associated with the jazz saxophonist, Charlie PARKER.

Bebung (*German*) literally "trembling," i.e. a VIBRATO effect caused by shaking a finger holding down a KEY (1) of a CLAVICHORD.

Bechet, Sidney (1897–1959) American jazz saxophonist and clarinettist, who settled in France in 1951. He never learned to read music, but became recognized as one of the greatest soprano saxophone virtuosos of the century.

Bechstein, Friedrich Wilhelm Karl (1826–1900) German piano manufacturer who, after working in Germany, France and England, established his own company in Berlin in 1856 and produced his first piano in 1859. Branches of his firm were subsequently formed in France, England and Russia. London's Wigmore Hall was originally named the Bechstein Hall.

Bedford, David (1937–) prolific English composer who was, for a time, a member of the pop group The Whole World. His best-known work is S*tar's End* (1974), a composition for electric instruments as well as orchestra.

Beecham, Sir Thomas (1879–1961) English conductor of international repute. His early ambition was to compose but he took up conducting instead. He founded the London Philharmonic Orchestra in 1932 and the Royal Philharmonic Orchestra in 1946. He was responsible for introducing many new operas to a British audience, for example, *ELEKTRA* by Richard STRAUSS in 1910, and was noted for his interpretations of BERLIOZ and DELIUS. He was knighted in 1914 and succeeded to his father's baronetcy in 1916.

Beethoven, Ludwig van (1770–1827) German composer and pianist of Flemish descent. He left school at the age of eleven and was initially taught music by his talented father. In 1792 he was noticed by HAYDN, who invited him to Vienna, but the two of them did not get on well together and Beethoven took lessons elsewhere. He made his first public appearance in Vienna in 1795, playing his B Flat Major Piano Concerto (Op. 19) and in 1800 he conducted his first symphony there. Apart from occasional excursions, Beethoven spent the rest of his life in Vienna composing a prodigious quantity of music. Yet he never found composing easy. In 1802 his increasing deafness may have led him to contemplate suicide; his struggle with his incurable ailment was expressed in the EROICA symphony (1804). By 1819 he was stone deaf and unmarried, although often in love; nevertheless it was during the last few years of his life that he composed some of his most profound works. His stature was recognized by his contemporaries, although they found his later music difficult.

Beethoven's influence on music is truly immense. He was a "subjective composer" whose works express great emotional intensity. He revolutionized the emotional range of the SYMPHONY and the SONATA FORM. Although much of his music reflects his tempestuous, restless nature, other pieces have a calmness that show a different side of his complex personality.

Beethoven's principal compositions include: nine symphonies; FIDELIO (opera); *The Creatures of Prometheus* (ballet); *Christus am Olberg* (oratorio); five piano concertos; the violin concerto; two Masses; numerous pieces of chamber music; thirty-two piano sonatas; ten violin sonatas; five cello sonatas; a horn sonata; and several songs.

Beggar's Opera, The a BALLAD OPERA by John GAY. It is essentially a play interspersed with songs to tunes of the day, and satirizes both contemporary politics and Italian operatic conventions. The musical arragement was by Johann Christoph PEPUSCH, who also wrote an overture. It was first performed in London in 1728.

Beiderbecke, "Bix" (Leon) (1903–31) an American jazz cornet player, pianist and composer. He was one of the few white jazz players to influence black musicians and his cornet playing was famed for its beautiful tone.

bel a unit used in the measurement of the intensity of SOUND, named after its inventor, Alexander Graham Bell (1847–1922). *See also* DECIBEL.

bel canto (*Italian*) literally "beautiful singing," a style of singing characterized by elaborate technique, associated with eighteenth-century Italian OPERA.

Bellini, Vincenzo (1801–35) an Italian composer who studied in Naples under the composer Nicola ZINGARELLI. He is famed for his operas which include *Il Pirata, La Sonnambula,* the fine, lyrical *NORMA,* and *I Puritani.*

bells (*orchestral*) cylindrical metal tubes (*tubular bells*) of different lengths which are suspended from a frame and struck with a wooden mallet.

belly the upper part of the body or soundbox of a stringed instrument.

Belshazzar's Feast an oratorio by William WALTON with words, taken largely from the bible, arranged by Sir Osbert Sitwell (1892–1969). It was first performed in Leeds in 1931. SIBELIUS wrote a piece on the same subject.

Belyayev, Mitrofan (1836–1904) Russian music publisher who was an enthusiastic sponsor of the "New" composers. BORODIN, RIMSKY-KORSAKOV and many others used to congregate at his house regularly on Fridays and collectively wrote *Les Vendredis* (*Fridays*) in his honour.

ben, bene (*Italian*) "well", as in *ben marcato* meaning "well marked", "well accented".

Benedicite (*Latin*) a CANTICLE known as the *Song of the Three Holy Children;* it is used during Lent as an alternative to the TE DEUM in the Anglican service of Morning Prayer.

Benedict, Sir Julius (1804–85) English composer and conductor who wrote many operas and oratorios but is best remembered for his opera *The Lily of Killarney* (1862). He was knighted in 1871.

Benedictus (*Latin*) (1) the second part of the SANCTUS of a Roman Catholic MASS. (2) the CANTICLE "Benedictus Dominus Israel "or "Blessed be the Lord God of Israel."

Benjamin, Arthur (1893–1960) Australian composer and pianist who was renowned for his humorous but accomplished style. His principal operas include *The Devil Take Her* (1931) and *Prima Donna* (1931). His popular *Jamaican Rumba* for two pianos (1938) is still widely played.

Bennet, John (*c*.1575–*c*.1614) English composer who wrote many of the best madrigals in English. He also composed hymns, and an anthem for the coronation of James I and VI, for five voices and instruments. His first book of madrigals, *To Foure Voyces*, was published in 1599 by BARLEY.

Bennett, Richard Rodney (1936–) English composer and pianist who is best known for the popular tunes from his film scores, such as *Far from the Madding Crowd* (1967) and *Murder on the Orient Express* (1974). But he has written a great variety of work, including his operas *The Mines of Sulphur* and *A Penny for a Song*, a piano concerto, a symphony, *Aubade* for orchestra, and ballets, for example, *Jazz Calendar* and *Isadora*.

Bennett, Sir William Sterndale (1816–75) English composer and pianist who was a friend of MENDELSSOHN and SCHUMANN and founded the Bach Society in 1849. His works include a symphony, four piano concertos, and songs. He was knighted in 1871.

Benvenuto Cellini an opera by BERLIOZ with a libretto by Léon de Wailly and Auguste Barbier. This was Berlioz's first opera and was based on the life of the famous Italian sculptor, with special reference to his love for Teresa and the casting of his great bronze sculpture of Perseus. When it was first produced in 1838, it received little acclaim but has since been recognized as a masterpiece.

Berberian, Cathy *see* **Berio, Luciano**.

berceuse (*French*) a cradle SONG.

Berg, Alban (1885–1935) Austrian composer who studied with SCHOENBERG and who was an exponent of ATONAL composition and the TWELVE-NOTE system. He established his reputation with his first opera, *Wozzeck*, in 1921 and went on to write significant concertos and chamber music. His second opera, LULU, was unfinished when he died, and a version of it was not performed until 1979.

Berg, Johann (d.1563) the founder of a music printing house in Nuremberg about 1531. He was succeeded by Ulrich Newber and Gerlach.

bergamasca (*Italian*) or **bergomask** (*English*) or **bergamasque** (*French*) (1) a popular sixteenth- and seventeenth-century dance from Bergamo in Italy. (2) a nineteenth-century dance in quick 6/8 TIME.

Berganza, Teresa (1935–) Spanish mezzo-soprano. She first trained as a pianist at the Madrid Conservatoire before starting a singing career which was to make her one of the leading performers of the twentieth century. Her début as Dorabella in Così FAN TUTTE was quickly followed by other successes, and in 1958 she was first heard in Britain at Glyndebourne and in 1959 at Covent Garden. Her brilliance is best expressed in the operas of MOZART and ROSSINI. She sang the part of Zerlina in Joseph Losey's film version of *Don Giovanni* (1979).

bergomask *see* **bergamasca**.

Bergonzi, Carlo (1924–) Italian tenor who made his début as a baritone in 1948 as Figaro in ROSSINI's BARBER OF SEVILLE. In 1951 he was acclaimed for his tenor role in *Andrea Chenier* by GIRODANO, since when he has had success worldwide, especially in the operas of VERDI.

Berio, Luciano (1925–) Italian composer and conductor who has applied AVANT-GARDE techniques to his works. He gained a reputation with *Circles* in 1960, a piece with text by e. e. cummings in which the female singer is given a certain amount of freedom with regard to which notes she sings. His output has been constant, and his experiments with ELECTRONIC music have produced *Mutations*, *Theme*, and *Chantas parallèles*. He has written a concerto for two pianos, orchestral pieces, stage music, and an opera, *Allez, Hop*. From 1950–66 he was married to the American soprano **Cathy Berberian** (1928–83), for whom many of his works were written, even after the marriage ended.

Berkeley, Sir Lennox Randal Francis (1903—89) an English composer who was influenced by STRAVINSKY and is best known for his symphonies and operas, for example *Ruth*, *Nelson*, *A Dinner Engagement*, and *The Castaway*. He also wrote an oratorio, *Jonah*, and a Stabat Mater. He was knighted in 1974. His son, **Michael Fitzhardinge Berkeley** (1948–) is also a composer and a presenter of music programmes on radio and television. His works include the oratorio *Or Shall We Die?*, a setting of words by the novelist Ian McEwan.

Berlin, Irving (originally **Israel Baline**) (1888–1989) American composer of Russian origin who was not technically knowledgeable but who nevertheless wrote some outstandingly successful songs. Among the best known are *Alexander's Ragtime Band*, *White Christmas* and *God Bless America*. He wrote most of the lyrics for his songs himself. His musicals, everlastingly popular, include *Top Hat*, *Annie Get Your Gun*, and *Call Me Madam*.

Berlioz, (Louis) Hector (1803–69) a French composer, conductor and critic. He was expected to follow in his father's footsteps and become a doctor but he soon gave up medicine and took lessons in composition instead. In 1827 he fell passionately in love with the Irish actress Harriet Smithson (whom he subsequently married but later left for Marie Recio), who was the inspiration for his first masterpiece, SYMPHONIE FANTASTIQUE (1830). Over the next ten years or so, he composed some of his most notable works but was invariably short of money. In 1858 he finished his most ambitious opera, *The* TROJANS, but ironically he never heard it performed in its entirety. He died an unhappy man, lonely and sick.

Berlioz's music is renowned for its extravagant style and startling rhythms; even during his lifetime he earned the reputation for being a ROMANTIC composer *par excellence*. However, much of his grand and extrovert music is balanced by more subtle works. It was as an orchestrator that he was most innovative.

His principal compositions include: BENVENUTO CELLINI (opera); *The Trojans* (opera); *Béatrice et Bénédict* (opera); SYMPHONIE FANTASTIQUE; *Harold in Italy* (viola and orchestra); *Romeo et Juliette* (dramatic symphony); and *Les Nuits d'été* (song cycle).

Berners, Lord (Gerald Hugh Tyrwhitt-Wilson) (1883–1950) English composer who was also a diplomat, author and painter. He is mainly remembered for his ballets, for example, *The Triumph of Neptune* and *A Wedding Bouquet*. He also wrote scores for the films *Champagne Charlie* and *Nicholas Nickleby*.

Bernstein, Leonard (1918–90) American conductor, composer and pianist. As a conductor, his specialities included the works of MAHLER, RAVEL and SIBELIUS; as a composer he achieved fame with such musicals as *West Side Story* and *On the Town*. He also wrote three symphonies, an opera, *Trouble in Tahiti*, an operetta, *Candide*, and music for the film *On the Waterfront* (1954).

Berwald, Franz Adolf (1796–1868) distinguished Swedish composer and violinist whose work included four symphonies, concertos, symphonic poems, and several operas, for example, *A Rustic Betrothal in Sweden*.

Besson, Gustave Auguste (1820–75) French manufacturer of BRASS musical instruments, who greatly improved the construction of the CORNET and the CONTRABASS CLARINET.

big band a large BAND, most commonly associated with the SWING era. Such bands were famed for the strong dance RHYTHMS they produced.

Billings, William (1746–1800) American who worked as a tanner and composed hymns, anthems and songs in his spare time. Although his knowledge of music was limited, he is considered to be the first "all-American" composer of any worth. His *New England Psalm-Singer* was published in 1770.

Billy Budd (1) an opera with an all-male cast by BRITTEN to a libretto by E. M. Forster (1879–1970) and Eric Crozier (1914–). It is based on Herman Melville's (1819–1891) story of a hapless mariner who is hanged for the murder of Claggart, the evil-minded Master-at-Arms. It was first performed in London in 1951. (2) an opera by Giorgio Ghedini (1892–1965) to a libretto by Salvatore Quasimodo, first performed in Venice in 1949.

bina an East Indian stringed instrument of the GUITAR family, the SCALE consisting of a series of small INTERVALS between a NOTE and its OCTAVE in the BASS family.

binary form a structure, common in BAROQUE

music, consisting of two related sections which were repeated. SONATA FORM evolved from it.

Birtwistle, Sir Harrison (1934–) English composer of operas and symphonies who has also occasionally dabbled with ELECTRONIC music. He trained in Manchester where he was a contemporary of Maxwell DAVIES and OGDON. He is noted for such works as *The Triumph of Time* (for orchestra), and the operas *Punch and Judy*, *Gawain*, *Yan Tan Tethera*, and *The Mask of Orpheus*. He was knighted in 1991.

bis (*French*) "twice," "again".

Bishop, Sir Henry Rowley (1786–1855) English composer and conductor who was the first British musician to be knighted (1842). He adapted a number of other composers' operas for the English stage, including MOZART's MARRIAGE OF FIGARO. Although he wrote many works himself, much of his work is forgotten, save his song *Home, Sweet Home*, a version of which appears in DONIZETTI's opera *Anna Bolena* (1830).

bissex a 12-stringed GUITAR invented by Vanhecke in 1770.

bitonality the use of two keys simultaneously.

Bizet, Georges (originally **Alexandre César Léopold Bizet**) (1838–75) French composer who is best known for his operas, for example, *The* PEARL FISHERS, IVAN THE TERRIBLE, CARMEN, and *The Fair Maid of Perth*, but who also wrote a symphony, undiscovered until many years after his death, and several songs. His deservedly popular *L'Arlésienne* suites were first composed as accompaniment to Alphonse Daudet's (1840–97) play but failed to capture an audience. He did not achieve the recognition he deserved in his lifetime.

Björling, Jussi (1911–60) Swedish tenor whose first role was Don Ottavio in MOZART'S DON GIOVANNI in Stockholm in 1930. Between 1938 and 1960 he sang to enthusiastic audiences at the METROPOLITAN OPERA, New York as well as the Italian opera houses and COVENT GARDEN. He was supreme in Italian opera, especially PUCCINI.

blanche (*French*) literally "white"; the French word for a MINIM.

Bliss, Sir Arthur (1891–1975) English composer who is noted for daringly adventurous works. Amongst his most famous pieces are *The Olympians* (opera), *Checkmate* and *Miracle of the Gorbals* (ballets), as well as *Rout* (a piece for soprano and ten instruments). He also wrote music for films, including H. G. Wells's (1866–1946) *Things to Come* and *Men of Two Worlds*. In 1953 he was appointed MASTER OF THE QUEEN'S MUSICK.

Bloch, Ernest (1880–1959) American composer who was born in Switzerland. His music is noted for being Jewish in character, for example *Hakdesh* (for baritone, chorus and orchestra), and his *Israel Symphony*, *American Symphony*, and *Schelomo*, a composition for cello and orchestra. He also wrote music for piano, strings, a violin concerto, and an opera, *Macbeth*.

block chords a harmonic procedure in which the NOTES of CHORDS are moved simultaneously in "blocks".

Blomdahl, Karl-Birger (1916–68) Swedish composer who wrote three symphonies and the opera,

Aniara (1959), which is set on a spaceship and contains ELECTRONIC effects.

Blow, John (1649–1708) English composer and organist at Westminster Abbey and at the CHAPEL ROYAL, where he was also appointed composer. He wrote numerous anthems and songs, and the masque, *Venus and Adonis*.

Blue Danube, The a famous waltz written by Johann STRAUSS (the younger) in 1867.

Bluebeard's Castle (Duke Bluebeard's Castle) an opera by BARTÓK to a libretto by B. Balazs, which was first performed in Budapest in 1918.

bluegrass a type of FOLK music originally from Kentucky, USA, (where Kentucky bluegrass grows); *see* COUNTRY AND WESTERN.

blues a twentieth-century Black American SONG or lamentation following an essentially simple form of twelve BARS to each verse. Blues music formed the basis for JAZZ; musicians favoured such instruments as the GUITAR and HARMONICA.

B Minor Mass a setting of the Latin MASS by J.S. BACH for soloists, chorus and orchestra, composed in 1733–8.

bocca chiusa (*Italian*) literally "closed mouth," i.e. humming.

Boccherini, Luigi (1743–1805) prolific Italian composer and acclaimed cellist, who became neglected and died in poverty in Madrid. His output was prolific and includes a total of 125 string quintets, 102 string quartets, cantatas, oratorios, 29 symphonies, and the opera, *Clementina*.

Boehm system an improved system of KEYS (2) and levers for the FLUTE (1) which is named after its German inventor, Theobald Boehm (1794–1881). The system is also applied to other instruments, for example, the clarinet.

Bohème, La an opera by PUCCINI to a libretto by Giuseppe Giacosa and Luigi Illica. The story tells of the love affairs between the student Rodolfo and the seamstress Mimi, which ends in tragedy with the death of Mimi, and between Marcello and Musetta, all set in the Latin Quarter of Paris. It was first performed in Turin, conducted by TOSCANINI, in 1896. LEONCAVALLO also wrote an opera of this name.

Böhm, Karl (1894–1981) Austrian conductor especially associated with the works of MOZART and Richard STRAUSS. He was conductor of the Munich Opera in the 1920s and director of the Vienna State Opera, 1943–45.

Boito, Arrigo (1842–1918) Italian composer and librettist who wrote the libretti for VERDI'S OTELLO and FALSTAFF. He also wrote an opera, *Mefistofele*, and another, *Nerone*, unfinished at his death, was performed in 1924 to little acclaim.

bolero (*Spanish*) a moderately fast Spanish dance in triple TIME. RAVEL'S *Bolero* (1928), a spiralling crescendo based on a repeated theme, was the music for a ballet choreographed by Vaslav Nijinsky (1890–1950).

Bologna the Italian city which was the seat of the first Italian school of music, founded by Pope Nicholas V in 1482. Later, many academies for the promotion of the arts and sciences, including music, were established there, as was an important Philharmonic Society.

bones a pair of small sticks (originally bones) that are held in the hands and clicked together rhythmically.

bongos pairs of small, upright Cuban DRUMS that are often found in dance BANDS. They are played with the hands.

boogie-woogie a JAZZ and BLUES style of piano playing in which the left hand plays a persistent bass RHYTHM while the right hand plays a MELODY.

bop short for BEBOP.

Boris Godunov an opera by MUSSORGSKY (who also wrote the libretto) which was first performed in its entirety in 1874. Considered one of the greatest of Russian operas, it tells the tragic story of Boris who, having assassinated Dimitri, the rightful heir, becomes Tsar of Russia. Gregory, a young monk, pretending to be Dimitri, rouses the people to his side. Seized by remorse and fear, Boris abdicates in favour of his son and dies.

Borodin, Aleksandr Porfiryevich (1833–87) Russian composer who was the illegitimate son of a Russian prince. As well as being a musician, he was a devoted and able scientist, which explains why his output of music was comparatively small. He was a member of the FIVE, and it was BALAKIREV who succeeded in weaning him from science to music. His most famous works include *In the Steppes of Central Asia* (tone poem), and PRINCE IGOR (an opera completed after his death by RIMSKY-KORSAKOV and GLAZUNOV).

bouche fermée (*French*) *see* **bocca chiusa**.

bouffe *see* **opéra bouffe**.

Boughton, Rutland (1878–1960) English com-

poser of operas, the most famous of which were
based on Arthurian legends, for example, *The
Immortal Hour*, immediately popular and performed first at Glastornbury in 1914, and *The
Birth of Arthur*.

Boulanger, (Juliette) Nadia (1887–1979) French
composer and conductor but who is mainly remembered for being an outstanding teacher of
COMPOSITION(3). Among her pupils were BERKELEY,
COPLAND and PISTON.

Boulez, Pierre (1925–) French composer, conductor and pianist who gave up a career as a
mathematician in order to study music. He is
reckoned to be one of the most important of AVANT-
GARDE composers and his most noted works include *Le Marteau sans maître* (for voice and chamber orchestra), and *Pli selon pli* (for soprano and
orchestra). He was chief conductor of the BBC
Symphony Orchestra (1971–75), the New York
Philharmonic Orchestra (1971–77), has conducted
WAGNER at BAYREUTH, and gave the first performance of BERG's LULU at the PARIS OPÉRA.

boulou an African HARP.

Boult, Sir Adrian Cedric (1889–1983) English
conductor who gained an international reputation after he conducted the first performance of
HOLST's suite *The Planets* in 1918. He conducted
many orchestras worldwide and had a particular
penchant for the works of English composers,
especially ELGAR, VAUGHAN WILLIAMS and WALTON.
He was conductor of the BBC Symphony Orchestra (1930–49) and was knighted in 1937.

bourrée (*French*) a lively French dance dating

from the seventeenth century.

bouzouki a Greek stringed instrument with a long, fretted neck. Its six strings are plucked, often to provide an emotionally charged ACCOMPANIMENT to songs. The sound of the bouzouki reached a worldwide audience with the film music of the Greek composer Mikis Theodorakis.

bow a wooden stick which is strung with horsehair and used to play instruments of the VIOLIN and VIOL families.

bowed harp a primitive VIOLIN, dating back to at least the twelfth century. It was held on the knee and played vertically.

bow hand usually the right hand.

bowing the technique of using a BOW to play an instrument. *See also* LEGNO.

Boyce, William (1711–79) English composer and organist whose works include twenty symphonies and numerous pieces of church and chamber music. He is most famous for writing "Heart of Oak," which was a song included in the music he wrote for *Harlequin's Invasion,* a pantomime by David Garrick (1717–79) first performed in 1759.

Brabançonne, La the Belgian national anthem, written in 1830.

brace the vertical line, usually with a bracket, which joins two STAVES of music to indicate that they are played together.

Brahms, Johannes (1833–97) German composer and one of the most influential of the nineteenth century. He had humble origins and was first taught by his father, a double-bass player. His ambitions to be a composer were encouraged by

LISZT and SCHUMANN, and his appointment as
director of music to the Prince of Lippe-Detmold
(1857) gave him time to concentrate on composing. It took him twenty years to write his first
symphony but when it was performed in Karlsruhe
in 1876, it was nicknamed "Beethoven's 10th"
and his reputation was assured. His second symphony was completed the following year.

Brahms's music was considered conservative by
many of his contemporaries but few composers
have managed to express deep emotions as eloquently. His symphonies and concertos are considered to be masterpieces.

Brahms's principal compositions include: four
symphonies, two piano concertos, a violin concerto, a concerto for violin and cello, *A German
Requiem* (chorus and orchestra), three piano sonatas and many outstanding pieces of chamber
music, especially noteworthy being the Clarinet
Quintet and the Clarinet Trio.

Brain, Dennis (1921–57) English horn player
who became the outstanding exponent of this
instrument in his day. BRITTEN wrote *Serenade*
(for tenor, horn and strings) especially for him.

Brandenburg Concertos six orchestral concertos by BACH which were written for Christian
Ludwig, Margrave of Brandenburg, in 1721.

branle (*French*) a French FOLK DANCE from the fifteenth century, which had a swaying movement.

brass band a type of BAND, particularly associated
with the north of England, which consists of BRASS
INSTRUMENTS and DRUMS only. Brass bands have
been popular in England since the beginning of

the nineteenth century.

brass instruments a family of WIND INSTRUMENTS which are made of metal but not always brass. Instruments with REEDS and those which used to be made from wood (such as the FLUTE) are excluded. A characteristic of the family is that sound is produced by the vibration of the lips which are pressed into a funnel-shaped MOUTHPIECE. A selection of NOTES can be produced by effectively lengthening the tubing, either with a slide (as in the TROMBONE) or with valves (as in the TRUMPET). Brass instruments include the trombone, CORNET, BUGLE, trumpet, French HORN, TUBA, and EUPHONIUM.

brava *or* **bravo** (*Italian*) literally "bravely done," cried in applause.

bravura (*Italian*) literally "bravery," as in a "bravura passage," a passage that demands a VIRTUOSO display by the performer.

break (1) in JAZZ, a short, improvised, SOLO passage. (2) the point in a vocal or instrumental range where the REGISTER changes.

Bream, Julian (1933–) virtuoso English guitar and lute player who has done much to revive interest in classical guitar music as well as introducing new works, for example, the Concerto for Guitar by VILLA-LOBOS. WALTON, BRITTEN, Richard Rodney BENNETT and TIPPETT wrote pieces especially for him. His interest in the lute led to recitals of music by DOWLAND and recordings of songs given by Peter PEARS with lute accompaniment.

breit (*German*) "broadly" or "grandly"; a term used to describe the manner in which a piece should be played.

Brendel, Alfred (1931–) Austrian pianist who lives in London and who has acquired an international reputation as a soloist. He is also highly respected as a musicologist, and his master-classes are immensely popular.

breve originally the short NOTE of music (*c.*thirteenth century), but as other notes have been introduced, it is now the longest note and is only occasionally used.

Brian, William Havergal (1876–1972) English composer who was largely self-taught. He wrote 32 symphonies, which sometimes demanded outrageously large orchestras, the opera *The Tigers*, and *By the Waters of Babylon* for chorus and orchestra.

Bride of Song a one-act operetta by Jules Benedict to the book by Henry Farnie, which was produced at COVENT GARDEN, London, in 1864.

bridge (1) a piece of wood that stands on the BELLY of stringed instruments and supports the strings. (2) a passage in a COMPOSITION (1) that links two important THEMES together.

Bridge, Frank (1879–1941) English composer, viola player, conductor and teacher. He wrote numerous works of all kinds, for example, four string quartets, songs, and *A Prayer,* for chorus and orchestra. BRITTEN was one of his pupils.

Brigg Fair the so-called "English Rhapsody" for orchestra by DELIUS; it is based on Lincolnshire FOLK SONGS.

brindisi (*Italian*) literally "a toast"; a drinking song in an opera during which toasts are often given.

71

brio (*Italian*) "vigour," so CON BRIO means "with vigour."

brisé (*French*) literally "broken"; a term which indicates that a CHORD should be played in ARPEGGIO fashion, or that music for stringed instruments should be played with short movements of the BOW.

Britten, (Edward) Benjamin (1913–77) an English composer, conductor and pianist who started to write music when he was five. He is one of the few twentieth-century composers who has succeeded in pleasing both "radical" and "conservative" audiences. Some of his greatest works were written in collaboration with the poet W. H. Auden and he wrote songs specifically for his friend and long-term companion, the tenor Peter PEARS, and a cello symphony for the cellist ROSTROPOVICH. He had a special gift for setting words to music, and his most impressive works are operas. He had a life-long love for the North Sea and the coastal town of Aldeburgh, where he lived and where he founded the ALDEBURGH FESTIVAL in 1948.

Britten's major works include the operas PETER GRIMES, *The* RAPE OF LUCRETIA, ALBERT HERRING, BILLY BUDD, *The* TURN OF THE SCREW, *A* MIDSUMMER NIGHT'S DREAM, and DEATH IN VENICE. He did, however, write numerous other pieces, notably *The Young Person's Guide to the Orchestra* (1946), SPRING SYMPHONY, and WAR REQUIEM (for the new Coventry Cathedral, 1962), and is considered to be one of the most influential of all twentieth-century composers.

broken octaves a term used to describe a passage of NOTES that are played alternately an OCTAVE apart; they frequently occur in piano music.

Brubeck, Dave (1920–) American JAZZ pianist and composer. He had a sophisticated style and is especially known for adapting CLASSICAL music for jazz.

Bruch, Max (1838–1920) German composer of Jewish origin. Among the posts he held was that of conductor of the Liverpool Philharmonic Society. His works include operas, three symphonies, three violin concertos, and *Scottish Fantasy*. Perhaps the best-known of all his works are his 1st Violin Concerto and his setting of *Kol Nidrei* for cello and orchestra.

Bruckner, Anton (1824–96) Austrian composer who is noted for his ten symphonies as well as his choral and chamber music. He also wrote organ music and pieces for male-voice choirs. He was influenced, and to some extent overshadowed by WAGNER. Many of his symphonies are essentially religious. Their original strength suffered, however, from contemporary criticisms, which forced Bruckner to make cuts and alterations in them. These versions are sometimes still played, but thanks to the International Bruckner Gesellschaft, the symphonies do now exist in their original form. He wrote three Masses, including *Grosse Messe* (a Mass in F minor), and numerous other sacred vocal works.

brunette (*French*) a folk love-song of the seventeenth and eighteenth centuries.

buccinator a muscle in the cheeks, development of which is important to players of WIND INSTRUMENTS.

bucina *or* **buccina** (*Latin*) a curved horn employed by ancient Romans for civil and military purposes.

buffa *see* **opéra bouffe**.

bugle a simple BRASS INSTRUMENT with a conical tube and a cup-shaped MOUTHPIECE which was widely used for giving military signals. *See also* LAST POST.

Bull, John (1563–1628) English organist and composer whose best-known works are keyboard and church music.

Bull, Ole Børneman (1810–80) Norwegian violinist and composer who was largely self-taught. He excelled when performing his own works.

bull roarer *see* **thunder stick**.

Bülow, Hans Guido von (1830–94) German pianist, conductor and composer who originally studied law. He is best remembered as a conductor who was greatly influenced by WAGNER (he conducted the first performances of TRISTAN UND ISOLDE and DIE MEISTERSINGER VON NÜRNBERG, both in Munich). As a pianist, he had an impressive repertoire.

Bumbry, Grace (1937–) American soprano (formerly mezzo-soprano) who made her début in AIDA in 1960. In 1961 she appeared at BAYREUTH, the first black singer to do so. She is especially noted for her interpretations of CARMEN, TOSCA and SALOME.

burla, burlesca (*Italian*) a short and jolly piece of music.

Bush, Alan Dudley (1900–) English composer and pianist. A Marxist, his works include the operas *Wat Tyler* and *Joe Hill*, several symphonies and choral works.

Busoni, Ferruccio Benvenuto (1866–1924) Italian composer, pianist, theorist and teacher. He lived most of his life in Germany and is remembered mainly for his operas, for example, *Die Brautwahl*, *Arlecchino*, and *Doktor Faust*, which, although it was unfinished at his death, was his most important work.

Butterworth, George (1885–1916) English composer whose musical skill and imagination are expressed and remembered in his rhapsody for orchestra, *A Shropshire Lad*, based on poems by A. E. Housman (1859–1936). His *Banks of Green Willow* for small orchestra illustrates his interest in English FOLK SONGS and their revival. A musical career of great talent and promise was cut short by his untimely death in World War I.

Buxtehude, Diderik *or* **Dietrich** (*c.*1637–1707) Danish composer and noted organist, much admired by BACH. He reinstituted the ABENDMUSICK concerts at Lübeck. His compositions include works for organ, church cantatas, and sonatas for orchestra.

buxus a boxwood FLUTE.

Byrd, William (1543–1623) English composer who was for a time an organist at Lincoln Cathedral and a Gentleman of the CHAPEL ROYAL, and later organist there. His compositions include Masses, anthems, and other church music.

Byzantine music music of the Christian Church of the Eastern Roman Empire which was established in AD 330 and lasted until 1435. It influenced Western church music.

C

C (1) the key-note or TONIC of the SCALE of C major.
(2) an abbreviation for CONTRALTO; *con* (with); *col,
colla* (with the).

c.c. abbreviation for *coll' arco,* meaning "with the
BOW," as opposed to PIZZICATO (with reference to
playing a stringed instrument).

cabaletta (*Italian*) a term for a simple ARIA with an
insistent RHYTHM, or an emphatically rhythmical
ending to an ARIA or DUET.

Caballé, Montserrat (1933–) Spanish soprano
whose dramatic singing has, since her début at
Basle in 1956, been heard in all the great opera
houses of the world. She has performed in the
operas of ROSSINI, PUCCINI, WAGNER and Richard
STRAUSS, and has been especially praised for her
singing of BELLINI and DONIZETTI roles. Throughout her career she has given memorable recitals,
often of Spanish songs, and made many recordings, notably as Fiordigli to Janet BAKER's
Dorabella in MOZART's COSÌ FAN TUTTE conducted
by Colin DAVIS.

cabinet organ *see* **American organ**.

cabinet pianoforte an upright PIANO.

caccia (*Italian*) literally a "hunt," as in *corno da*

76

caccia, hunting horn. It can also mean a fourteenth-century hunting poem about country life set to music.

Caccini, Giulio (*c.*1550-1618) Italian singer and composer who was a member of the Florentine group, the Camerata, which helped to establish opera. He wrote many songs and the early opera *L'Euridice.*

cachucha a Spanish solo dance in 3/4 time, resembling the BOLERO.

cacophony a discordant muddle of SOUND or DISSONANCE.

cadence literally a "falling," a term used to describe the concluding PHRASE at the end of a section of music.

cadenza (*Italian*) literally "cadence," but it has come to have two specific meanings: (1) an elaborate ending to an operatic ARIA. (2) a flourish at the end of a PASSAGE of SOLO music in a CONCERTO.

Cage, John (1912-92) American composer and pianist who is famed for his experimental works which do not conform to standard musical practice. He has incorporated elements of chance into his compositions as well as ELECTRONIC and environmental sounds. His works include *Music of Changes* (for "prepared" piano), *4' 33",* which consists of 4 minutes 33 seconds of silence, *Radio Music* for one to eight radios, and *Imaginary Landscape* for twelve radios with two players to each radio.

calando (*Italian*) literally "diminishing," i.e. in both volume and speed.

calcando (*Italian*) "pressing forward," i.e. a term

used to indicate an increase in speed.

Callas, Maria (originally **Maria Kalogeropoulou**) (1923-77) a soprano of Greek origins but who was born in the USA. She became the most celebrated singer of her day and was famed for her acting ability as well as her outstanding voice. Among her many memorable performances are those of Norma in Bellini's opera of that name, Violetta in LA TRAVIATA, and Tosca.

calypso a kind of song with SYNCOPATED RHYTHMS from the West Indies, notably Trinidad; calypso LYRICS are usually witty and topical, and are often vehicles for political satire.

Calzabigi, Ranieri da (1714–95) Italian writer and librettist of the operas of GLUCK.

cambiata (*Italian*) an abbreviation for *nota cambiata*, CHANGING NOTE.

camera (*Italian*) literally a "room," but in musical terms it refers to a type of music that can be performed in a place other than a church, music hall, or opera house, etc; *see* CHAMBER MUSIC.

campanelli (*Italian*) *see* **glockenspiel**.

campanology the art of bell-ringing or the study of bells.

Campion (Campian), Thomas (1567-1620) English poet and songwriter who was also a physician and lawyer. He published several books of lute songs and many MASQUES for performance at court.

cancan a Parisian music-hall dance of the late nineteenth century in quick 2/4 time. Famous examples of the dance are found in OFFENBACH'S operettas, in particular ORPHEUS IN THE UNDERWORLD.

cancel (*US*) *see* **natural**.

cancrizans (*Latin cancer*, "crab") literally "crab-like," a type of music that makes sense if it is played backwards; RETROGRADE MOTION.

Cannabich, Christian (1731-98) German violinist, composer and conductor. His conducting was particularly admired by MOZART.

canon a COUNTERPOINT composition in which one part is imitated and overlapped by one or more other PARTS, for example, a SOPRANO lead with a TENOR follow-up. In a "strict" canon, the imitation is exact in every way.

cantabile (*Italian*) literally "song-like"; it is a term applied to instrumental pieces indicating that they should be played in a singing style.

cantata originally a piece of music of the BAROQUE period that is sung (as opposed to a SONATA, a piece which is played). It has come to be a term used to describe a vocal or CHORAL piece, with an instrumental accompaniment. German cantatas were generally religious works. In many ways, the form is similar to OPERA and ORATORIO, but it tends not to be so elaborate.

Cantelli, Guido (1920–56) Italian conductor whose conspicuous talent rapidly brought him international renown. From 1949, his début in New York, followed in 1950 by his appearance at the Edinburgh Festival, until his appointment to La SCALA, Milan, he was hailed, not least by TOSCANINI, as unique in his time. His death in an air crash at the age of thirty-six was a tragedy for the musical world.

canticle a HYMN that has words from the bible, other than a PSALM.

cantino (*Italian*) a VIOLIN's E string.

canto.(*Italian*) the upper VOICE (2) PART in concerted music, which carries the MELODY.

cantor (*Latin*) a "singer"; nowadays the term refers to the chief singer in a CHOIR (2) or the lead singer of liturgical music in a synagogue. Formerly it also meant the PRECENTOR, the person in charge of music at a cathedral or a monastic or collegiate church; the principal of a college of church music; or the head of a musical institution.

cantoris in cathedrals where ANTIPHONAL singing was practised, the PRECENTOR, or CANTOR, usually had his stall on the north side of the CHOIR (1) facing the altar, and this was called the *cantoris* side, as opposed to that on the south side where stood the dean's stall, known therefore as the *decani* side.

cantus mensurabilis (*Latin*) a "measured song." The practice of dividing music into MEASURES (1) of equal duration by means of BARS seems to have been a gradual growth of the fourteenth and fifteenth centuries to which many musicians contributed, but for which none was solely responsible.

cantus firmus (*Latin*) "fixed song," i.e. a MELODY in POLYPHONIC music, often taken from PLAINSONG, with long NOTES (1) against which COUNTERPOINT tunes are sung.

canun a Turkish ZITHER.

canzone, canzona, canzon literally "song"; a vocal work, or an instrumental piece that is modelled on music for the VOICE.

canzonet (1) a short kind of CANZONE. (2) a type of

MADRIGAL or a simple SOLO SONG.

caoinan (*Gaelic*) an Irish funeral song or wail.

capo, da *see* **da capo**.

capotasto (*Italian*) the "head of the fingerboard," i.e. the raised part or "nut" at the top of the FINGERBOARD of a stringed instrument that defines the lengths of the strings. A moveable capotasto, comprising a wood or metal bar that can be clamped to the fingerboard, is occasionally used on fretted instruments to shorten all the strings at the same time, thus raising the PITCH.

cappella, a *see* **a cappella**.

capriccio (*Italian*) "caprice"; a short, lively piece.

Capuleti e I Montecchi, I *see* **Romeo and Juliet.**

Carey, Henry (*c.*1690–1743) English composer of "Sally in our Alley," which featured in *The* BEGGAR'S OPERA, and numerous other songs and cantatas, for which he wrote the verses as well, possibly including "GOD SAVE THE KING." He wrote and composed the music for quantities of dramatic farces and burlesques, among them *Chrononhotonthologos*, *The Dragon of Wantley*, and *Nancy*, revived as *The Press Gang* and *True Blue*. He was possibly the illegitimate son of George Savile, Marquis of Halifax, and his own posthumous son, **George Savile Carey** (1743–1807) sang and acted, and advanced his father's claim to the authorship of "God Save the King."

carillon (1) a set of bells, usually in a bell tower, which can be played by electrical or mechanical means to produce a tune. (2) an ORGAN STOP which produces a bell-like sound.

Carissimi, Giacomo (1605-74) Italian composer,

particularly of church music. He is noted for his oratorios, for example *Jephte* and *Jonas Baltazar*.

carmagnole a French Revolutionary song beginning "*Madame Veto avait promisé*," and with the refrain, "*Dansons la carmagnole, vive le son du canon.*"

Carmen an opera by BIZET to a libretto by Henri Meilhac and Ludovic Halévy. It tells the tragic story of the sergeant of the guard, Don José, who falls in love with the coquettish gypsy girl, Carmen. Bewitched by her dark beauty, he deserts and allows himself to be lured to the mountain haunt of her smuggler comrades. The fickle Carmen, soon tiring of Don José, taunts him with her new conquest, Escamillo, the toreador. Don José's pleadings are in vain, and at last, beside himself with jealousy, he knifes her in the back just as the crowd is heard roaring its joy at the toreador's victory in the bullring. It was first performed in Paris in 1875, since when it has been the best loved of all French operas.

Carmina Burana (Songs from Beuren) an oratorio or cantata by Carl ORFF first performed in Frankfurt in 1937. The mainly Latin text is based on medieval poems about women, drink and love.

Carnegie Hall a famous concert hall in New York endowed by the philanthropist and millionaire, Andrew Carnegie (1835-1919), who was born in Scotland but made his fortune in the USA.

Carnival of the Animals (Le carnaval des animaux) a popular satirical suite by SAINT-SAËNS, composed in 1886 but not published until after the composer's death. Each of the fourteen movements depicts a different animal.

carol originally, any medieval English song with a refrain, but now generally a song associated with Christmas.

Carpenter, John Alden (1876-1951) successful American businessman who was also a noted composer. His works include *Krazy Kat*, a jazz pantomime, ballets, for example *The Birthday of the Infanta* (1918) and *Skyscrapers* (1926), and two symphonies.

Carreras, José (1946-) Spanish tenor, one of the most respected and admired of the late twentieth century. He studied in Barcelona, where he first appeared in VERDI'S NABUCCO, and it is particularly in Verdi roles that he has since excelled, although his Don José in CARMEN is supreme. In the late 1980s he successfully combated serious illness to return to the stage with his fine lyrical voice in no way diminished.

cartellone (*Italian*) the prospectus of an opera season.

Carter, Elliot (1908-) major American composer of ballets, chamber music, symphonies, and a piano concerto. He held many teaching posts at prestigious American colleges, and his works include *Variations for Orchestra*, *Symphony of Three Orchestras*, and *Penthode*.

Caruso, Enrico (1873-1921) legendary Italian tenor who made more than 600 appearances at the New York METROPOLITAN OPERA HOUSE. His singing, strong and effortless and lyrically pure, is considered by many never to have been surpassed. He was the first tenor to make recordings, which earned him a handsome fortune.

Casali, Giovanni Battista (d.1792) Italian composer of church music and the operas *Campasbe* (1740) and *Antigone* (1752). He was chapelmaster at St John's Lateran, Rome, from 1759, until his death.

Casals, Pablo (1876-1973) Catalan cellist, conductor and composer whose worldwide performances did much to raise the status of the cello as a solo instrument. He made his home in Puerto Rico in 1956. His compositions include the oratorio *El pessebre* (*The Manger*).

Casella, Alfredo (1883-1947) Italian composer, conductor, teacher and pianist who was also an author. He was passionate about modern Italian music and he helped to establish the Venice Biennale festivals. His works include operas, for example, the one-act operas, *Il Deserto tentato* (*The Desert Probed*) and *La Favola d'Orfeo* (*The Tale of Orpheus*), and the full-length opera *La Donna serpente* (*The Serpent Woman*) and the ballet *La Giara* (*The Jar*). His publications included works on BACH, BARTÓK, BEETHOVEN and STRAVINSKY.

cassation an eighteenth-century term for instrumental music devised for open-air performance, similar to the SERENADE (2).

Casse-Noisette, a *see* **Nutcracker, The**.

castanets a Spanish PERCUSSION INSTRUMENT comprising two shell-like pieces of wood which are clicked together by the fingers. In orchestras, they are occasionally shaken on the end of sticks.

castrato (*Italian*) an adult male singer with a

SOPRANO or CONTRALTO voice produced by castration before puberty. Castrati were popular singers in the seventeenth and eighteenth centuries. The practice was abandoned during the nineteenth century. MOZART wrote for a castrato role in his IDOMENEO, as did MONTEVERDI in ORPHEUS and *The* CORONATION OF POPPEA.

catch a ROUND for three or more VOICES. The words are often humorous and frequently contain puns, for example, *Ah, how Sophia* which, when sung, sounds like "Our house afire." The first collection of catches to be printed was in 1609, *Pammelia: Musicke's Miscellanie* by Thomas RAVENSCROFT. They were also popular with PURCELL.

Caters Changes rung on nine bells.

Cavalieri, Emilio de' (*c.*1550-1602) amateur Italian composer of the Medici court in Florence. He wrote four MUSIC DRAMAS which heralded the way for the oratorio form. His best-known work is the morality play *La rappresentazione de anima e di corpo* (*The Representation of Soul and Body*).

Cavalleria Rusticana (Rustic Chivalry) MASCAGNI's first opera was written for, and won, a competition for one-act operas, and its first night in Rome in 1890 was an event rarely equalled in opera. So rapturously was it received that Mascagni became famous overnight. Based on a play by Giovanni Verga, the hot-blooded story is of Sicilian love, jealousy, betrayal and revenge against a rural background—a tragedy flawlessly illustrated by inspired music. Its sensational popularity brought imitations of the one-act form, only one achieving real success, LEONCAVALLO's *I*

Pagliacci. To this day the latter is performed with *Cavalleria Rusticana* as part of a double bill, affectionately known as *"Cav and Pag."*

Cavalli, Pietro Francesco (originally **Pier Caletti-Bruni**) (1602-76) an Italian composer who wrote more than forty operas as well as church music. He was one of the first composers to inject humour and exaggerated drama into his operas, for example, *L'Ormindo*, *La Callisto*, and *Egisto*. These have been successfully performed in recent times.

cavatina (*Italian*) a short and often slow SONG or instrumental piece.

Cavendish, Michael (c.1565–1628) English composer of songs for lutes and of madrigals, a volume of which was published in 1598. He also composed "Ayres for four Voyces," 1599; and, with nine other composers, *The Whole Booke of Psalmes*, published in 1592.

CB an abbreviation for *contrabasso* (DOUBLE BASS).

cebell a seventeenth-century English dance similar to the GAVOTTE.

Cecilia, St the patron saint of music who was martyred in the second or third century. Since the sixteenth century music festivals to commemorate her have been annual events. Her feast day is 22 November.

ceilidh (*Gaelic*) a gathering at which SONGS, FOLK music and dances are performed; ceilidhs are particularly associated with Scotland and Ireland.

celesta a small keyboard instrument in which HAMMERS are made to strike metal bars suspended over wooden resonators; the sound produced has an ethereal, bell-like quality. TCHAIKOVSKY included a celesta in the" Dance of the Sugar-Plum Fairy" in his ballet *The* NUTCRACKER.

cello *see* **violoncello**.

cembalo (*Italian*) (1) a DULCIMER. (2) an abbreviation of *clavicembalo*, which is the Italian for HARPSICHORD.

Cesti, Antonio (1623-69) Italian opera composer who was originally a friar but was released from his vows in 1658. He was musical director at the Medici court in Florence until 1652. He then served the Habsburgs in Austria, and in 1667 wrote his longest opera, *Il pomo d'oro* (*The Golden Apple*), in honour of the marriage of Leopold I. His works helped to develop the operatic form, for example, *Orontea*.

cetera (*Italian*) a CITTERN or ZITHER.

CF abbreviation for CANTUS FIRMUS.

Chabrier, Alexis Emmanuel (1841-94) French composer who worked as a civil servant for eighteen years and who was largely self-taught. He was a devotee of WAGNER, whose influence can be heard in some of his operas, especially *Gwendoline*. Later operas, French in style and full of melody, wit and charm, include *L'Etoile* and *Le Roi malgré lui*. His most famous piece is his lively orchestral rhapsody, *España*.

chaconne (*French*) a slow dance in triple time that is thought to have originated in Mexico.

Chaikovsky, Piotr llyich *see* **Tchaikovsky**.

Chaliapin, Fedor Ivanovich (1873-1933) Russian bass who had formidable stage presence as well as a magnificent voice. From 1896 in Moscow his reputation grew in Russia and then throughout Europe, where his singing of bass roles in Italian as well as Russian opera was soon unrivalled. He left Russia after the Revolution of 1917 and settled in France, where he became a naturalized citizen. Between 1921 and 1925 he was a member of the METROPOLITAN OPERA New York. Of his many outstanding roles, he is best remembered for his Boris Gudunov.

chalumeau (*French*)) (1) a generic term for a type of REED-PIPE. (2) a term now used for the lower REGISTER (2) of the CLARINET.

chamber music originally, chamber music was a term used to describe any type of music that was suitable for playing in a room of a house as opposed to a church or concert hall. However, it has come to mean music for a small number of instruments (for example, flute and piano) or group of performers (for example, STRING QUARTET, SEXTET, etc.), with one instrument to each part.

chamber orchestra a small orchestra, sometimes solely of stringed instruments, for performing CHAMBER MUSIC.

chamber organ a small ORGAN.

Chaminade, Cécile (1857-1944) French pianist and composer who is best known for her songs and piano works, although she did write a number of more ambitious pieces, for example *Konzertstück* for piano and orchestra, and *Les Amazones*, a lyric symphony for chorus and orchestra.

champêtre (*French*) "rural" or "rustic."

change-ringing an English method of ringing a

peal of church bells; the bells are rung in an established order, which then passes through a series of changes.

changing note *or* **cambiatta** a dissonant PASSING NOTE which is a third away from the preceding note, before being resolved.

chanson (*French*) a song for either a SOLO VOICE or a CHOIR (2). In some contexts it can also mean an instrumental piece of song-like quality.

chant a general term for a type of music which is sung as part of a ritual or ceremony. It is a term which is used particularly for unaccompanied singing in religious services.

chanter the pipe of a BAGPIPE, on which the MELODY is played.

chanterelle (*French*) literally the "singing one", i.e the highest string on a bowed, stringed instrument (for example, the E string on a VIOLIN).

Chapel Royal the body of musicians and clergymen who serve a British monarch in his or her court. It also refers to the building in St James's Palace where services are held.

character piece a term used by composers for a short instrumental piece, such as may attempt to describe a specific mood. Examples are SCHUMANN's *Fantasiestücke*, *Nachtstücke*, and *Albumblätter*.

Charles, Ray [Ray Charles Robinson] (1930–) an American singer, pianist and songwriter. Originally a blues and jazz singer, he became one of the most popular singers in the world with songs such as "I Can't Stop Loving you."

charleston a ballroom dance, similar to the FOX-TROT, which was evolved by black Americans of the Southern USA.

Charpentier, Gustave (1860-1956) French composer whose works include instrumental pieces and songs. His most memorable piece, however, is *Louise,* an opera concerning the low-life of Paris, set to romantic music.

Charpentier, Marc-Antoine (1634-1704) French composer of stage and church music but whose most impressive works were the operas, *Les Amours d'Acis et de Galatée* and *Médée.* He wrote for Molière's troupe and enjoyed the patronage of the royal household.

Chausson, Ernest (1855-99) a French composer of romantic operas and orchestral pieces, including *Le Roi Arthur* (opera) and his *Poème* for violin and orchestra.

Chávez (y Ramirez), Carlos (1899-1945) noted Mexican composer and conductor whose work was much influenced by Indian folk music and folklore, for example *Sinfonía India* and *Xochipilli-Macuilxochitl* (ballet).

Cherubini, (Maria) Luigi (Carlo Zenobia Salvatore) (1760-1842) Italian composer who settled first in London then in Paris in 1788. He wrote operas, for example, *Médée, Les Deux Journées, Faniska* and *Ali Babar,* and other works. He was much admired by BEETHOVEN, whose FIDELIO story closely followed that of *Médée* in its study of feminine psychology, and of *Les Deux Journées* in its stress on democratic values.

chest voice the lower REGISTER (2) of VOICE (1), so called because NOTES seem to emanate from the chest. *Compare* HEAD VOICE.

chevalet (*French*) the BRIDGE of a stringed instrument.

chiaro, chiara (*Italian*) "clear," "distinct."

Child of Our Time, A an oratorio in three parts composed in 1941 by Sir Michael TIPPETT, who also wrote the libretto, the theme of which is the Nazi persecution of the Jews. It was first performed in 1944 in London and won great respect.

Chisholm, Erik (1904–65) Scottish composer and from 1930 conductor of the Glasgow Grand Opera Society. Thanks to him, British audiences were introduced to operas such as *The* TROJANS and *Béatrice et Bénédict* by BERLIOZ, and IDOMENEO by MOZART. He was appointed professor of music at Cape Town University in 1946. His compositions include two symphonies, piano and violin concertoes, and an opera trilogy, *Murder in Three Keys*.

chitarrone (*Italian*) a large LUTE.

choir (1) the place, defined by special seats or "choir stalls", in a large church or cathedral where singers are positioned. (2) a body of singers, such as a male-voice choir, church choir. (3) (US) a section of the orchestra, for example "brass choir".

choir organ the section of an ORGAN that is played from the lowest MANUAL and is soft enough to accompany a church CHOIR (2).

choirbook a large medieval volume that (usually) included both words and music and was designed to be read by various members of a CHOIR (2) while it was stationed on a centrally placed lectern.

Chopin, Frédéric François (originally **Fryderyk Franciszek Chopin**) (1810-49) Polish-born com-

Chopin

poser and pianist who was the son of a French father and Polish mother. He was a prodigy, taking his first music lessons at six, composing at seven and giving recitals at eight. He settled in Paris in 1831 and, although he had already gained a worthy reputation as a pianist, he earned a living as a teacher to aristocratic families and this allowed him time to concentrate on composing. He became friendly with the leading musicians of his era (such as LISZT, MENDELSSOHN, BERLIOZ) and fell in love with the novelist George Sand (Amandine Aurore Dupin), who devotedly nursed him when he began to suffer from tuberculosis, the disease from which he was to die. Whilst he was living with Sand (they never married), he composed his most impressive works. When their relationship broke up in 1848, he toured Britain to earn money but died the following year.

As well as being an exuberant, virtuoso pianist, Chopin was an outstanding composer, especially of keyboard music. He advanced the concept of the NOCTURNE, as expressed by FIELD, and developed subtle and unconventional HARMONICS in his compositions for piano. His reputation as a ROMANTIC, in every sense of the word, did, for a time, hinder him in being accepted as an innovative composer (although nobody has ever doubted his talent as a pianist).

Chopin's principal works include: pieces for piano and orchestra, two concertos, *Variations on Là ci darem la mano*; piano solos, four Ballades), twenty-seven Etudes; three Ecossaises, fifty-one Mazurkas, nineteen Nocturnes, twelve Polonaises, preludes, scherzos, sonatas, waltzes, and many chamber music works and songs.

choral (1) an adjective used to describe music that involves a CHORUS (1), for example CHORAL SYMPHONY.

chorale a HYMN-tune of the Lutheran Church, but dating back to the fifteenth century.

chorale cantata a CANTATA that was written to be performed in a (Lutheran) church.

Chorale Fantasia (1) a work by BEETHOVEN (Op. 80) for piano, chorus and orchestra. (2) a setting by HOLST for soprano, chorus, organ, brass, strings and percussion of words by Robert Bridges (1844–1930).

Choral Service an Anglican church service which is sung or chanted throughout.

choral symphony (1) a SYMPHONY in which a CHORUS (1) is used at some point (or, indeed, a symphony written entirely for voices). (2) the popular name of BEETHOVEN's symphony no. 9 in D Minor, which ends with "An die Freude" ("Ode to Joy") for chorus and soloists.

chord a combination of NOTES played simultaneously, usually not less than three.

chordophone any instrument in which stretched strings are vibrated to produce sound, for example, a VIOLIN.

chorus (1) a body of singers. *See* CHOIR. (2) music written for a body of singers (usually to follow an introductory piece). (3) a REFRAIN that follows a SOLO verse.

Christmas Oratorio the name given to a series of six church CANTATAS by J. S. BACH (1734).

"Christmas" Symphony Another nickname given

to HAYDN's "LAMENTATION" SYMPHONY.

Christus am Olberge BEETHOVEN's first choice of name for the work now known as the *Christ on the Mount of Olives*.

Christoff, Boris (1919–) Bulgarian bass of exceptional quality of tone, who has sung at La SCALA, COVENT GARDEN, in Russia, and in New York. He is famed worldwide for his dramatic Boris in BORIS GODUNOV.

Christus Felix MENDELSSOHN's oratorio to words by Chevalier Bunsen was begun 1844, laid aside until the completion of *Elijah*, resumed in 1847 but never finished. Eight numbers were published after Mendelssohn's death, and these were sung in 1852 at the Birmingham Festival.

chromatic (from Greek *chromatikos,* "coloured") a term used to describe NOTES which do not belong to a prevailing SCALE, for example, in C major all SHARPS and FLATS (1) are chromatic notes. The "chromatic scale" is a scale of twelve ascending or descending SEMITONES; and a "chromatic CHORD" is a chord that contains chromatic notes. *See also* TWELVE-NOTE MUSIC.

ciaccona (*Italian*) *see* **chaconne**.

Cilèa, Francesco (1866-1950) Italian composer, teacher and administrator. He trained in Naples and is best known for his successful operas, including and *L'Arlesiana* (*The Woman of Arles*), taken from the same play by Alphonse Daudet (1840–97) for which BIZET wrote a score, and *Adriana Lecouvreur*. The leading tenor parts in both operas were created by CARUSO in 1897 and 1902.

Cimarosa, Domenico (1749-1801) Italian composer of operas, whose first opera, *Le Stravaganze del Conte* (*The Count's Eccentricities*), was performed in 1772 in Naples. In St Petersburg he became MAESTRO DI CAPELLA to Catherine II in 1787, and in 1791 spent a year in Vienna in the service of Leopold II. His most successful opera, *Il Matrimonio segreto* (*The Secret Marriage*), based on a play by David Garrick, was performed there, and on its first night was given a second performance on the order of Leopold. Of more than sixty popular operas that he wrote, this one can still be seen. He also wrote Masses and oratorios.

cimbal, cimbalom *see* **dulcimer**.

circular breathing the technique of sustaining a NOTE when playing a WIND INSTRUMENT by breathing in through the nose while sounding the note.

citole a medieval instrument and ancestor of the CITTERN.

cittern a pear-shaped stringed instrument of the GUITAR family popular from the sixteenth century to the eighteenth century It was similar to the LUTE except that it had a flat back and wire strings, and was easier to play.

Clair de lune a piano piece by DEBUSSY, which forms the third movement of the *Suite Bergamasque*, composed 1890-95.

clappers virtually any kind of PERCUSSION INSTRUMENT comprising two similar pieces that can be struck together, for example BONES, spoons, sticks.

Clapton, Eric (1945–) English guitarist and composer, who is widely recognized as one of the most influential rock guitarists. He played with the Yardbirds (1963–65) and the "super group" Cream (1966–68).

clarinet a single-REED WOODWIND instrument dating back to the seventeenth century. It has a cylindrical tube and nowadays comes in two common sizes: B flat and A. It is an instrument common to both CLASSICAL music and JAZZ.

Clarke, Jeremiah (*c*.1673-1707) English composer who was, for a time, organist at St Paul's Cathedral in London. His compositions include many anthems and pieces for harpsichord, but he is best remembered for "The Prince of Denmark's March", otherwise known as the TRUMPET VOLUNTARY (formerly attributed to PURCELL).

clàrsach (*Gaelic*) a small harp of the Scottish Highlands and Ireland.

classical (1) a term used to describe a certain form of music which adheres to basic conventions and forms that are more concerned with carefully controlled expression rather than unrestrained emotion. (2) a term used to describe "serious" music as opposed to popular music.

clavecin (*French*) *see* **harpsichord**.

claves Short sticks that are held in the hand and clicked together to emphasize a BEAT (1) or RHYTHM. They originated in Cuba.

clavicembalo (*Italian*) *see* **harpsichord**.

clavichord a keyboard instrument dating from the fifteenth century in which the strings are struck by a brass "tangent" and can be made to sound a note of variable PITCH until the KEY (1) is released. However, the sound is soft and the keyboard is limited; the instrument fell out of favour with the introduction of the PIANO.

clavier (1) a practice keyboard which makes no sound save clicks. (2) any keyboard instrument that has strings, for example, the CLAVICHORD, the HARPSICHORD, the PIANO.

clef a symbol positioned on a line of a STAVE which indicates the PITCH of the line and consequently all the NOTES on the stave. Three clefs are commonly used: ALTO (TENOR), TREBLE and BASS.

Clementi, Muzio (1752-1832) Italian composer and pianist whose works exploit the potential of the piano (as opposed to the harpsichord). He knew MOZART, BEETHOVEN and HAYDN and taught John FIELD in London. He wrote many symphonies, some 60 piano sonatas, and *Gradus ad Parnassum*, 100 studies for the piano.

"Clock" Symphony the nickname of HAYDN's Symphony No. 101 in D Major, so called because of the "tick-tock" rhythm of the second movement.

close harmony HARMONY in which the NOTES of the CHORDS are close together. In singing, this means that each VOICE remains fairly close to the MELODY.

Coates, Eric (1886-1957) an English composer and viola player whose orchestral works, for example, *Countryside*, *The Three Bears* and the *London Suite*, are light but well crafted. He wrote more than 100 songs and marches, such as *The Knightsbridge March* and the march for the film (1955) *The Dam Busters*.

Cockaigne a concert overture by ELGAR subtitled "In London Town" and dedicated to "my friends the members of British orchestras."

coda (*Italian*) literally a "tail," meaning a PASSAGE

at the end of a piece of music which rounds it off.

codetta (*Italian*) a "little tail," i.e. a shorter version of a CODA.

col legno (*Italian*) *see* **legno**.

col, coll', colla, colle (*Italian*) literally "with the," so *col basso* means "with bass"; *colle voce*, "with voice."

Coleridge-Taylor, Samuel (1875-1912) English composer whose mother was English and father was from Sierra Leone. He wrote famous settings for poems by Henry Longfellow (1807–82), for example, *Hiawatha's Wedding Feast* and *The Death of Minnehaha,* and also composed orchestral, stage and chamber music.

coloratura (*Italian*) the florid ornamentation of a melodic line, especially in opera.

colour the TONE-quality of instruments and voices.

Coltrane, John [William] (1926–67) American jazz saxophonist. A virtuoso on the tenor and soprano saxophones, he became one of the most influential and popular jazz musicians of his generation.

combination tone a faint (third) NOTE that is heard when two notes are sounded simultaneously; also called a "resultant tone."

combo an abbreviation of "combination," especially a collection of musicians that make up a JAZZ BAND.

comic opera an OPERA that has an amusing plot, or (sometimes) an opera that includes some spoken dialogue.

common chord a MAJOR or MINOR CHORD, usually consisting of a keynote and its third and FIFTH.

comodo (*Italian*) "convenient," as in *tempo comodo*, meaning at a "convenient speed."

compass the musical RANGE of a VOICE (1) or instrument.

composer an author of music.

composition (1) a work of music. (2) the putting together of sounds in a creative manner. (3) the art of writing music.

compound interval an INTERVAL which is greater than an OCTAVE.

compound time musical TIME in which each BEAT (1) in a BAR is divisible by three, for example 6/8, 9/8 and 12/8 time.

computer-generated music music that is created by feeding a formula or program into a computer, which then translates the program into sounds.

Comus a MASQUE by the poet John Milton (1608–74) with music by Henry LAWES. It was first performed in 1634.

con amore *see* **amore**.

con anima *see* **anima**.

con animo *see* **animo**.

con brio *see* **brio**.

concert a public performance of secular music other than an OPERA or BALLET.

Concertgebouw (*Dutch*) literally a "concert building," but usually taken to mean Amsterdam's main concert hall, completed 1883.

concert grand a large GRAND PIANO that is used in concert halls.

concertina a type of ACCORDION, hexagonal in shape, with small studs at each end which are used as keys.

concertmaster (*US*) the first violinist, or leader of an orchestra.

concerto (*Italian*) (1) originally, a work for one or several voices with instrumental ACCOMPANIMENT. (2) a work for several contrasted instruments. (3) an orchestral work in several movements, containing passages for groups of SOLO instruments (*concerto grosso*). (4) a piece for a solo instrument and an accompanying orchestra.

Concerto de Aranjuez a concerto for guitar and orchestra by RODRIGO, which was first performed in 1940.

concert overture an orchestral piece of one MOVEMENT, similar to an opera OVERTURE, but written solely for performance in a concert hall. It originated in the nineteenth century. Examples are Mendelssohn's HEBRIDES and Tchaikovsky's ROMEO AND JULIET.

concert pitch the internationally agreed PITCH, according to which A above middle C (in the middle of the TREBLE CLEF) is fixed at 440 hertz (cycles per second).

Concertstück, Konzertstück (*German*) a short CONCERTO.

concitato (*Italian*) "agitated."

concord a combination of sounds (such as a CHORD) that are satisfactory and sound agreeable. The opposite of DISSONANCE.

concrete music *see* **musique concrète**.

conducting the art of directing and controlling an ORCHESTRA or CHOIR (2) (or operatic performance) by means of gestures. As well as indicating the speed of a piece, a conductor, who often uses a

BATON to exaggerate his or her arm movements, is also responsible for interpreting the music.

conga (1) a tall, narrow DRUM which is played with the hands. (2) an entertaining dance in which the participants form a long, moving line one behind the other.

conjunct a succession of NOTES of different PITCH.

conservatory a school that specializes in musical training. The term originates from the kind of charitable institutions for orphans, called *conservatorii* in sixteenth- and seventeenth-century Italy, where music was taught to a high standard.

consort an old spelling of the word "concert," meaning an ENSEMBLE of instruments, for example, a consort of VIOLS.

Contes d'Hoffmann, Les *see* **Tales of Hoffmann**.

continuo (*Italian*) an abbreviation of *basso continuo*. *See* FIGURED BASS.

contrabass (1) (adjective) an instrument that is an OCTAVE lower than the normal BASS of the family, for example, contrabass TUBA. (2) (noun) a DOUBLE BASS.

contralto the lowest female VOICE, which usually has a range of about two OCTAVES.

contrapuntal relating to COUNTERPOINT.

contrary motion *see* **inversion**.

contratenor the fourteenth- and fifteenth-century word for a VOICE with approximately the same range as a TENOR.

contredanse (*French*) a French corruption of "country dance," i.e. a lively dance.

Coperario, John (*c*. 1575-1626) English composer and noted player of the lute and viola da gamba. His name was originally John Cooper but he changed it because Italian music was fashionable.

Copland, Aaron (1900-90) American composer, conductor and pianist who was also an influential teacher (BERNSTEIN being among his pupils). He championed the cause of modern music and wrote several books on the subject. He was also determined to write music that was characteristically American. In this genre, his best-known works include the ballets *Billy the Kid, Appalachian Spring* and *Rodeo*, and *Fanfare for the Common Man*. He also wrote symphonies, a piano concerto, and chamber music.

Coppélia a ballet with music by DELIBES which was first performed in 1870.

cor (*French*) *see* French horn *under* **horn**.

cor anglais (*French*) literally "English horn," but it is neither English nor a HORN. It is in fact an ALTO OBOE pitched a FIFTH below the standard oboe.

coranto (*Italian*) *see* **courante**.

Corbett, William (d.1747) English composer who wrote incidental music to Shakespeare's plays, and concertos and sonatas. He played the violin at the London Opera, and collected Italian music and violins during a sojourn in Italy. He returned to England in 1740, and played in the royal orchestra.

corda (*Italian*) a "string," as in "piano string"; the term *una corda* literally means "one string," an indication to use the "soft" PEDAL on the PIANO.

Corelli, Arcangelo (1653-1713) Italian violinist

and composer who spent much of his early life in France and Germany as a virtuoso performer. His most important pieces include sonatas (for example, twelve *Sonate a tre*) and twelve *Sonate da camera a tre*.

Cornelius, Peter (1824-74) German composer and writer who was a friend of WAGNER and LISZT. His works include the operas *The Barber of Baghdad* and *The Cid*.

cornet (1) a BRASS INSTRUMENT with three valves that has a quality of TONE (3) lying between a HORN and a TRUMPET; it has great flexibility and is often used in MILITARY and JAZZ BANDS. (2) an ORGAN STOP used for playing flourishes.

cornett (*French*) an obsolete WIND INSTRUMENT dating from the Middle Ages. It comprised a tube of wood, pierced with seven holes which were covered by the fingers and with a cup-shaped MOUTHPIECE.

Coronation Concerto the name given to MOZART's Piano Concerto in D Major which was said to have been played at the coronation of Leopold II in 1790.

Coronation Mass MOZART's Mass in C Major, so called because it was associated with the annual crowning of a statue of the Virgin near Salzburg in Austria.

Coronation of Poppaea, The *see* **Incoronazione de Poppea, L'**.

coranach (*Gaelic*) a lament sung at Scottish funerals.

Così fan tutte (*Women are all the same*) an opera by MOZART to a libretto by Lorenzo da Ponte.

which has the subtitle, *"La scuola degli amante"* (*The School for Lovers*). It was first performed in Vienna in 1790 and relates the story of two sisters, Fiordiligi and Dorabella, tricked by their soldier fiancés into unfaithfulness, so proving to the men's satisfaction—and that of their scheming friend Don Alfonso—that it is always so and "women are all the same."

cotillion a popular ballroom dance of the early nineteenth century.

cottage piano a small upright PIANO.

Cotrubas, Ileana (1939–) Romanian soprano whose distinctive voice was first heard in Britain at GLYNDEBOURNE in 1969 when she sang Mélisande and then in 1971 at COVENT GARDEN as Tatyana in Eugene Onegin. At La SCALA in 1975 she understudied Mirella Freni, and her Mimi was a triumph, and with her later outstanding successes—in THE MARRIAGE OF FIGARO, DON PASQUALE, and RIGOLETTO, among others—her reputation and popularity were assured.

counterpoint the combination of two or more independent melodic lines that fit together to create a coherent SOUND texture. The CLASSICAL (1) conventions of HARMONY are based on counterpoint.

counter-subject a MELODY, found in a FUGUE, that is CONTRAPUNTAL to the main THEME (SUBJECT), i.e. after singing the subject, a VOICE (2) carries on to sing the counter-subject while the answer is sung.

counter-tenor the highest natural male VOICE (1) (not to be confused with FALSETTO).

country and western a generic term for a form of

twentieth-century American folk music, originating from the south-east of the USA, with Nashville, Tennessee, as its traditional home. It is usually played by small BANDS using FIDDLES, GUITARS, BANJOS and DRUMS etc. The songs are typically of a sentimental, sometimes tragic, nature. Lively BLUEGRASS music is a form of country and western.

country dance a dance once popular in rural England, whence it spread to France and Italy as CONTREDANSE and *contraddanza*. It consisted of four- or eight-measure PHRASES which might be in either triple or DUPLE TIME.

Couperin, François ("le Grand") (1668-1733) French composer and the most important member of a family of musicians. He was an organist and wrote music for the harpsichord. His book *L'Art de toucher le clavecin*, published in 1716, gave instructions on how to play his harpsichord pieces and had an influence on BACH.

couplet (1) the same as DUPLET. (2) a two-note SLUR. (3) a SONG in which the same music is repeated for every STANZA.

courante (*French*) short for *danse courante* or "running dance," a lively Baroque dance in triple time.

Covent Garden Theatre an opera house in London. The first theatre on the site, built in 1732, was for plays and was destroyed by fire in 1808. The second theatre was renamed the Royal Italian Opera in 1847 because all operas then were sung in Italian. In 1856 it, too, burned down. The third and present building was erected in 1858 and in 1892 became the Royal Opera House. It is the home of the Royal Ballet and the Royal Opera Companies.

cow bell as used as a PERCUSSION INSTRUMENT in an orchestra, it is an ordinary square cow bell with the clapper taken out. It is played with a drumstick.

Coward, Sir Noel (1899-1973) English playwright, songwriter, singer and actor, noted in particular for his witty songs, such as "Mad Dogs and Englishmen." He wrote songs and scores for a number of revues and musicals, for example, *Bitter Sweet*, *Cavalcade*, *Words and Music*, as well as stage plays.

Cowell, Henry Dixon (1897-1965) American composer, pianist, teacher and writer who was largely self-taught but nevertheless rose to become a revered experimenter. He developed a technique of playing what he called "tone clusters" on the piano, which involved hitting the keyboard with a fist or elbow. He wrote twenty symphonies, a piano concerto, chamber music, two ballets, *The Building of Banba* and *Atlantis*, and the opera *O'Higgins of Chile*.

Cramer, Johann Baptist (1771-1858) German-born composer and pianist who came to live in London where he gained a high reputation. He is most noted for his piano pieces and his book of *Studies,* which he wrote to pass on his skills and which is still used by young pianists today.

Creation, The (Die Schöpfung) an ORATORIO by HAYDN to a text by Baron van Swieten (a translation of an English libretto, including biblical passages from the Book of Genesis and from John

Milton's great poem *Paradise Lost*).

"Creation" Mass the nickname for a Mass in B flat major by HAYDN.

credo (*Latin*) "I believe," the first word in the Roman Catholic Creed.

crescendo (*Italian*) "increasing," i.e. getting gradually louder.

Creston, Paul [originally **Joseph Guttoveggio**] (1906–) American self-taught composer of Italian origin. His works include five symphonies, choral pieces and concertos, some of which were written for uncommon instruments (such as the harp, accordion, marimba, trombone).

Cristofori, Bartolomeo (1655-1731) Italian instrument maker who first devised the HAMMER mechanism for the PIANO.

croche (*French*) a QUAVER.

Croft, William (1678-1727) English composer who was for a time organist at Westminster Abbey. He is best known for his odes and anthems, especially the hymn-tune "St Anne" to which is sung "O God our Help in Ages Past."

crook (1) a detachable section of tubing that was inserted into a BRASS or WOODWIND INSTRUMENT between the MOUTHPIECE and the body of the instrument to give it a different KEY (by increasing the length of the air-column). Performers often had as many as twelve crooks but the introduction of valved instruments in the 1850s virtually dispensed with their necessity. (2) a curved metal tube between the mouthpiece and the body of large wind instruments such as the BASSOON and BASS CLARINET.

crooning a soft, sentimental style of singing, often to DANCE MUSIC. Bing CROSBY was a noted "crooner."

Crosby, Bing (Harry Lillis Crosby) (1904–77) American singer and actor. His relaxed, jazz-influenced style of singing or CROONING made him one of the most popular and imitated singers of the twentieth century. His recording of Irving BERLIN's "White Christmas" (1942) is often said to be the best-selling record of all time.

cross rhythms rhythms that appear to have conflicting patterns and are performed at the same time as one another.

Cross, Joan (1900—) English soprano, who was one of the greatest of the twentieth century. She was particularly associated with the works of BRITTEN. Her deep interest in and love of English opera led to the founding of the English Opera Group and the National School of Opera.

Crosse, Gordon (1937-) English composer whose works include pieces for children, for example, *Ahmet the Woodseller*, and four operas, including *Purgatory* and *Potter Thompson*.

crotchet (*US* "quarter note") a NOTE with a quarter of the time value of a whole note (SEMIBREVE).

crumhorn *see* **Krumhorn**.

csárdás *see* **czárdás**.

cuckoo a short PIPE with a single finger hole; it gives two notes that imitate the sound of the bird.

cue a catchword or note on a score, used to indicate the entrance of a voice or instrument.

Cui, César Antonovich (1835-1918) Russian composer, critic and member of The FIVE. He trained as a military engineer and rose to the rank of general, while still composing. He wrote fifteen operas, including *The Captive of the Caucasus*, *William Ratcliffe*, *The Saracen* and *Mam'zelle Fifi*, but is best remembered for his witty writings (he became a music critic in 1864).

curtain music *see* **act tune**.

curtall a small BASSOON of the sixteenth and seventeenth centuries.

Curzon, Sir Clifford (1907–82) English pianist who was well known for his skilled playing of the classics—Beethoven, Schubert, Brahms and, above all, Mozart.

cycle a series or sequence of pieces of music, by a single composer, which have a common THEME or idea.

cymbalo *see* **dulcimer**.

cymbals PERCUSSION INSTRUMENTS comprising two metal plates which are held in the hands and clashed together. They are mounted on stands for JAZZ and POPULAR MUSIC DRUM KITS, where they are operated by pedals or struck with sticks.

czárdás a Hungarian dance with two parts (a slow section and a fast section) that alternate.

Czerny, Karl (1791-1857) Austrian-born composer and piano teacher who was taught by BEETHOVEN and in turn taught LISZT. He published many influential books on piano playing.

czimken a Polish dance, similar to the COUNTRY DANCE.

D

D (1) the second NOTE of the SCALE of C major. (2) abbreviation for DOMINANT, and for doctor (as in D.Mus., Doctor of Music).

da capo (*Italian*) "from the head"; it is an instruction to repeat the beginning of the piece. Abbreviation: DC.

Dallapiccola, Luigi (1904-75) Italian pianist and composer whose work includes anti-fascist songs, for example, *Canti di prigionia* ("Songs of Captivity") and several operas, including *Il Prigioniero,* (*The Prisoner*) and *Ulisse* (*Ulysses*), and two ballets.

dal segno (*Italian*) "from the sign," i.e. go back to the point in the music marked by the relevant symbol and repeat the music which follows it. abbreviation: DS. (*See* APPENDIX).

damp to stop the vibrations of an instrument by touching it, or part of it, for example the strings of a HARP, the skin of a DRUM.

Dämpfer (*German*) *see* **mute**.

Damrosch, Walter Johannes (1862-1950) American composer and conductor of German birth, who was particularly noted for conducting works by WAGNER. He was conductor of the METROPOLITAN

110

OPERA, New York (1885–91, 1900–1902), founded his own company, the Damrosch Opera Company, and was a pioneer of symphonic radio broadcasting. He composed songs, two cantatas, and operas, the best-known of which include *Cyrano de Bergerac*, *The Scarlet Letter*, and *The Man Without a Country*. His brother, **Frank Heino Damrosch** (1859–1937), and his father, **Leopold Damrosch** (1832–85), were also notable conductors and musicians.

dance music if not the original FORM of music in a country, dance has played an important part in the origin of form. It is conceivable that the first idea of RHYTHM, whether in poetry or music, was suggested by dance; and it is certain that all PERCUSSION INSTRUMENTS were invented and employed to mark the steps in dancing. Since dancing was a religious rite as well as a social diversion with primitive peoples, the first attempts at singing were probably guttural grunts, rising or falling in tone as the dancers became more excited and their movements more rapid, or slackening as their vigour diminished. American Indian dance and that of tribal Africa are of this type. Dancing formed part of the religious ritual of the Jews, Greeks, and Romans, but there soon came to be a distinction between the religious dances and those meant for social entertainment. Ancient secular dances were largely gymnastic and intended for exercise, or mimetic to convey emotion by gesture; and the various dances in Greece were so highly specialized that there is reason to believe they included a form of entertainment closely corresponding to the modern *ballet d'action,* which developed in Italy in the sixteenth century.

During the early ages of Christianity, dancing was not wholly discouraged, but probably because of the pagan origin of dance and its connection with pagan worship rhythm was ignored in the songs used in Christian worship. At any rate, secular music became rhythmic long before church music, which had reached its final perfection in form in the sixteenth century. As secular songs were nearly always in some dance rhythm, leaders of rebellion against the religious authority of Rome would adapt their HYMNS and CHORALES to popular music, and this soon reacted on the older church music.

There is a remarkable similarity in the dance rhythms of all European races, however different they may be in name. In various forms, these rhythms have perpetuated themselves in the SONATA and SYMPHONY from the earlier orchestral SUITES, which were merely various dances brought together so as to give an agreeable sense of variety. Modern composers, even more than those of the classic period, borrow freely from the dance tunes of every nation, and the WALTZ has taken its place along with the GAVOTTE, SARABANDE, SCHERZO, CONTREDANSE, and MINUET in the severest forms of music.

Dankworth, John (1927–) English composer and jazz musician who started his musical career as a clarinettist. His popular Johnny Dankworth Seven combination was followed by a full-scale jazz orchestra founded in 1953, which became world famous and constantly featured his wife, the well-known singer Cleo Laine. His many compositions include such works as *Zodiac Variations* for his orchestra, a piano concerto, a string quartet, an opera-ballet, *Lysistrata*, and film scores for, among others, *Saturday Night and Sunday Morning* (1960), *The Servant* (1963), *Accident* (1967) , and *10 Rillington Place* (1970).

Daphnis et Chloë a ballet by RAVEL, based on a Greek legend, which was commissioned by the impresario Sergei Diaghilev (1872–1929)with choreography by Michel Fokine (1880–1942). It was first performed in 1912 and includes pieces for chorus as well as orchestra.

Dargomizhsky, Alexander Sergeivich (1813-69) Russian composer who was largely self-taught. His works include the operas *The Russalka* and *The Stone Guest*, unfinished at his death but completed by CUI in 1872. He also wrote songs and orchestral fantasias.

Davies, Sir Peter Maxwell (1934—) English composer and one of the MANCHESTER SCHOOL. Many of his compositions are influenced by medieval techniques. Since 1971 he has lived in the Orkney Islands, which have provided inspiration, especially by way of the works of the Orkney poet, George Mackay Brown (1921–), in his settings of *From Stone to Thorn* for soprano and chamber ensemble, and *Solstice of Light* for choir and organ. As well as writing operas, notably *Taverner*, and orchestral pieces, he has also composed film music, for example for Ken Russell's *The Devils* (1971).

Davies, Sir Henry Walford (1869–1941) Welsh composer and organist, who became MASTER OF

THE KING'S MUSICK in 1934. He is best known and remembered for his music for festivals. In 1974 he wrote *Everyman* for the Leeds Festival, and in 1908 *Solemn Melody* for the tercentenary of the birth of the poet John Milton. In 1917 he was appointed Director of Music to the Royal Air Force, and in 1918 wrote the well-known and stirring *Royal Air Force March-past*. He was knighted in 1922.

Davis, Carl (1937–) American composer who came to England in 1960. His highly successful scores for films and television include, for television, *The Naked Civil Servant* and *The World at War*. He was specially commissioned to write the music for the brilliant silent cinematic epic of 1927, Abel Gance's *Napoléon*. The score for another silent classic, D. W. Griffiths's *Intolerance*, followed. In 1981 he wrote the music for the film *The French Lieutenant's Woman*.

Davis, Sir Colin (1927-) English conductor who is especially associated with the works of MOZART, STRAVINSKY, BERLIOZ and TIPPETT. He was knighted in 1978.

Davis, Miles (1926-91) black American jazz trumpeter and band leader who was a devotee of Charlie PARKER. He was one of the most influential of all contemporary jazz players and was especially well known for his "cool" style. He made numerous recordings, which include *Sketches of Spain* and *Miles Ahead*.

DC *see* **da capo**.

Death and the Maiden (Der Tod und das Mädchen) a SONG by SCHUBERT to words by

Matthias Claudins, composed in 1817; also a string quartet in D minor by Schubert, which incorporates VARIATIONS on this song or LIED.

Death and Transfiguration (Tod und Verklärung) a SYMPHONIC POEM by Richard STRAUSS. It was first performed in 1889.

Death in Venice an opera by BRITTEN to a libretto, based on the novel by Thomas Mann (1875–1955), by Myfanwy Piper.

Debussy, Claude Achille (1862-1918) French composer who was one of the most influential of his era. He lived in Russia and Italy before settling in his native France and was friendly with the IMPRESSIONIST painters, whose ideals he admired and whose style he attempted to imitate in music. The poet Stéphane Mallarmé (1842–98) was also a friend and he "illustrated" his poem in *Prélude à l'après-midi d'un faune;* the orchestral piece considered to be one of his greatest. His opera *Pelléas et Mélisande* took him ten years to write and was partly inspired by his reaction to the music of WAGNER. His work is powerfully suggestive, but is nevertheless meticulously constructed.

Debussy's principal works include: NOCTURNES, *La Mer, Printemps* and PRÉLUDE À L'APRÈS MIDI D'UN FAUNE (orchestral pieces); *Suite bergamasque, Pour le piano* and *Études* (for piano); *L'Enfant prodigue* (choral work); and PELLÉAS ET MÉLISANDE (opera). He also wrote various pieces of chamber music and many songs.

début (*French*) "beginning," i.e. a first appearance.

decani *see* **cantoris**.

decibel one tenth of a BEL, a unit for measuring

SOUND. A decibel represents the smallest change in loudness that can be detected by the average human ear.

deciso (*Italian*) literally "decided," i.e. with decision or "play firmly".

decrescendo (*Italian*) "decreasing," i.e. getting gradually softer.

de Falla *see* **Falla, Manuel de**

degree a step of a SCALE; the position of each NOTE on a scale is identified by its degree.

Delibes, (Clément Philibert) Léo (1836-91) French composer of opera and organ pieces who was also a teacher. His best known works include the ballet, COPPÉLIA and the opera LAKMÉ.

delicatamente (*Italian*) "delicately."

delicato (*Italian*) "delicate."

Delius, Frederick (1862-1934) English composer, born of German parents who had settled in Bradford. His father refused to admit to his son's musical talents and pushed him into a career as a businessman. He lived in Florida as an orange-grower for a time, but returned to Europe and became friendly with many artists and composers, including RAVEL and the painter Paul Gauguin (1849–1903).

He visited Norway and became a close friend of GRIEG, who greatly influenced his compositions. In Britain, his music was slow to be recognized but was championed by Sir Thomas BEECHAM. Delius was happily influenced by the music he heard wherever he travelled and hints of SPIRITUALS and Norwegian folk songs are evident in some of his works. He is considered a ROMANTIC composer and his works tend to be robust, frequently demanding large orchestras.

His principal works include: *Over the hills and far away, Appalachia,* BRIGG FAIR, and ON HEARING THE FIRST CUCKOO IN SPRING (for orchestra); A VILLAGE ROMEO AND JULIET, and *Fennimore and Gerda* (opera); and several choral works and pieces of chamber music.

Deller, Alfred George (1912–79) English COUNTER-TENOR who prompted a revival of interest in early English songs, especially those of PURCELL and DOWLAND, and also of seventeenth-century lute songs and madrigals. To promote these, he formed the Deller Consort in 1948. Musicians who composed for his voice include BRITTEN, who wrote the part of Oberon in *A* MIDSUMMER NIGHT'S DREAM for him, FRICKER, and RUBBRA.

Dello Joio, Norman (1913-) American composer, pianist and organist. He has written operas, including *The Ruby* and *The Trial at Rouen*, as well as organ, choral and piano music.

Del Mar, Norman (1919-) English conductor particularly associated with twentieth-century music. He is a guest conductor with many international orchestras.

de Reszke, Jean *see* **Reszke, Jean de.**

de Sabata, Victor *see* **Sabata, Victor de.**

descant (1) a soprano part, sometimes improvised, sung above a HYMN TUNE while the tune itself is sung by the rest of the congregation or CHOIR (2). (2) (spelt **discant** by music scholars) a general term for all forms of POLYPHONY used from the 12th century. It replaced the still earlier diaphony or organum, in which a second or more PARTS progressed with the principal or SUBJECT by SIMILAR MOTION, and by permitting CONTRARY MOTION, paved the way for the development of COUNTERPOINT. Discant was soon defined by a set of rules, the object of which was to enable a singer to improvise a part to a subject, but improvisation or *Contrappunto alla mente* must soon have given way to written descant. Descant was double, triple, or quadruple, according to the number of parts added. Descant was also the name of the part added to the TENOR MELODY or CANTUS FIRMUS, or to the first part, if there were several. The descant was written above the tenor on its own CLEF.

Deutschland über alles (Germany beyond Everything) the German national anthem written just before the revolution of 1848 and sung to a tune by HAYDN. *See* EMPEROR'S HYMN.

deux temps (*French*) In 2/2 TIME. *Valse à deux temps* is a WALTZ which has only two dance steps to every three BEATS (1) of the BAR.

development the expansion or changing in some way of parts of a THEME of music that have already been heard, for example, by varying the RHYTHM or elaborating the PHRASE to give it new impetus.

Devil's Opera MACFARREN's two-act opera to words by F. Macfarren was first performed in 1838, at the COVENT GARDEN Opera House, London.

Diabelli, Anton (1781-1858) Austrian composer and founder of a firm of music publishers. He was a friend of BEETHOVEN and HAYDN and wrote many simple piano pieces himself. He is, however, best known for inviting a number of composers to write variations on a waltz tune of his own. Beethoven wrote 33, which have subsequently become known as the *Diabelli Variations*.

Diamond, David Leo (1915-) American composer whose works include eight symphonies as well as concertos for piano, violin and cello. *Rounds,* for string orchestra, is probably his best-known piece.

diapason (1) the term given to a family of ORGAN STOPS which are largely responsible for the TONE (3) of the instrument. (2) (*French*) a TUNING FORK; *diapason normal* means the same as CONCERT PITCH.

diatonic belonging to a SCALE. The diatonic NOTES of a major scale consist of five TONES (1) (T) and two SEMITONES (S), arranged TTSTTTS. *Compare* CHROMATIC.

Dibdin, Charles (1745-1814) self-taught English composer who wrote successful short operas, for example *The Padlock*, and numerous songs, one of the best known being "Tom Bowling." He also wrote a book, *The Musical Tour of Mr Dibdin*.

Dido and Aeneas an opera by PURCELL, first performed in 1689. The story, taken from Virgil, concerns the events leading up to the suicide of Dido, Queen of Carthage, after being deserted by Aeneas.

Dies Irae ("Day of Wrath") a part of the REQUIEM MASS, with a PLAINSONG MELODY which has often been used by ROMANTIC composers such as BERLIOZ, LISZT, and RACHMANINOV.

dièse (*French*) sharp.

Dietrich, Albert Hermann (1829–1908) German composer who wrote the successful three-act opera *Robin Hood*, a symphony in D minor, the concert overtures *Normannenfahrt* and *Rheinmorgen*, among other works for chorus and orchestra, incidental music to *Cymbeline*, and chamber music. He was a pupil of SCHUMANN and a friend of BRAHMS. He wrote *Recollections of Brahms* (1899) with J. V. Widmann. He was court chapelmaster at Oldburg and royal professor at Berlin.

digital (1) One of the KEYS on the keyboard of a PIANO or ORGAN. (2) In sound recording, a method of converting audio or analogue signals into a series of pulses according to their voltage, for the purposes of storage or manipulation.

diminished interval a PERFECT or MAJOR INTERVAL reduced by one SEMITONE by flattening the upper NOTE or sharpening the lower one.

diminished seventh chord a CHORD which covers a MINOR SEVENTH diminished by one SEMITONE, i.e. C-B flat diminished to C-A. (This is in fact equivalent to a major sixth, but the term "diminished seventh" is often used.) It is frequently employed as a means of TRANSITION (1) into another KEY.

diminished triad a MINOR TRIAD in which the FIFTH is flattened (diminished), for example in the KEY of C major, C-E-G flat.

diminuendo (*Italian*) "diminishing," i.e. getting gradually quieter.

diminution the shortening of NOTE TIME-values, so that a MELODY is played more quickly, usually at double speed.

d'Indy *see* **Indy, Vincent d'**.

direct a sign placed at the end of a line or page of old music that indicates the PITCH of the following NOTE or notes.

discant *see* **descant**.

discord a CHORD or combination of NOTES which creates an unpleasant or jarring sound that needs to be resolved.

dissonance the creation of an unpleasant sound or DISCORD.

Dissonance Quartet a string quartet in C major by MOZART, composed in 1785, so named because of the dissonance of the opening section.

divertimento (*Italian*) an eighteenth-century term for a piece of music that was intended to be a light entertainment, i.e. a diversion. MOZART wrote many divertimenti.

divertissement (*French*) (1) a short ballet incorporated into an opera or play. (2) a short piece that includes well-known tunes taken from another source. (3) a DIVERTIMENTO.

divisé (*French*) *see* **divisi**.

divisi (*Italian*) "divided"; a term used to indicate that, where a PART is written in double NOTES, performers should not attempt to play all the notes but should divide themselves into groups to play them. It is particularly used in music for STRINGS.

division (1) a seventeenth-century type of VARIATION in which the long NOTES of a MELODY were split up into shorter ones. (2) an obsolete term for long vocal RUNS used by composers such as BACH and HANDEL.

Dixie a song of national interest in the USA,

121

although "Dixie's Land" refers to the Southern States only. It was first made known in 1859 or 1860 by Bryant's Minstrels, and was announced as a "walk around" by Daniel Emmett. In 1861 a song of the same name and to the same tune, words by Albert Pike, went the rounds of the Confederate Army, and became very popular. The title may have been adoped in compliment to a New York slaveholding family named Dixie.

"Dixieland" a simple form of traditional JAZZ which originated in New Orleans at the start of the twentieth century.

do (*Italian*) *see* **doh**.

dodecaphonic Relating to dodecaphony, the TWELVE-NOTE SYSTEM of composition.

"Dog" Waltz *see* **Minute Waltz**.

doh the spoken name for the first NOTE of a MAJOR SCALE in TONIC SOL-FA.

Dohnányi, Ernö *or* **Ernst von** (1877-1960) Hungarian composer and pianist who travelled the world giving recitals and eventually settled in the USA. His compositions tended to follow the German, rather than Hungarian, tradition, and he is best known for his *Variations on a Nursery Theme* (for piano and orchestra). He also wrote three operas, *The Tenor*, *Aunt Simona*, and *The Tower of Voyvod*, and three symphonies, amongst other pieces.

dolce (*Italian*) "sweet" or "gentle."

dolcissimo (*Italian*) "very sweet."

dolente (*Italian*) "sorrowful."

Dolmetsch, Arnold (1858–1940) French-born

musician and early-instrument-maker and-restorer of Swiss origin, who settled in England in 1914 at Haslemere, where he set up his workshop. He made and restored such old instruments as harpsichords, clavichords, lutes, viols, and recorders. He and family members performed, and in 1950 he established an annual festival for the playing of early music on original instruments. It is because of his efforts that the recorder is so popular today. His son, **Carl Dolmetsch** (1911–), continued the management of the workshop and also became the leading recorder player of the day.

doloroso (*Italian*) "sorrowfully."

dominant (1) the fifth NOTE above the TONIC of a MAJOR or MINOR SCALE. (2) the name given to the RECITING NOTE of GREGORIAN CHANTS.

Domingo, Placido (1941-) Spanish tenor of international repute and immense popularity, who is particularly well known for performing in Italian operas, although he has a repertoire of more than 40 roles. His dramatic portrayal of romantic heroes is superb in roles such as Cavaradossi in TOSCA, Rodolf in *La* BOHÈME, and Othello.

Don Carlos an opera by VERDI to a French libretto by François Joseph Méry and Camille du Locle. The story tells of Don Carlos, the heir to the Spanish throne, who falls in love with Elisabeth de Valois, who is destined to marry his father. It was first performed in 1867.

Don Giovanni (full title: *Il dissoluto punito, ossia Don Giovanni*, The Rake punished, that is, Don Juan) a comic opera by MOZART to a libretto by

Don Pasquale

Lorenzo da Ponte. The story concerns the amorous adventures of the legendary Don Juan, who at last meets a dramatic demise by the hand of the statue of a vengeful father. It was first performed in 1787.

Don Pasquale a comic opera by DONIZETTI, who also wrote the libretto with Ruffini. The story tells of an old bachelor, Don Pasquale, who is tricked into a false marriage contract in a successful plot that will persuade him to allow his nephew to marry his beloved.

Don Quixote (1) a tone poem by Richard STRAUSS, based on the novel by the Spanish writer Miguel de Cervantes Saavedra (1547–1616), first performed in 1898. (2) an opera by MASSENET, first performed in 1910. (3) a suite by TELEMANN.

Donizetti, Gaetano (1797-1848) a prolific Italian composer who wrote no fewer than 75 operas, some serious, others comic. Many of his compositions are considered superficial, but some are perennial favourites, in particular DON PASQUALE, LUCIA DI LAMMERMOOR, LUCREZIA BORGIA, and *La Favorita*.

doppio (*Italian*) "double," as in *doppio movimento*, meaning "twice as fast."

Dorian mode a term applied to the ascending SCALE which is played on the white keys of a PIANO beginning at D.

dot a MARK used in musical NOTATION. When it is placed after a NOTE, it makes the note half as long again; when it is placed above a note it indicates STACCATO.

124

dotted note *see* **dot**.

double (1) a word used to describe certain instruments that are built an OCTAVE lower than normal, for example a double BASSOON (also called a "contrabassoon") is built an octave lower than a standard bassoon. (2) a term used to describe a type of VARIATION found in seventeenth-century French instrumental music in which MELODY NOTES are embellished with ornamentation.

double bass the largest and lowest-pitched of the bowed string instruments. It used to have three strings but now it has four (sometimes five).

double counterpoint COUNTERPOINT in which the two PARTS can change places, i.e. the higher can become the lower and vice versa.

double fugue (1) a FUGUE with two SUBJECTS. In one type of double fugue both subjects are introduced at the start; in another type the second subject appears after the first and the two are eventually combined.

Dowland, John (1563-1626) English composer and lute player who was famous as a performer during his lifetime and who is now considered to be a great and innovative composer of songs. He published four volumes of airs and a celebrated collection of twenty-one instrumental pieces called *Lachrimae*. His son, **Robert Dowland** (*c*.1585–1641), followed in his father's footsteps and also became a noted lutenist and composer.

down-beat the downward movement of a conductor's BATON or hand which usually indicates the first BEAT of a BAR.

down bow in the VIOLIN or other stringed instrument, the drawing down of the BOW over the strings giving the greatest volume of TONE (3).

Doxologia Magna (*Latin*) the "Gloria in Excelsis Deo." *See* GLORIA.

D'Oyly Carte, Richard (1844-1901) English impresario who brought together GILBERT and SULLIVAN and subsequently founded the D'Oyly Carte Opera Company to perform their operas, for which he built the Savoy Theatre in London.

Dream of Gerontius, The an ORATORIO by ELGAR which, along with the *Enigma Variations*, established his reputation as a great composer. Set to the words of a poem by Cardinal Newman, its first performance, conducted by Hans RICHTER in Birmingham, was a disappointment due to lack of rehearsal, but two years later, in 1902, in Düsseldorf it was a triumph. It has been regarded ever since as a masterpiece among oratorios.

Dreigroschenoper, Die *see* **Threepenny Opera**.

drone a PIPE that sounds a continuous NOTE of fixed PITCH as a permanent BASS. The BAGPIPES, for example, have several drone pipes. Also, a similar effect produced by stringed instruments fitted with "drone strings".

drum a PERCUSSION INSTRUMENT of which there are numerous types, including BASS DRUM, SIDE DRUM, TABOR, TENOR DRUM and TIMPANI. Most drums consist of a hollow metal or wood cylinder over which is stretched a skin. Sound is produced by beating the skin with drumsticks or with the hands.

drum kit a set of DRUMS and CYMBALS that are arranged in such a way that they can all be played by one person sitting on a stool. Some of the instruments (such as the BASS DRUM) are played with a foot PEDAL, but most are struck with sticks or wire brushes. Drum kits are used by JAZZ and POP drummers and can vary enormously in size.

Drum Roll Symphony the name given to HAYDN's Symphony No. 103 in E Flat Major, which twice features a KETTLEDRUM in the first movement.

DS abbreviation for DAL SEGNO.

due corde (*Italian*) literally "two strings"; a term used in VIOLIN music indicating that a PASSAGE that could theoretically be played on one string should nevertheless be played on two to produce the desired effect.

duet a combination of two performers or a composition for such a pair, for example, piano duet.

Dufay, Guillaume (*c.*1400-74) Flemish composer who was the most important of his time. Although he wrote some secular songs, he is best known for his church music and masses, for example *L'Homme armé*, based on a secular folk song.

Dukas, Paul (1865-1935) French composer and critic who was at first influenced by the works of WAGNER but became increasingly drawn to the IMPRESSIONIST movement. His output was comparatively small but includes some of the most important works of the early twentieth century, such as the scherzo for orchestra, *The* SORCERER'S APPRENTICE, the opera *Ariadne and Bluebeard*, and the ballet *La Péri*.

dulcimer *or* **cymbalo** an ancient instrument which was introduced to Europe from the East in the Middle Ages. It consists of a shallow box over which strings are stretched. The instrument is placed on the knees and the strings are struck with small HAMMERS. In the USA, an instrument similar to the ZITHER is sometimes called a dulcimer.

dulcitone a keyboard instrument containing TUNING FORKS which are struck with HAMMERS, as in a PIANO.

Dumbarton Oaks Concerto a concerto in E flat major for fifteen instruments by STRAVINSKY. It is so called because it was first performed, in 1938, at Dumbarton Oaks, the estate in Washington, DC, belonging to the American patron Robert Woods Bliss, who commissioned it.

dumka a Slavonic folk BALLAD or lament, which may have a fast middle section.

Dunstable, John (*c*.1385-1453) English musician, astrologer and mathematician of whose early life very little is known. However, he is considered one of the most important composers of the fifteenth century and was probably one of the first to write instrumental accompaniments to church music.

Duparc, Henri (1848–1933) French composer and pianist who, owing to ill health from an early age, composed little. His fifteen songs, however, set mainly to poems by Charles Baudelaire (1821–

67), notably "Invitation au voyage," are of the highest quality and established his reputation for sheer lyricism.

duple time a form of musical TIME in which the number of BEATS in a BAR is a multiple of two, for example 2/4 (2 CROTCHETS) and 6/8 (6 QUAVERS in two groups of three).

duplet a group of two NOTES of equal value which are played in the time normally taken by three.

Du Pré, Jacqueline (1945-1987) celebrated English cellist who was renowned worldwide for her interpretation of ELGAR's Cello Concerto. In 1967 she married the conductor Daniel BARENBOIM, but her life was cut tragically short by multiple sclerosis.

dur (*German*) "major," as in MAJOR KEY.

Dussek, Jan Ladislav (originally **Dusik**) (1760-1812) Czech pianist and composer who earned a reputation as a virtuoso performer in his own lifetime. He was a prolific composer and his works include twenty-eight piano sonatas and fifteen piano concertos as well as many sonatas for violin and flute.

Dvořák, Antonin (1841-1904) a Czech composer of modest origins who learned to play the violin at an early age. He went on to become a viola player with the Prague National Theatre, with which he stayed for eleven years. His talent for composing was encouraged by BRAHMS, who helped to get some of his pieces published. He travelled to England, where he was fêted, and to the USA, where he stayed for three years. In the USA he was influenced by black music, reflected in the AMERICAN QUARTET, and this, coupled

129

with homesickness, inspired him to write his most famous, and last, symphony, the 9th, entitled FROM THE NEW WORLD. When he eventually returned to Czechoslovakia, he concentrated on writing symphonic poems and operas. All Dvořák's work is carefully constructed, yet fresh and exciting. BRAHMS, SMETANA and WAGNER influenced his work, but so too did his love of folk music.

His principal works include operas such as *The Devil and Kate*, *Armida*, and, most popular of all, the story of the water sprite *Rusalka* with its beautiful aria "O Silver Moon"; choral works—a Stabat Mater, *The Spectre's Bride*, and a Te Deum; nine symphonies, the magnificent cello concerto; many chamber music compositions, piano pieces, among them the well-known *Slavonic Dances*, and songs.

Dylan, Bob [originally Robert Allen Zimmerman] (1941–) American FOLK and ROCK singer and songwriter. Influenced by Wood GUTHRIE, he became the most prominent "protest" folksinger in the 1960s with sonts such as "The Times They Are A-Changing'." He later took up rock music.

dynamic accents ACCENTS which correspond to the regular RHYTHM of a piece of music, as indicated by the TIME SIGNATURE.

Dyson, Sir George (1883-1964) English composer and teacher who for a time studied in Italy and Germany. His works include one symphony and several cantatas, such as *The Canterbury Pilgrims*. He was knighted in 1941.

E

E the third note (MEDIANT) of the SCALE of C major.

écossaise abbreviation of *danse écossaise*, i.e. "Scottish dance," although in fact the term has little to do with Scottish dancing and merely refers to a quick dance in 2/4 TIME.

Egk, Werner (1901-83) German composer and conductor who was influenced by STRAVINSKY. His important works include the operas PEER GYNT, *Irish Legend* and *The Government Inspector*. He also wrote ballet and choral music.

Eighteen-Twelve (The Year 1812) a concert overture by TCHAIKOVSKY, written in 1882 to commemorate the seventieth anniversary of Napoleon's retreat from Moscow. It includes *La* MARSEILLAISE and optional parts for cannon, church bells and a MILITARY BAND.

eighth-note (US) a QUAVER.

Eine kleine Nachtmusik, *see* **Kleine Nachtmusik, Eine.**

Einem, Gomried von (1918-) Austrian composer who was born in Switzerland. He is most noted for his operas *Danton's Death* and *The Old Lady's Visit*, performed at GLYNDEBOURNE in 1973, and the ballet *Princess Turandot*. He has also written orchestral and choral pieces.

electronic instruments a generic term for instruments that convert electrical energy into sound, such as the SYNTHESIZER.

Elektra an opera in one act by Richard STRAUSS to a libretto, based on Sophocles's *Electra*, by Hugo von Hofmannsthal (1874–1929). The story concerns the consuming desire for revenge of Elektra on her mother, Clytemnestra, for the death of her father, Agamemnon. Given the axe that slew their father, Orestes, brother of Elektra, kills both Clytemnestra and her husband and former lover, Aegisthus. Elektra in her mad joy dances ever more frenziedly to her death. The opera was first performed in 1909.

Elgar, Sir Edward William (1857-1934) English composer who had no formal musical training but learned from his father, who ran a music shop and was a part-time piano tuner. For a time Elgar earned a living teaching the violin, and it was not until his famous piece for orchestra, ENIGMA VARIATIONS, was first performed in London in 1899 that his reputation as a composer was assured. The next fifteen years of his life were the most fruitful, and he wrote many impressive works, among them the oratorios *The* DREAM OF GERONTIUS and *The Kingdom*; two symphonies, and the violin and cello concertos. The work for which he is most popularly known, No. 1 of the set of five POMP AND CIRCUMSTANCE Marches, popularly known as "Land of Hope and Glory", was first performed in 1901. He was knighted in 1904 and created a baronet in 1931.

Although Elgar was an overtly ROMANTIC composer, he was an undoubted master of orchestration. His Roman Catholic faith and his love of England were lasting influences throughout his life. Unlike many of his contemporaries, Elgar realized the potential of the gramophone and he made several recordings of his own work.

His principal works include: *The Apostles, The Dream of Gerontius* (oratorios); *Coronation Ode, The Spirit of England* (choral works); FALSTAFF (a tone poem); the Violin Concerto and the Cello Concerto; *Enigma Variations*. In addition, he wrote many pieces for orchestra, chorus and organ. He was appointed MASTER OF THE KING'S MUSICK in 1924.

Elisir d'Amore, L' (The Love Potion) an opera by DONIZETTI to a libretto by F. Romani. The story tells of a poor youth who buys a love potion (elixir) from a quack doctor; this turns out to be nothing more than wine, but love results none the less. The beautiful tenor aria "Una furtiva lagrima" is a highlight of the opera.

Ellington, Edward Kennedy "Duke" (1899-1974) American jazz composer, pianist and band leader whose experiments with jazz (such as his jazz impressions of classical pieces) opened up new horizons for the genre. He was called "Duke" because of his aristocratic air. His most memorable compositions among the hundreds he wrote include *Mood Indigo, Take the "A"-Train, Concerto for Cootie* and *Creole Rhapsody*.

embouchure (1) the mouthpiece of a BRASS or WIND INSTRUMENT. (2) the correct tensioning of the lips and facial muscles when playing woodwind and brass instruments to create good TONE (3).

Emperor's Hymn Joseph HAYDN's setting of a hymn written by Lorenz Leopold Haschka embodies the patriotic feeling aroused in Austria by the excesses of the French Revolution. It was first sung on February 12, 1797, at the Emperor's birthday and became the Austrian national anthem. *See also* DEUTSCHLAND ÜBER ALLES.

encore (*French*) literally "again"; the call from an English audience (the French equivalent is in fact BIS) for more music. If the performance does continue, the additional music is also known as an "encore."

end pin *see* **tail pin**.

Enescu, George (1881–1955) Romanian composer who studied in Vienna and at the Paris Conservatoire under the directorship of Gabriel FAURÉ. There he won first prize for the violin and went on to become a virtuoso violinist widely known both for his playing and as a conductor. His compositions are redolent of Romanian national music and include three symphonies, two Romanian rhapsodies, and chamber music. He also wrote an opera, *Oedipe*.

enharmonic intervals INTERVALS that are so small that they do not exist on keyboard instruments; an example is the interval from A sharp to B flat.

Enigma Variations (**Variations on an Original Theme**) a famous work for orchestra by ELGAR, first performed in 1899. The enigma may be an unheard theme (possibly the Scottish ballad "Auld lang syne"), and thirteen of the variations are dedicated to friends whose personalities he attempted to portray in the music; the fourteenth is devoted to himself.

ensemble (*French*) literally "together"; a term meaning a group of players or singers, a MOVEMENT in OPERA for several singers, or the precision with which such a group performs together.

Entführung aus dem Serail, Die (The Abduction from the Harem) a comic opera with spoken dialogue by MOZART to a libretto by Gottlieb Stephanie after a play by Christoph Friedrich Bretzner. Constanze and her maid Blonde are imprisoned in the palace of the Pasha Selim. The plan to rescue them by their lovers Belmonte and Pedrillo is foiled by the vigilance of Osmin, the steward of the palace, who has fallen in love with Blonde. But the Pasha, although discovering Belmonte to be the son of an old enemy, shows mercy, and all four are set free. The opera was first performed in 1782.

entr'acte (*French*) the music played between the acts of a play or OPERA. *See also* ACT TUNE, INTERLUDE, INTERMEZZO.

episode (1) in A FUGUE, a PASSAGE that connects entries of the SUBJECT. (2) in A RONDO, a contrasting section that separates entries of the PRINCIPAL THEME.

equal temperament a convenient, but technically incorrect, way of tuning a keyboard in which all SEMITONES are considered equal, for example F sharp and G flat are taken to be identical NOTES when theoretically they are not. Such a system makes complex MODULATIONS practicable.

equal voices

equal voices works for women's or men's or boys'
VOICES (2) are said to be for equal voices, and when
male and female voices are used in combination
they are said to be mixed.

Erlkönig (The Erl-King) a setting of Goethe's
ballad by SCHUBERT, who wrote it when he was
eighteen.

Ernani VERDI's fifth opera was first produced in
Venice in 1844, and presentations in the next two
years in London and New York assured Verdi's
future popularity abroad as well as in Italy. The
libretto is based on a drama by the French novelist Victor Hugo (1802–85), who strongly dis-
approved of its interpretation. The story is a
tangle of three-cornered rivalry for the hand
of Donna Elvira, conspiracy and uprising against
the king of Spain, and old Spanish honour,
which brings about the tragic suicide of the
heroic Ernani in the hour of his triumph.

Eroica (*Italian*) the popular, abbreviated title of
BEETHOVEN's Symphony No. 3 in E Flat Major,
composed and given its first performance in 1804.
It was originally entitled *Sinfonia grande
Napoléon Bonaparte*, but Beethoven was so an-
noyed that Napoleon proclaimed himself emperor
(in 1804) that he changed the name to *Sinfonia
eroica, composa per festeggiare il sovvenire d'un
grand' uomo* ("Heroic Symphony, composed to
celebrate the memory of a great man").

escapement the mechanism in a PIANO which
releases the HAMMER, allowing a string to vibrate
freely after it has been struck.

espressivo (*Italian*) "expressively."

esquisse (*French*) a "sketch," a title sometimes given to short instrumental pieces.

Estampes (*French*) (**Engravings**) a set of three piano pieces by DEBUSSY, which were first performed in 1904.

estampie (*French*) a form of dance accompanied by song, dating from the thirteenth and fourteenth centuries, which may constitute the oldest type of instrumental composition in Western music.

Esther an ORATORIO by HANDEL with words by Alexander Pope (1688–1744) and John Arbuthnot (1667–1735), based on Racine. It was originally composed as the MASQUE *Haman and Mordecai*, but the Bishop of London refused to allow a religious story to be performed on stage so Handel expanded it into an oratorio, which was first performed in 1732.

estinto (*Latin*) literally "extinct," i.e. as soft as possible.

étude (*French*) a "study" or piece of music evolved from a single PHRASE or idea. Studies are also written purely as exercises to improve technique or FINGERING.

Eugene Onegin an opera by TCHAIKOVSKY, who also wrote the libretto (from Aleksandr Pushkin; 1799–1837) in conjunction with Konstantin Shilovsky. The story concerns Tatiana, a romantic young girl who falls in love with the worldly-wise and wary Onegin, who rejects her. Twenty-six years later Tatiana, now married and a brilliantly assured woman of the world, is faced with Onegin's love for her. Although her feelings for him have never changed, she tells the grief-stricken Onegin that she must remain true to her husband, Prince Gremin. The opera was first performed in 1879, by students.

euphonium a large BRASS INSTRUMENT, a tenor TUBA, which is mainly used in BRASS and MILITARY BANDS.

eurhythmics a system of teaching musical RHYTHM by graceful physical movements. It was invented in 1905 by Émile JAQUES-DALCROZE, whose training institute was founded in Dresden in 1910 .

Evans, Sir Geraint (1922-92) Welsh baritone and opera producer of international repute. He was particularly famous for his roles in MOZART operas—as Leporello in DON GIOVANNI and Figaro in *The* MARRIAGE OF FIGARO—and also as VERDI's Falstaff. He was knighted in 1969.

evensong *see* **Nunc Dimittis**.

exposition (1) in the SONATA FORM, the first section of a piece in which the main THEMES are introduced before they are developed. (2) in FUGUE, the initial statement of the SUBJECT by each of the PARTS.

expressionism a term borrowed from the visual arts which implies the expression of inner emotions.

extemporization *see* **improvisation**.

F

F (1) the fourth note (or SUBDOMINANT) of the scale of C major. (2) in abbreviations, *f* means *forte* (loud); *ff*, *fortissimo* (very loud) and *fp, forte piano* (loud and then soft).

fa In the TONIC SOL-FA, the fourth degree in any major scale.

faburden literally "false bass" or "drone," the lowest of three voices in the English fifteenth-century improvised harmonization of PLAINSONG melody.

Façade an "entertainment" by WALTON, for six instruments (flute, clarinet, saxophone, trumpet, cello, percussion) and a narrator, of a series of poems by Edith Sitwell. It was first performed in 1923. Today it is played in orchestral form in two suites or performed as a ballet.

fado (*Portuguese*) a type of melancholy song with a guitar accompaniment.

Fairy Queen, The an operatic MASQUE with music by PURCELL. The words, which include spoken dialogue, are based on Shakespeare's *Midsummer Night's Dream*. It was first performed in 1692.

Falla, Manuel de (1876-1946) a Spanish com-

139

poser and pianist who was first taught the piano by his mother. He won a prize from the Madrid Academy of Fine Arts for his opera *La vida breve* (Life is Short) in 1905, but it was not performed. For a time he lived in Paris where he met, amongst others, RAVEL and DEBUSSY, who both influenced his compositions. He returned to Spain until the beginning of the Spanish Civil War when he left for Argentina, where he died. His work is full of Spanish vitality but he was rarely satisfied with his own work and his output was small.

His principal compositions include the ballets, *El amor brujo* (LOVE THE MAGICIAN), *El sombrero de tres picos* (The Three-cornered Hat); a work for piano and orchestra, *Noches en los jardines de Espana* (NIGHTS IN THE GARDENS OF SPAIN); and the piano piece *Fantasia betica*.

false relation in harmony, the occurrence of a note bearing an ACCIDENTAL, which is immediately followed, in another part, by the same note which does not bear an accidental, or vice versa.

falsetto (*Italian*) an adult male voice, used in the register above its normal range. It has often been used, to comic effect, in operas.

Falstaff (1) a comic opera by VERDI to a libretto by A. Boito (after Shakespeare's *Merry Wives of Windsor* and *Henry IV, Parts 1 and 2*) which tells of the revenge of two merry wives who, with the help of others, turn the tables on the faithless, prank-playing, obese knight—first by a ducking in the Thames, and next by a concerted attack on him in the forest at midnight. This was Verdi's last opera and was first performed at La Scala in

1893. (2) a symphonic study in C minor by ELGAR.

Fanciulla del West, La *see* **Girl of the Golden West, The**.

fancy *see* **fantasia**.

fandango a lively Spanish dance, thought to be South American in origin, in triple time. It is usually accompanied by guitar and castanets. Composers who have included or adapted the fandango form include GLUCK in his *Don Juan* ballet, MOZART in *The Marriage of Figaro*, and RIMSKY-KORSAKOV in his *Capriccio Espagnol*.

fanfare a flourish of trumpets, or other instruments (for example, the organ) that imitate the sound of trumpets.

fantasia (*Italian*) a piece in which the composer follows his imagination in free association rather than composing within a particular conventional form; when such a piece is played, it can sound as if it is being improvised. It is also a composer's adaptation or use of another's theme or of a known song, for example. VAUGHAN WILLIAMS's *Fantasia on a theme by Thomas Tallis*.

Fantasie (*German*), **fantaisie** (*French*) a FANTA-SIA.

Farewell Symphony (*Abschiedssymphonie*) HAYDN's symphony no. 45 in F sharp minor. Haydn intended the piece to be a hint to his patron, Prince Esterhazy, that his orchestra needed a holiday. In the last movement, the performers stop playing and leave one by one until just two violinists are left.

Fauré, Gabriel Urbain (1845-1924) a French composer, organist and teacher who was a pupil of SAINT-SAENS. He later taught composition (to RAVEL, among others). The last twenty years of his life were marred by deafness. He particularly excelled at writing songs and, although some of his pieces were influenced by WAGNER, they were all unmistakeably French.

His principal works include: *Promethée* and *Penelope* (operas); PELLÉAS ET MÉLISANDE (incidental music); *Ballade* (for piano and orchestra); and many songs, among them *La Chanson d'Eve* and *Le Jardin clos,* which are often heard. His Requiem Mass, today frequently performed and recorded, has become one of his best-known compositions. It demonstrates his strong religious faith and mixes plainsong and melodic, almost operatic, melodies to great effect.

Faust an opera by GOUNOD to a libretto by J. Barbier and M. Carré (after Goethe's *Faust*). Faust the philsopher pines for the gift of youth and is granted his desire by Satan (Mephistopheles) in return for his soul. With the help of Mephistopheles, Faust pursues the beautiful Marguerite. Having won her love, he betrays and deserts her. In prison for killing her child, Marguerite is visited by Faust and Mephistopheles. Realizing the latter's evil, she implores the mercy of God, and followed by Faust, who has recanted, both are borne to Heaven. It was first performed in 1859 and, rich in melody of arias, duets, chorus and ballet, remains one of the most popular of all operas.

Faust Overture, A an orchestral overture by WAGNER, first performed in 1844.

Faust Symphony, A a symphony for orchestra and chorus by LISZT, performed in 1857.

fauxbourdon (*French*) a fifteenth-century continental technique of improvising a bass part for a PLAINSONG melody.

Favorite, La (*La Favorita*), an opera by Donizetti to a libretto by Alphonse Royer, Gustave Vaëz and SCRIBE, tells the story of Ferdinand, a novice, who falls in love with Leonora, unknown to him the mistress of the king of Spain. He renounces his vows and declares his love for Leonora who has him brought blindfold to the island where she lives. Fearful of Ferdinand discovering her relationship with the king, Leonara at last persuades him to accept a commission in the army. Returning from the war a national hero, Ferdinand asks for Leonora's hand. The king, threatened with excommunication, reluctantly agrees to give up Leonora, and Ferdinand, still ignorant of her former live, marries her. Hearing at last the truth, Ferdinand retires in despair to his monastery. The opera had its first performance in Paris in 1840, and in 1843 was performed in London in English.

Feldman, Morton (1926-) an American composer who was greatly influenced by CAGE and the paintings of the abstract expressionists, such as Jackson Pollock, whose work he has attempted to emulate in music. He has experimented with alternative forms of music and music notation and his most noted pieces include *Projections* (chamber music) and *Vertical Thoughts* (keyboard pieces).

feminine cadence an ending in which the final chord occurs on a weak beat of the bar and not the more usual strong beat.

Ferguson, Howard (1908-) a Northern Irish composer and teacher who became a teacher at the Royal Academy in London. His works include the ballet *Chauntecleer, Diversions on Ulster Airs* for orchestra, as well as chamber and piano music.

fermata (*Italian*) *see* **pause**.

Ferrabosco, Alfonso (1543-88) an Italian composer who came to live in England when he was young and served at the court of Queen Elizabeth. He wrote several madrigals, motets and pieces for lute. He left England in 1578 upon being appointed to serve the Duke of Savoy, but his son Alfonso (*c.*1575-1628) remained and was employed as a violinist by James I. He composed music for MASQUES, and some fine instrumental music.

Ferrier, Kathleen (1912-53) an English contralto who was probably the most famous of her generation. The part of Lucretia in BRITTEN's opera RAPE OF LUCRETIA was written for her, and in 1946 she made her opera debut with its premiere at Glyndebourne. Her fame was assured with her singing of the role of ORPHEUS in Gluck's *Orféo* at Glyndebourne in 1947 and at Covent Garden in 1953. She was best known and loved for her song recitals, especially of BRAHMS and WAGNER, and was often accompanied by the conductor Bruno WALTER. She was made a CBE in 1953 but her brilliant career was cut short when she died of cancer shortly later that year.

festival of music now usually a regular event, often annual or biannual, for the performance and celebration of music. The first was held in Italy and was given by the combined musicians of the courts of Pope Leo X and Francis I of France at the meeting of their employers in Bologna in 1515. Originally, festivals were occasional affairs, held to celebrate some important event in a royal family. The first regularly recurring festival was probably that of the Vienna *Tonkünstler-Societät*, but the practice has since spread throughout the world. The best-known is the annual Salzburg festival.

ff *see* **F** (2).

fiddle (1) a generic term for a range of primitive stringed instruments played with a bow, as used in parts of Asia, Africa and Eastern Europe. (2) a colloquial term for a violin, especially in folk music.

Fidelio (full title: *Fidelio, oder Die eheliche Liebe,* Fidelio, or Married Love) BEETHOVEN's only opera, originally to a libretto by J. Sonnleithner. The story tells of the rescue of Florestan, a prisoner of Pizarro, by his wife Leonora, who is disguised as a jailer named Fidelio. Her fears and the dangers she must overcome before reaching her husband in the deepest of the prison dungeons are further compounded by the daughter of the jailer, Rocco, falling in love with her in her guise as a man. Beethoven wrote four LEONORA overtures for the opera. It was first performed, in the first of its three versions, in 1805 to an unethusiastic audience, but was hailed as an outstanding success when it was given in its final version in 1814.

Field, John (1782-1837) an Irish pianist and composer who was an apprentice to CLEMENTI. He travelled all over Europe demonstrating pianos and earned the reputation of being a virtuoso performer. He eventually settled in Russia, where he died. He invented the NOCTURNE form, which CHOPIN later developed. He composed more than twenty of these pieces as well as writing seven piano concertos and four sonatas.

fife a small flute still used in "drum and fife" bands.

fifth an INTERVAL of five notes (the first and last notes are counted) or seven semitones, for example, from C to G.

figure a short musical phrase that is repeated in the course of a composition.

figured bass the bass part of a composition which has numerical figures written below the notes to indicate how the harmony above should be played. It is, in effect, a type of musical shorthand in which the bass line and melody are written down while the numbers indicate which chords should be played. The system was used during the seventeenth and early eighteenth centuries.

fila la voce (*Italian*) to prolong a tone, swelling and diminishing it by degrees.

fin (*French*) "the end."

finale (*Italian*) (1) the last movement of a work. (2) the concluding section of an opera act.

Fingal's Cave (*alternative title* "The Hebrides") an overture in B minor by MENDELSSOHN, said to have been inspired by a visit to the Isle of Staffa.

It was first performed in 1832.

fingerboard the wood attached to the neck of stringed instruments of the viol and guitar families, against which the strings are stopped by pressing with the fingers.

fingering a type of notation that indicates which fingers should be used to play a piece of music.

Finlandia an orchestral tone-poem by SIBELIUS, nationalistic in character, containing melodies which resemble Finnish folk tunes. It was first performed in 1900 as an orchestral piece on its own. When first performed in 1899 it was as the finale of a set of patriotic "Tableaux from the Past." *See also* nationalism.

fino (*Italian*) "as far as," so *fino al segno* means "as far as the sign."

Finzi, Gerald (1901-56) an English composer who is best known for his musical settings of poems by Thomas Hardy, and for *Dies natalis,* for voice and strings.

fiochetto (*Italian*) "slightly hoarse."

fioco (*Italian*) "hoarse."

fioritura (*Italian*) "flowering," i.e. an embellishment.

fipple flute *see* **flageolet; recorder**.

Firebird, The a ballet with music by STRAVINSKY and choreography by Fokine and based on a Russian fairytale. It was the first of Stravinsky's ballets to be specially written for Diaghilev and the Ballets Russes, and was an immediate success. It was first performed in 1910.

Fireworks Music the popular title of HANDEL's *Music for the Royal Fireworks*, a suite of eight movements. It was originally composed for a wind band as an accompaniment to the fireworks display in London's Green Park, celebrating the Peace of Aix-la-Chapelle in 1749. Handel subsequently added string parts.

firing ringing all the bells in a tower together as an expression of joy, and of mourning, when muffled.

Fischer-Dieskau, Dietrich (1925-) a German baritone and conductor who is especially admired for his huge repertoire, including the *Lieder* of SCHUBERT and WOLF, BEETHOVEN, BRAHMS and STRAUSS. He was also outstanding in operatic roles, including Falstaff, Don Giovanni and Wozzeck.

Fitzgerald, Ella (1918–) an American jazz singer whose highly praised vocal range, rhythmic subtlety and clarity of tone mader her one of the most popular singers of her day. She toured widely, notably with BASIE, ARMSTRONG and ELLINGTON.

Fitzwilliam Virginal Book a highly important manuscript collection of keyboard music of the late sixteenth and early seventeenth centuries. There are 297 musical pieces covering most of the notable composers of the period.

Five, The the name given to a group of nationalistic nineteenth-century Russian composers who were known in Russia as *moguchaya kuchka* (The Mighty Handful). The five were RIMSKY-KORSAKOV, BALAKIREV, BORODIN, CUI, and MUSSORGSKY.

flageolet a small, end-blown FLUTE with six holes, four in front and two at the back, popular in the seventeenth century.

Flagstad, Kirsten (1895-1962) a Norwegian soprano who was especially famous for singing WAGNER roles. She first sang at the age of eighteen, and her first appearance outside Norway was at Bayreuth in 1933, when she sang Sieglinde in DIE WALKÜRE. Her beautiful and powerful voice made her every performance exceptional right up to her stage farewell in 1951 when she sang Isolde.

flamenco a generic term for a type of Spanish song from Andalusia, usually sad and often accompanied by guitar and dancing. Flamenco guitar playing relies heavily on the strumming of powerful, dynamic rhythms.

flat (1) a note which is lowered by one semitone as indicated by the flat sign (*see* Appendix). (2) a note (or notes) produced at too low a pitch and hence "out of tune."

Fledermaus, Die (The Bat) an operetta by Johann STRAUSS the Younger to a libretto by C. Haffner and R. Genée. Full of melody, comedy and confusion, the action takes place both inside and outside a gaol, the title referring to a fancy-dress costume which has a crucial effect on the plot. The operetta was first performed in 1874 and remains one of the most popular of Strauss's light operas.

Fliegende Hollander, Der *see* **Flying Dutchman, The**.

Flight of the Bumble-Bee, The the orchestral interlude in RIMSKY-KORSAKOV's opera *The Legend of the Czar Saltan,* which describes how a prince becomes a bee. It has been arranged for many different instruments.

Flotow, Friedrich von (1812-83) a German composer, popular in his own lifetime, who is best known for his operas such as *Alessandro Stradella* and MARTA (Martha). The latter, set in England in the time of Queen Anne, is the only one still performed today.

flue pipes all ORGAN pipes that have narrow openings, or flues, into which air passes; the other pipes are REED PIPES.

Flügelhorn (*German*) a soprano brass instrument invented by Adolphe SAX, similar to a bugle in shape, but with three pistons.

flute (1) the tranverse or German flute is a member of the WOODWIND family of instruments, although these days it is normally made of silver or other metal. One end of the instrument is stopped and sound is produced by blowing across the mouthpiece formed around an aperture cut into the side of the instrument at the stopped end. The pitch is controlled by means of a lever system. (2) the English flute is a beaked, end-blown, wind instrument with finger holes, now more usually called the RECORDER.

Flying Dutchman, The (*Der Fliegende Holländer*) an opera by WAGNER, who also wrote the libretto, in which the power and drama of the music were a foretaste of his later and even more eloquent genius. It tells the story of the Flying Dutchman, who is condemned by the Devil to wander the seas for ever, but allowed to step on shore every seven years to seek a woman whose love until death will free him. His meeting with Senta and their love for each other is thwarted by Senta's former lover, and the Dutchman sets sail once more. Senta, beside herself and vowing her undying love, casts herself from a cliff into the sea, and the Dutchman is redeemed by the love of Senta. It was first performed in 1843.

folia (*Portuguese*) "the folly," a wild and noisy Portuguese dance.

folk dance any dance, performed by ordinary people, in a pre-industrial society, that has evolved over the years and gained a traditional form. Folk dances differ widely in character and some have symbolic significance, such as war dances, fertility dances etc.

folk song properly, any song that has been preserved by oral tradition. Many composers and pop musicians have written new compositions that imitate old folk songs.

Force of Destiny, The *see* **Forza del Destino, La**.

forlana (*Italian*) an Italian dance from northern Italy that is especially associated with Venetian gondoliers.

form the structure of a composition. The basic elements of musical composition which define a given piece's form are repetition, variation and contrast. Examples of recognized forms include FUGUE, RONDO, SONATA FORM, etc.

forte (*Italian*) "loud"; abbreviation *f*.

fortepiano (*Italian*) an early word for PIANOFORTE. Not to be confused with *forte piano* (loud then soft).

fortissimo (*Italian*) "very loud." abbreviation *ff*.

Forty-Eight, The the popular name of BACH's forty-eight *Preludes and Fugues*, also called *The*

Well-Tempered Clavier.

forza (*Italian*) "force," so *con forza* means "with force."

Forza del Destino, La (The Force of Destiny) an opera on a grand scale by VERDI, with a libretto by Piave from a drama by the Duke of Rivas, it comes towards the end of the composer's middle period. The action takes place in Spain and Italy, and the story concerns Don Alvaro, about to elope with his beloved Leonora, who is discovered by her father, the Marquis, and who accidentally kills him. As he dies, the Marquis curses his daughter and adjures his son, Don Carlo, to avenge him. The lovers flee, Leonora in male garb to a monastery, Don Alvaro to the wars, hotly pursued by her brother. The two men then later meet on the battlefield, and as neither recognizes the other they strike up a friendship. Finding out Don Alvaro's true identity at last, Don Carlo resumes the pursuit, which ends before a cave where Leonora is hiding. A duel is fought, Don Carlo is vanquished, Leonora emerges from the cave and is stabbed to death by her brother before he dies. Don Alvaro in despair throws himself over a precipice.

forzato (*Italian*) "forced."

Foss, Lukas [originally Fuchs] (1922-) a composer of German parentage who settled in the United States in 1937. He has written several operas (for example *The Jumping Frog of Calaveras County*), two symphonies, two piano concertos, the oratorio *A Parable of Death*, *Recordare* for orchestra and *Round a Common Centre*.

Foster, Stephen Collins (1826–64) an American composer of popular songs. He was self-taught and wrote more than 200 songs with such appeal that they quickly became regarded almost as folk songs. They include "My old Kentucky Home," "Beautiful Dreamer," "Camptown Races," "Jeannie with the Light Brown Hair" and "Oh! Susanna."

Four Last Songs (*Vier letzte Lieder*) Four short, but exquisitely executed settings of poems for soprano and orchestra by Richard STRAUSS. They were his last compositions and were first performed in 1950.

Fournier, Pierre (1906–86) French cellist, one of the most talented of the age. His performances of works by BACH, BEETHOVEN and BRAHMS, and the cello concertos of ELGAR and DVORAK were norteworthy, and composers, among them POULENC and MARTINU, wrote works for him.

Four Seasons, The (*Le quattro stagioni*) a set of four beautifully evocative and perennially popular violin concertos by VIVALDI, depicting the seasons' changes of aspect and mood.

fourth an INTERVAL of four notes (including the first and last) or five semitones, for example C to F.

foxtrot a dance, originating in the USA, in duple time. It first became popular in the ballroom from about 1912 and was at the height of its popularity in the 1930s and 1940s, by which time it had acquired two variations, the quick and the slow foxtrot.

fp abbreviation for FORTE PIANO (*Italian*), meaning

"loud then soft."

Français, Jean (1912-) a French composer of operas, ballets and orchestral works, for example *Les Demoiselles de la nuit* (ballet), and *La Maine de Gloire*, an opera in four acts. He has also written chamber music, including a quintet for flute, harp and string trio.

Franck, César Auguste (1822-90) a Belgian composer and organist whose work is marked by its chromatic and romantic style. In his lifetime, it was as an organist of outstanding talent that he was hailed, and his playing gained for him the French Légion d'Honneur in 1885. His principal compositions include: *Ruth, La Tour de Babel, Rébecca* (oratorios); *Hulda, Ghiselle* (operas); and his brilliant *Variations symphoniques* (for piano and orchestra) for which he is probably most famed.

Frankel, Benjamin (1906–73) an English composer and violinist who was well known as an exponent and arranger. From the 1940s onwards, he wrote scores for more than one hundred films, among which are *The Years Between*, *A Kid for Two Farthings*, and *The Battle of the Bulge*. His serious music includes a violin concerto, eight symphonies, and sonatas for violin and viola.

Frankl, Peter (1935-) a Hungarian-born pianist who has been a British citizen since 1967. He is a member of a chamber music trio and is a renowned concert hall soloist.

Franz, Robert (1815-92) a German composer, admired by SCHUMANN and LISZT, who wrote more than 250 songs. He became deaf in 1868 and was forced to give up his music.

Frederick the Great (1712–86) Prussian king, composer and flautist who maintained a flourishing musical establishment at his court. Musicians who were members included Carl Philipp BACH, who served the king for a large part of his life. Frederick wrote more than a hundred compositions for the flute. Following a visit to the court in 1747, Johann Sebastian BACH dedicated *The Musical Offering* to the king. Frederick also established the Berlin Opera.

Freischütz, Die (The Freeshooter) Carl Maria von WEBER's operatic masterpiece, which is generally regarded as the first of the ROMANTIC operas. The music is melodic, dramatic, atmospheric and overall brilliantly expressive of the romantic-cum-supernatural story of Max the forester whose skill as a marksman has deserted him. As he must win a shooting contest to gain the hand of his beloved Agathe, he is persuaded to make a pact with the Devil in return for seven magic bullets. It was first performed in Berlin in 1821.

free reed a type of REED found in such instruments as the ACCORDION and HARMONICA. It consists of a small metal tongue that vibrates freely in a metal slot when air is blown over it. The pitch of the reed is determined by its thickness and length.

French horn *see* **horn**.

French sixth *see* **augmented sixth**.

Freni, Mirella (1935–) Italian soprano who, since her debut as Micaëla in CARMEN in 1955 and as Zerlina in DON GIOVANNI at Glyndebourne in 1960, has become enormously popular. Later she starred in, among others, *La* TRAVIATA, *La* BOHÈME, AÏDA, and OTELLO. She has also made notable recordings with the conductors ABBADO and Sinopoli.

Frescobaldi, Girolamo (1583-1643) an Italian composer who was one of the outstanding organists of his era. For much of his life he was organist at St Peter's Rome. He wrote many keyboard pieces, toccatas, arias and madrigals.

fret (*French*) one of a series of thin pieces of metal fitted into the wooden fingerboard of a stringed instrument to make the stopping of strings easier and more accurate. Each fret represents the position of a specific note. Frets are found on guitars, mandolins and banjos.

Fricker, Peter Racine (1920–90) an English composer who came to prominence in 1947 when he won the Alfred Clements Prize with a wind quintet. His symphony no. 1 won him the Koussevitsky Prize in 1950. In 1953 he followed Michael TIPPETT as director of music at Morley College, London. In 1965 he became a professor at the University of California. His music does show some influence of STRAVINSKY, BARTOK and SCHOENBERG. Other compositions are a violin concerto, a second and third symphony, *Fanfare for Europe* for trumpet, choral works, and *Sinfonia in Memoriam Benjamin Britten*.

Friml, Rudolf (1879–1972) Czech composer and pianist who went to the United States in 1906. He wrote music for the piano, including concertos and chamber music, but he is chiefly remembered for his operettas, immensely popular and frequently filmed. Some of the best known are *The*

Firefly, *Rose Marie*, and *The Vagabond King*.

"Frog" Quartet the nickname of HAYDN's string quartet in D major (1787); it is so called because the theme in the last movement sounds like croaking.

From the House of the Dead (*Z Mrtvého Domu*) JANACEK's last opera, which he did not quite complete himself. It used the theme of Dostoyevsky's *Memoirs from the House of the Dead* to present a powerful and compelling study of life in a Siberian prison camp.

From the New World the title of DVORAK's symphony no. 9 in E minor, composed in 1893. It was written while Dvorak was in the USA and is his impression of the country. It shows influences of black American music and the music of the American Indians.

front man the person who stands at the front of the stage during a performance of JAZZ and who is therefore the focus of the audience's attention. He or she is often, but not always, the leader or singer of the band.

frottola (*Italian*) literally "little mixture"; a type of Italian POLYPHONIC song that was popular in the fifteenth century.

fugue a contrapuntal composition for two or more parts (commonly called "voices") which enter successively in imitation of each other. The first entry is called the "SUBJECT" and the second entry (a fifth higher or lower than the subject) is called the "ANSWER." When all the voices have entered, the EXPOSITION is complete and is usually followed by an EPISODE which connects to the next series of subject entries. A COUNTER-SUBJECT is a melodic accompaniment to the subject and answer, and is often in DOUBLE COUNTERPOINT. A fugue may be written for voices, instruments or both. The form dates back to the seventeenth century. Possibly the greatest exponent of the fugue was Johann Sebastian BACH, and his *Art of Fugue* is the fullest statement of the form.

full close *see* **cadence**.

full organ a term used in ORGAN music to indicate that all the loud stops are to be used together.

funk a form of heavily syncopated, rhythmic black dance music, originating in the United States. The adjective, often used in JAZZ terminology, is *funky*.

fuoco (*Italian*) "fire," so *con fuoco* means "with fire."

Für Elise (For Elise) a BAGATELLE in A minor for piano by BEETHOVEN, written *c*.1810. The word "Elise" on the manuscript may have been an erroneous transcription of Therese; Beethoven was in love with Therese von Brunswick, among whose papers the score was found.

furioso (*Italian*) "furious."

Furtwängler, Wilhelm (1886–1954) German conductor and composer who was and is considered to be one of the great conductors of the twentieth century. Although he was not without critics of some of his treatment of German composers, he was generally thought to be unsurpassed in the operas of Wagner. After posts in Zurich, Strasbourg, Lübeck and Mannheim, he became conductor first of the Leipzig Gewandhouse Orchestra then of the Berlin Philharmonic, a post he held for twenty-three years, until 1945. He frequently conducted at Bayreuth and also at Salzburg. His somewhat equivocal attitude to the Nazi regime in Germany caused animosity, but his musical genius helped him to override this after World War II. As a composer his works include two symphonies, a piano concerto, chamber music and a *Te Deum*.

Fux, Johann Joseph (1663-1741) an Austrian composer, organist and theorist who specialized in church music. He was appointed court musician by Joseph I in 1700 and was intermittently Kapellmeister at St Stephen's Church in Vienna. He wrote over 400 works, including ten oratorios, fifty masses, and eighteen operas, one of which, *Costanza fortezza*, was written to mark the coronation of Charles VI as king of Bohemia in 1723.

fz abbreviation for FORZATO.

G

G the fifth note (or DOMINANT) of the scale of C major.

Gabrieli, Andrea (*c*.1517-86) an Italian organist and composer of madrigals, motets, Masses and instrumental pieces. His nephew, **Giovanni Gabrieli** (*c*.1557-1612), was also a noted composer, organist and teacher, who studied with his uncle. He became one of the greatest Venetian composers of motets.

Gade, Niels Wilhelm (1817-90) a Danish composer, organist and violinist, who travelled to Italy and Germany, where he was encouraged by MENDELSSOHN. His output was influenced by Mendelssohn and SCHUMANN, and his principal works include eight symphonies, six overtures and several cantatas, for example *The Crusaders*.

galant (*French*) "polite"; a term applied to certain graceful styles of court music, especially of the eighteenth century.

galanterie an eighteenth-century German term for a keyboard piece in the GALANT style.

galliard (*French*) a lively court dance, usually in triple time, which dates back to the sixteenth century.

galop a lively dance in duple time that originated in Germany and was popular in the nineteenth century.

Galway, James (1939-) a Northern Irish flautist and composer who has done much to popularize the flute with his many recordings and television appearances. Before he embarked on a solo career, he was principal flautist with several of the world's leading orchestras, notably the Berlin Philharmonic Orchestra. He has made many fine recordings, which include works by Johann Sebastian BACH and MOZART, as well as contemporary composers.

gamba abbreviation of VIOLA DA GAMBA.

gamelan a type of traditional orchestra found principally in Indonesia and South-East Asia. Although such an orchestra includes strings and woodwind instruments, it is the array of gongs, drums, chimes, xylophones and marimbas that produces the unique and highly complex rhythms of gamelan music. DEBUSSY was especially influenced by gamelan.

gamut (1) the note G on the bottom line of the bass clef. (2) an alternative (now obsolete) word for the key of G. (3) the whole range of musical sounds, from the lowest to the highest.

Garcia, Manuel (1775–1832) Spanish tenor whose singing career began in Seville and who was famous in his lifetime for his performances in ROSSINI operas, especially in the role of Count Almaviva in *The* BARBER OF SEVILLE, which he was the first to sing in 1816. He appeared many times both in Paris and in London, where he started a es, as well as in Italy. He intro-

school for singers, as well as in Italy. He introduced an Italian company to America for the first time, and thanks to him a New York audience saw MOZART's *Don Giovanni*. This company included his three children, all singers of renown: his daughter **Maria Malibran** (1808–36) was a contralto with a soperadded soprano register, which she used with such intelligence and spirit that she became the most celebrated female singer of her age. She died from injuries that she had concealed in order to sing after being thrown from a horse. His daughter **Pauline Viardot-Garcia** (1821–1910) was a mezzo-soprano with a great range, a composer and teacher who had a distinguished career before devoting herself to teaching and composition. Her works include songs, pieces for violin and three operas. His son **Manuel Garcia** (1805–1906) was a bass, and also a teacher. He was the first to investigate the voice scientifically and in the process invented the laryngoscope. From 1829 he devoted himself to teaching, his pupils including Jenny LIND, Mathilde MARCHESI and STOCKHAUSEN.

gavotte an old French dance, originally of the upper Alps, in 4/4 time, which usually starts on the third beat of the bar. It was favoured by LULLY in his ballets and operas and has been revived in the twentieth century by such composers as PROKOFIEV and SCHOENBERG.

Gay, John (1685-1732) an English poet and playwright who is best known for writing the words of the BEGGAR'S OPERA.

Gazza Ladra, La *see* **Thieving Magpie, The**.

Garden, Mary (1877–1967) Scottish soprano who was brought up in the US where she studied singing in Chicago. Her studies continued in Paris, where in 1900 she made a memorable debut when, due to the illness of the leading soprano in LOUISE, she replaced her. Two years later, at the request of Debussy she created the role of Mélisande in the first performance of PELLÉAS AND MÉLISANDE. Appearances in London followed, and in 1907 she returned to the US to sing the title role in MASSENET's opera *Thaïs* in its first performance in New York. From 1910 to 1931 she sang with the Chicago Opera Company and took over its directorship 1921–22, which financially was not a success. Charming and vivacious and enormously popular, other roles in which she shone included, Richard STRAUSS's SALOME, MANON and CARMEN.

gedämpft (*German*) "muted."

Gedda, Nicolai (1925–) Swedish tenor who since his debut in 1952 has sung and excelled in a wide variety of roles in all the leading opera houses. His first appearance at Covent Garden was in 1955 as the Duke of Mantua in RIGOLETTO. He was outstanding in the title role of BENVENUTO CELLINI in 1961 and came to be highly regarded and associated with French opera in general, although his appearances and recordings have embraced almost the entire tenor range. He also is esteemed as an interpreter of songs, in particular those of FAURÉ.

Geige (*German*) "fiddle" or "violin."

Geistertrio (*German*) (The Ghost Trio) the nickname of BEETHOVEN'S piano trio in D major. It is so called because of the sinister character of the slow movement, which Beethoven intended to use in an opera version of *Macbeth*.

Geminiani, Francesco (*c*.1679-1762) an Italian violinist who lived in Paris, London and Dublin. He had a highly successful solo career and wrote a ballet (*La foresta incantana*) and several impressive sonatas, trios and concertos. His book *The Art of Playing on the Violin*, was the first of its kind.

gemshorn *or* **chamois horn** (1) an early type of recorder made from the horn of an animal. It fell out of favour in the sixteenth century. (2) an organ stop with a light tone.

Generalpause (*German*) a rest of one or more bars for all the members of an orchestra.

Gerhard, Roberto (1896–1970) a Spanish composer of Swiss-French parentage. A student of GRANADOS and PEDRELL, and later SCHOENBERG, he was teacher of music and librarian at Barcelona from 1929 to 1938. He came to Britain after the Spanish Civil War, where he remained until his death. He was a leading exponent of SERIALISM, and among his compositions are an opera, *The Duenna*, based on the opera-play by Richard Sheridan (1751–1816), four symphonies, two ballets, *Algerías* and *Don Quixote*, a concerto for eight instruments that included an accordion, and a setting of *The Akond of Swat* by Edward Lear (1812–88) for mezzo-soprano and two percussionists.

German, Sir Edward [originally Edward German Jones] (1862-1936) a Welsh composer who is best known for the incidental music he wrote for Shakespeare's plays, for example *Henry VIII*. He also composed the operettas *Merrie England* and *Tom Jones*. He was knighted in 1928.

Germani, Fernando (1906–) Italian organist and composer, he is regarded as one of the leading organists of this century. From 1948 to 1959 he was organist at St Peter's Rome, and has given recitals worldwide.

German sixth *see* **augmented sixth**.

Gershwin, George (1898-1937) an American composer and pianist who wrote songs for many musical shows, often in conjunction with his lyricist brother, **Ira Levin** (1896–1983), such as *Lady, Be Good, Funny Face* and *Girl Crazy*. His most famous concert piece is *Rhapsody in Blue* for piano and jazz orchestra. He also wrote An American In Paris, a rhapsody for orchestra that later was featured in a highly successful film, together with several of his best-known songs, and the opera PORGY AND BESS, whch was first performed in 1935 and is enjoyed worldwide to this day.

Gesualdo, Carlo (*c*.1560-1613) an Italian composer and lutenist who was also Prince of Venosa. He wrote outstanding madrigals and motets which were far in advance of their time. He gained a certain notoriety for ordering the murder of his wife and her lover. STRAVINSKY was just one twentieth-century composer who was captivated by his compositions.

Gevaert, François Auguste (1828–1908) Belgian composer and musical historian and theorist who was appointed musical director of the Paris Opéra in 1867 and in 1871 director of the Brussels Conservatoire. His operas and operettas were successful in his lifetime, but he is best remembered for the treatises he wrote on instrumentation, orchestration and harmony, and his editions of early music, notably *Gloire d'Italie*.

Ghedini, Giorgio Federico (1892–1965) Italian composer. He taught at the conservatoires of Turin, Parma and Milan, composing between 1939 and 1956 a series of operas, among them *Billy Budd* in 1949 and, inspired by Max Beerbohm (1872–1956), *The Happy Hypocrite* in 1956. He also wrote works for orchestra, including a symphony, piano concertos, chamber and church music, and transcriptions of music by Johann Sebastian Bach, Monteverdi and Frescobaldi.

Ghiauvorov, Nicolai (1929–) Bulgarian bass who made his debut in 1955 as Don Basilio in *The* Barber of Seville, since when he has become internationally known as one of the great bass voices of the twentieth century. He has been particularly excellent in the roles of Mephistopheles in Gounod's Faust, Verdi's King Philip in Don Carlos, and peerless as Boris in Mussorgsky's Boris Godunov.

"Ghost" Trio *see* **Geistertrio.**

Giannini, Vittorio (1903–66) American composer of operas, concertos for piano and organ, a *Stabat Mater*, and a symphony entitled *In Memoriam Theodore Roosevelt*. He wrote nine operas in all, among them *Lucidia*, *The Scarlet Letter* (after the novel by Hawthorne), *The Taming of the Shrew* (based on Shakespeare's play), and *The Servant of Two Masters* (based on the play by Goldoni), which was performed the year after his death.

Gianni Schicchi a one-act comic opera by PUCCINI, the third of the TRITTICO. Implored by the family of the newly dead Buoso Donati to revoke his will, leaving a fortune to a monastery, the cunning lawyer, Schicchi, takes advantage of them by hiding the body and pretending to be Donati. He dictates a new will bequeathing the bulk of the fortune to himself. The angry relatives are helpless, but to please his own daughter, who is in love with Donati's nephew, Schicchi gives the house to the lovers.

Gibbons, Orlando (1583-1625) an important English composer and organist who wrote motets, madrigals and stately anthems (for example, *This is the Record of John*). His son, **Christopher Gibbons** (1615–76), was also an organist and composer of note.

Gibbs, Cecil Armstrong (1889-1960) an English composer who is best known for his songs. He also composed an opera as well as a choral symphony, *Odysseus*.

Gibson, Sir Alexander (1926–) Scottish conductor, who worked at Sadler's Wells 1954–59 as conductor then music director. In 1959 he became principal conductor of the Scottish National Orchestra, a post he held for the next twenty-five years. In 1962 he was prime mover in founding Scottish Opera, of which he was artistic director until 1984. Under his directorship the company gave many fine performances, notably of the RING

cycle, *The* Trojans by Berlioz, Pelléas et
Mélisande by Debussy, and the first British production of *Volo di Notte* by Dallapiccola, an opera
based on the St Exupéry novel *Vol de Nuit*. Thanks
to him, interest in and enthusiasm for music was
rekindled and energized in Scotland. For his
valuable contributions to the music scene, he was
knighted in 1977.

giga (*Italian*) *see* **gigue**.

Gigli, Beniamino (1880–1957) Italian tenor. One
of the finest who ever lived, he has been described
as "*the* tenor" and was hailed in New York in the
1930s as the successor to Caruso. He sang all over
the world, his longest engagement being twelve
seasons as the Metropolitan New York. His voice,
always beautiful, was heard at its peak in *La
Bohème*, *L'Africaine*, Ponchielli's *La Gioconda*,
as Cavaradossi in Tosca, and in Giordano's *Andrea
Chénier*, and thanks to his many recordings it can
still be appreciated today.

gigue (*French*) a lively dance or jig.

Gilbert, William Schwenk (1836–1911) a British writer whose successful collaboration, as librettist, with the composer Arthur Sullivan produced a string of highly successful and ever-
popular comic operas.

Gillespie, "Dizzy" (1917-93) an American jazz
trumpeter and band leader, with a distinctive
trumpet, the bell of which stuck out at an angle.
He was a virtuoso performer of bebop. He earned
his nickname "Dizzy" because his playing reached
such virtuoso heights.

Ginastera, Alberto (1916-) an Argentinian composer whose earlier works had a traditional and nationalistic flavour. In later works he has explored modern techniques and styles. He is particularly well known for his operas, *Don Rodrigo, Bomarzo* and *Beatrix Cenci,* but he has also written ballets, concertos and several pieces for voice and orchestra.

Gioconda, La (The Joyful Girl) PONCHIELLI's best-known opera is based on Victor Hugo's play *Angelo, Tyrant of Padua* and was first produced in 1876 in Milan. La Gioconda is a ballad or street singer in love with Enzo, a man of noble birth disguised as a seaman. Enzo has lost his love, Laura, to the powerful noble Alvise. But upon seeing and recognizing Laura again despite the mask she wears, Enzo finds his love for her is as strong as before. Barnaba, an evil spy of the Inquisition, wants La Gioconda for himself. Repulsed by her, Barnaba has her old blind mother imprisoned for witchcraft. She is saved by the supplications of Laura. La Gioconda, who has recognized Enzo's love for Laura, decides to kill her. But discovering that it was Laura who has had her mother set free, she helps the lovers to escape by promising herself to Barnaba, but when Barnaba presents himself, she stabs herself with a dagger.

giocoso (*Italian*) "merry."

gioioso (*Italian*) "joyful."

Giordano, Umberto (1867-1948) an Italian composer of the VERISMO kind of operas, for example, *Mala vita, Andrea Chenier*, a tragedy set at the time of the French Revolution and *Fedora*.

Girl of the Golden West, The (*La Fanciulla del*

West) an opera by PUCCINI to a libretto by G. Civinini and C. Zangarini. Set in the Wild West at the time of the Gold Rush, the story tells of Minnie, the owner of a bar in a mining camp, who falls in love with Dick Johnson, a bandit. He is discovered to be hiding in the loft of Minnie's cabin by Jack Rance, the sheriff, who is also in love with Minnie. Rance agrees to play poker with Minnie for Johnson's freedom. Minnie cheats and wins the game. Johnson goes free but is later captured in the forest and condemned to be hanged by Rance and the miners. Minnie rides to the scene to plead for his life. The men relent and Minnie and Johnson go off together to start a new life. The opera was first performed in New York in 1910 with CARUSO singing the part of Johnson.

gittern the old English name for a kind of four-stringed GUITAR played with a plectrum.

Giulini, Carlo Maria (1914–) Italian conductor with an international reputation in both concert hall and opera house. His distinguished career, starting in 1946 as musical director of Radio Italiano, led in 1953 to his appointment as musical director of La Scala, Milan, and from 1958 to 1967 he was guest conductor at Covent Garden. From 1969 to 1972 he was co-conductor with Sir Georg SOLTI of the Chicago Symphony Orchestra and was music director of the Los Angeles Philharmonic Orchestra 1978–84. In 1982 he was again at Covent Garden conducting *Falstaff*, the opera that had first introduced him to Britain in 1955 when he directed the Glyndebourne Company at the Edinburgh Festival.

giusto (*Italian*) "exact," as in *tempo giusto*, which can mean either "strict time" or "appropriate speed".

Glass, Philip (1937-) an American composer, a pupil of Nadia BOULANGER and Ravi SHANKAR, whose work shows the influence of oriental music and SERIALISM. His music tends to use minimal themes, repeated over and over again, but the overall effect is often richly textured, with great poise. His work includes pieces for voice and a broad variety of instruments, as well as the operas *Einstein on the Beach* and *Akhnaten, Glass Pieces*, a ballet, incidental music and film scores.

glass harmonica at its simplest, a set of goblets that are played by rubbing a moistened finger around the rims. This idea was taken further by the American scientist and statesman Benjamin Franklin (1706-90), who invented a glass harmonica in which a gradated series of glass bowls is fixed to a rotating spindle and played with the fingers. Both BEETHOVEN and MOZART wrote music for the instrument, which produces a high-pitched humming sound.

Glazunov, Alexander Konstantinovich (1865-1936) a Russian composer who was a pupil of RIMSKY-KORSAKOV. His first symphony, written when he was seventeen, was hailed as a masterpiece but he never entirely fulfilled his promise. In all, he wrote eight symphonies and seven quartets, and other compositions include the ballet *Raymonda*.

glee a simple, unaccompanied composition for male voices in several sections.

glee club a club formed for the purpose of singing GLEES. The first glee club had its beginning in meetings held in a private house in London in 1783, at which part songs were sung after dinner. It was organized as the Newcastle Coffee House and 1787 and lasted until 1857. Glee clubs became very popular in the USA.

Glière, Reinhold Moritzovich (1875-1956) a Russian composer of Belgian descent. His most important works include the opera *Shah Senem* and the ballet *Red Poppy*.

Glinka, Mikhail Ivanovich (1804-57) a Russian composer, influenced by folk-music. His best known works are his operas *A Life for the Tsar (Ivan Susanin)* and *Ruslan and Ludmilla*. He composed numerous other works including orchestral pieces and chamber music.

glissando (*Italian*) "sliding"; a rapid sliding movement up or down a scale.

Glockenspiel (*German*), **Campanelli** (*Italian*) literally "a play of bells," an instrument, produced in a variety of sizes, comprising steel bars of different lengths that are arranged like a keyboard; each bar sounds a different note. Played with hammers, it produces sounds that have a bell-like quality. It is used in orchestras and military bands (in which it is held vertically).

Gloria (*Latin*) the first word of *Gloria in excelsis Deo* (Glory to God in the highest), the hymn used in both Roman Catholic Masses and in Anglican services. Many composers have set it to music. It is also the first word of the doxology *Gloria Patri* (Glory be to the Father), sung after a psalm.

Gloriana BRITTEN's opera was commissioned for Elizabeth II's coronation in 1953 and first presented in her presence at a gala performance. The libretto, by William Plomer (1903–73) is based on Lytton Strachey's *Elizabeth and Essex*.

glottis the aperture in the LARYNX by which the voice is controlled.

Glover, Jane (1949–) British conductor and musicologist, who first conducted at the Wexford Festival in 1975, followed by appearances at Glyndebourne, where in 1980 she became chorus master. In 1984 she was appointed artistic director of the London Mozart Players, and in 1988 conducted at Covent Garden. Television appearances include a series of programmes on the history of the orchestra and one programme on MOZART's life.

Gluck, Christoph Willibald [von] (1714-87) a German composer who, after studying and working in Prague, Rome, London and Paris, eventually settled in Vienna. He is best known for his operas, especially ORFÉE ET EURIDICE, which revolutionized the Italian style of opera by simplifying it and relating the music to the drama. In a later opera, *Alceste*, Gluck set down in a preface his intentions and aims. In all, he wrote some 100 operas (many are now lost) and he had a profound influence on the works of MOZART and BEETHOVEN. He also wrote ballets and assorted pieces of miscellaneous music.

Glyndebourne a small, but prestigious, opera house established by John Christie (1882-1962) on his estate near Lewes, in the heart of the

English countryside. An annual opera festival has been held there since 1934. A new building to house the opera is in the process of construction.

Gobbi, Tito (1915–84) an Italian baritone who was one of the greatest singing actors of the twentieth century. He had a reputation as a professional that was second to none, and he reached the height of his powers in such roles as Scarpia in PUCCINI's *Tosca* and VERDI's *Falstaff*. He also appeared in twenty-six films.

God Save the Queen/King the British national anthem and possibly one of the best-known tunes in the world. However, the authorship of both the tune and the words remains obscure.

Golden Cockerel, The (*Le Coq d'Or*) Rimsky-Korsakov's last opera, which was banned in his lifetime owing to alleged adverse references to the tsar, Nicholas II. The libretto is based on a poem by Pushkin. King Dodon, weak, lazy and unwilling to deal with affairs of state, and surrounded by enemies threatening his kingdom, is offered by the Astrologer a golden cockerel with magic powers. It will foretell the future and also warn of approaching danger by crowing from the highest spire. The delighted king, relieved of all responsibilities, takes to his bed. When the cockerel sounds the alarm Dodon sends his two sons. They do not return, and when the cockerel crows again the king sets out himself to find both sons dead and his army sadly harassed. On a hillside is a tent that Dodon fears holds a fearsome enemy, but from it steps a beautiful woman, the queen of Shemakha. She agrees to be the king's bride, but on their triumphal return the Astrologer demands the queen as payment for the magic bird. Furious, Dodon kills the Astrologer and in turn is killed by the cockerel. Darkness falls over the kingdom, and both bird and queen vanish.

Gondoliers, The an operetta by SULLIVAN with a libretto by GILBERT. The tale concerns the Duke of Plaza Toro and two gondoliers who find themselves jointly reigning as kings. It was first performed at the Savoy Theatre, London, in 1889.

gong a PERCUSSION INSTRUMENT that originated in the Far East. Gongs are made in many sizes and shapes, but an orchestral gong consists of nothing more than a large sheet of metal with a pronounced rim. Sound is produced by striking it with a hammer.

Goodman, Benny (1909-86) an American jazz clarinetist who formed the original SWING band in 1934. Although jazz was his first love, he was also a notable classical player and gave virtuoso performances of MOZART concertos. Pieces by BARTOK and COPLAND were commissioned by him.

Goossens, Eugene (1893-1962) an English conductor and composer who worked all over the world, championing the cause of modern music. His works include the operas *Judith* and *Don Juan de Manara,* as well as two symphonies, the oratorio *Apocalypse*, and various pieces of incidental and chamber music. His brother, **Leon Goossens** (1897–1988), was a distinguished oboist, and his father, **Eugène Goossens** (1867–1958), was an influential conductor, with the Carl ROSA company and at Covent Garden.

gopak *or* **hopak** a Russian folk dance originally from the Ukraine, set to lively music in 2/4 time.

gorgheggi (*Italian*) trills.

gosba an Arabian FLUTE.

gospel song a type of popular religious song originated by black American slaves who sang hymns to pulsating BLUES rhythms. Such songs, which are still sung fervently today in religious services, were one of the originating forces of JAZZ.

Götterdämmerung *see* **Ring des Nibelungen, Der**.

Gottschalk, Louis Moreau (1829-69) an American composer and pianist who earned fame as a virtuoso performer whilst travelling the globe. He also composed memorable pieces, such as *The Aeolian Harp* and *The Dying poet* for piano.

Gould, Glenn (1932–82) a Canadian pianist with an international reputation and a very broad repertoire. He was noted in particular for his interpretation on the piano of works by Johann Sebastian BACH.

Gould, Morton (1913-) an American composer, conductor and pianist, who composed a concerto for tap dancer and orchestra. He also wrote three symphonies, *Cowboy Rhapsody*, a ballet *Fall River Legend*, and several musicals including *Delightfully Dangerous* and *Billion Dollar Baby*.

Gounod, Charles François (1818-93) a French composer whose original ambition was to become a priest. He lived in England for a period and was the first conductor of the Royal Albert Hall Choral Society, renamed in 1888 the Royal Choral Society. He is best known for his opera FAUST, although he wrote many other pieces, including cantatas, oratorios and symphonies. Apart from *Faust*, he wrote eleven other operas, none of which came up to the *Faust* standard, although *Mireille* has charm and lyrical simplicity.

Gow, Nathaniel (1763–1831) Scottish composer, trumpeter and violinist, who belonged to a musical family. His collections of dance tunes he published himself. His best-known tune was written for the song "Caller Herrin'."

GP an abbreviation of GENERALPAUSE.

grace note an ornamental, extra note, usually written in small type, used to embellish a melody.

gradation by degrees of the SCALE.

Gradus ad Parnassum (Steps to Parnassus) (1) a work on counterpoint by FUX. (2) a collection of piano studies by CLEMENTI.

Grainger, Percy Aldridge [originally George Percy] (1882-1961) an Australian-born composer and pianist who settled in the USA in 1914. He was influenced by GRIEG into collecting folk songs and is best known for composing the orchestral pieces *Country Gardens* and *Handel in the Strand, Shepherds Hay*, and *Molly on the Shore*.

Granados [y Campiña], Enrique (1867-1916) a Spanish composer, pianist and conductor. Much of his work, which includes seven operas and two symphonic poems, has a distinctly Spanish flavour. His best work is *Goyescas*, piano pieces based on Goya paintings and tapestries. This music also was used in a opera performed in New York in 1916.

grand a term that, when prefixed to a SONATA,

SYMPHONY or CONCERTO, means in complete classic form; when prefixed to ORCHESTRA it means complete; when used of PIANO works it means of the largest proportions, volume, and form; in OPERA it means of serious purport and sung throughout. *See also* GRAND OPERA.

grandioso (*Italian*) "in an imposing manner."

grand opera a term originally used to distinguish serious opera, sung throughout, from opera that contained some spoken dialogue. The term is now also used to describe a lavish production.

grand orchestre (*French*) a full orchestra.

grand orgue (*French*) a great ORGAN (as opposed to a swell organ, etc).

grand piano *see* **pianoforte**.

Grappelli, Stephane (1908–) a French JAZZ violinist, a founder member of the Quinttete du Hot Club de France (1934–39), noted for his highly individual, sliding style. He has made any recordings and performed with Yehudi MENUHIN.

Graun, Karl Heinrich (1704–59) a German composer and singer. He wrote some thirty operas (for example, *Montezuma*) as well as cantatas, church music and piano concertos. His brother, **Johann Gottlieb Graun** (*c*.1702–71), was also a noted composer and violinist.

grave (*Italian*) "Slow" or "solemn".

grazia (*Italian*) "Grace".

grazioso (*Italian*) "Gracefully".

Great C Major Symphony the name given to SCHUBERT's symphony no. 9; so called to distinguish it from his shorter 6th symphony, also in C major.

great stave a STAVE created by pushing the stave with the treble clef and the stave with the bass clef closer together so that both clefs can be located on one exaggerated stave.

Greensleeves an old English tune that probably dates from the reign of Henry VIII. It is referred to in Shakespeare's play *The Merry Wives of Windsor*, and became a favourite song with the Cavaliers in the English Civil War. The tune was adapted by VAUGHAN WILLIAMS in his orchestral work *Fantasia on Greensleeves*, originally part of his opera *Sir John in Love*.

Gregorian chant a term that refers to the large collection of ancient solo and chorus PLAINSONG melodies preserved by the Roman Catholic Church. They are named after Pope Gregory I (c.540-604) but date from about 800. Until recently they were sung at specific ceremonies, such as baptism, Mass, etc.

Grieg, Edvard Hagerup (1843–1907) a Norwegian composer who started writing music at the age of nine. He travelled all over Europe, visiting England and Italy, where he met LISZT. Grieg remains perennially popular with twentieth-century audiences for his lyricism and atmospheric writing and his PEER GYNT (for orchestra) has frustrated cognoscenti, who have peristently panned it, by being a regular favourite. Much of Grieg's music gains its strength from its use of national idiom and, without doubt, he remains the most prominent of all Norwegian composers. His works include violin sonatas, piano pieces, choral works, compositions for orchestra (including *The Holberg Suite*), and many songs. His piano concerto is probably, apart from *Peer Gynt*, his best-known work and remains one of the most popular in the concert hall today.

Griffes, Charles Tomlinson (1884–1920) an American composer who was influenced by IMPRESSIONISM in music, particularly by the French composers. His works include the symphonic poem *The Pleasure Dome of Kubla Khan* and the dance drama *The Kairn of Koridwen*.

Grosse Fuge a fugue in B flat major for string quartet by BEETHOVEN. It was published as a separate work (Op. 133).

ground bass a BASS line that is constantly repeated throughout a composition, as a foundation for variation in the upper parts.

Grove, Sir George (1820–1900) an English scholar, editor and writer on music. He edited *The Dictionary of Music and Musicians,* the authoritative music dictionary that, many editions later, still bears his name. He was also the first director of the Royal College of Music. He was knighted for his achievements in 1883.

Groves, Sir Charles (1915–92) an English conductor of outstanding merit, and a noted champion of British music. He conducted many of the world's leading orchestras, including the Bournemouth Symphony Orchestra and the Royal Liverpool Philharmonic Orchestra. He was for two years music director of Welsh National Opera and of English National Opera 1978–79. He was knighted in 1973.

Grumiaux, Arthur (1921-86) a Belgian violinist

of international repute whose playing was especially admired by fellow violinists for its classical purity.

grupetto (*Italian*) literally, a "little group"; a general term used to describe various ORNAMENTS of one or more decorative notes.

G string the fourth STRING on the VIOLIN; the third on the VIOLA, CELLO, and GUITAR; and the first on the DOUBLE BASS.

Guarneri *or* **Guarnerius** a famous family of violin-makers who were based in Cremona. The first member was Andrea, who was a pupil of NICOLA AMATI (with STRADIVARI). The greatest was Giuseppe (1687-1744).

guddok a Russian FIDDLE.

Guido Arezzo *or* **Aretinus** *see* **Aretinian syllables**.

guitar a plucked STRING instrument, which may have been introduced to Spain from North Africa. Unlike the LUTE, it has a flat back and usually carries six strings suspended over a fretted finger-board (twelve-string guitars were favoured by certain BLUES musicians, such as LEDBETTER). The acoustic ("soundbox") guitar has been played by classical, flamenco and folk musicians for generations, but the electric guitar is a comparatively new development. The body may be hollow (or "semi-acoustic") or solid, with "pick-ups" (electrically motivated resonators that respond to the vibration of the strings) mounted under the BRIDGE. The vibrations received by the pick-ups have to be electrically amplified or else they are virtually featureless. Electric guitars have a huge COMPASS, which has been exploited by JAZZ, POP and ROCK musicians.

Guntram an opera by Richard STRAUSS to a libretto he wrote himself. It was the first opera he wrote and was first performed at Weimar in 1894. Its plot concerns two thirteenth-century German knights who have taken vows of fidelity and obedience and of the love of one, Guntram, for Freihild.

Gurney, Ivor Bertie (1890-1937) an English composer and poet who suffered terribly during World War I. He never recovered his health and was eventually confined to a mental hospital, but he composed some memorable works, including the song-cycle for tenor and strings *Ludlow and Teme*.

gusto (*Italian*) "taste," so *con gusto* means "with taste."

Guthrie, Woody [originally Woodrow Wilson Guthrie] (1912–67) an American folksinger and writer. His songs, which attack racial bigotry and the economic exploitation of the poor and immigrants, include "This Land is Your Land" and "Pastures of Plenty," and were a strong influence on such 1960s "protest" singers as BAEZ and DYLAN.

H

H (*German*) B natural.

habanera (*Spanish*) a dance of Cuban origin with a powerful, SYNCOPATED RHYTHM; it is, however, most usually associated with Spain.

"Haffner" Symphony the Symphony in D by MOZART, so called because it was written for the Haffner family.

Haitink, Bernard (1929-) Dutch conductor with an international reputation and formidable repertoire, including, in particular, MAHLER. He has been a regular conductor at Glyndebourne and Covent Garden and was created an honorary KBE in 1977.

Halévy, Jacques François (1799-1862) French composer of operas and ballets, the most notable being *La Juive* (*The Jewess*; opera). He was also a teacher and instructed both GOUNOD and BIZET.

Hale *or* **Halle, Adam de la** *see* **la Hale, Adam de**.

half note (US) a MINIM.

half step (US) a SEMITONE.

Hallé, Charles (1819-95) German-born conductor and pianist who settled in Manchester in 1848 and founded the internationally famous Hall

Orchestra in 1857. He was knighted in 1888.

Hallelujah Chorus the name of several pieces of music, the most famous being that written by HANDEL which brings Part II of MESSIAH to a close.

halling a lively Norwegian dance, in 2/4 TIME, during which men leap high into the air.

hammer that part of the PIANO mechanism which strikes the strings; a mallet for playing the DULCIMER; the clapper of a BELL.

Hammerstein, Oscar (II) (1895-1960) American lyricist, responsible for numerous highly successful Broadway MUSICALS, written in collaboration first with Jerome KERN, then with Richard RODGERS.

Hammond, Dame Joan (1912–) New Zealand operatic soprano. Her recording of Puccini's Turandot was the first classic record to sell over a million copies.

Hammond organ the brand name of an electric ORGAN first produced by the Hammond Organ Company, Chicago, in 1935. The sound it produces is electronically manufactured and attempts to reproduce the sound of the PIPE ORGAN. It cannot be said to succeed in this, but its unique temperament has been exploited by JAZZ, POP and music-hall musicians the world over.

Hampton, Lionel (1913–) an American jazz vibraphonist and band leader. He began his career with Benny GOODMAN's bands in the late 1930s, and became renowned for his exuberant personality and gift for bringing skilled musicians together in bands of his own.

handbells bells, of various pitch, that are held

in the hands of a group of performers and rung in sequence to create a tune.

Handel, George Frideric [originally **Georg Frie-drich Händel**] (1685-1759) German-born com-poser who settled in England and took English nationality. His father was a barber-surgeon who sent his son to study law at Halle University, but the young Handel rebelled and became a violinist at the Hamburg Opera House, where his first operas, *Almira* and *Nero,* were produced. He lived in Italy for three years but settled in London in 1712. He readily found favour with the English court of Queen Anne and, subsequently, George I. His talent was allowed to flourish in England and he wrote some twenty operas. However, he even-tually abandoned the writing of "Italian" operas for commercial reasons, and instead composed oratorios. This process led to MESSIAH, possibly his greatest, and certainly his most well known, piece of music. During the last years of his life he was troubled with blindness.

Handel succeeded in amalgamating Italian and German styles and traditions with his own nota-ble originality. In his oratorios, in particular, he has given the world some of the most stupendous and magnificent music ever written. His princi-pal works include: the operas *Almira, Rodrigo, Agrippa, Rinaldo, Allessandro, Orlando, Arianna, Atlanta, Imeneo;* the *St John Passion;* the orato-rios SEMELE, *Esther, Israel in Egypt,* MESSIAH, *Samson, Hercules,* the *Triumph of Time and Truth;* the secular choral works ACIS AND GALATEA, *Ode for St Cecilia's Day;* the orchestral pieces

WATER MUSIC, FIREWORKS MUSIC; and many other pieces for harpsichord and chamber orchestras, in addition to songs and cantatas.

Hansel and Gretel an opera by HUMPERDINCK to a libretto by the composer's sister, Adelheid Wette. The story is taken from the tale by the Brothers Grimm. It was first performed in 1893.

hardanger fiddle a Norwegian VIOLIN used in FOLK music. It is somewhat smaller than an ordinary violin, and has four SYMPATHETIC STRINGS.

harmonica a small, FREE-REED instrument commonly called the "mouth organ." Although it is a small and apparently inconsequential instrument (often considered a toy), many BLUES and FOLK musicians have illustrated its potential by exploiting its emotive power. *See also* ADLER.

harmonic minor MINOR SCALE containing the minor sixth with the MAJOR SEVENTH, in which ascent and descent are without alteration.

harmonics the sounds that can be produced on stringed instruments by lightly touching a string at one of its harmonic nodes, i.e. at a half-length of a string, quarter-length and so on.

harmonium a small, portable REED-ORGAN which developed in the nineteenth century. Air is pumped to the REEDS (which are controlled by STOPS and KEYS) by PEDALS worked continuously by the feet.

harmony (1) the simultaneous sounding of two or more NOTES, i.e CHORDS. A harmonious SOUND is an agreeable or pleasant sound (CONCORD); but harmonization may also produce sounds which, to some ears at least, are unpleasant (*see* DISCORD).

(2) the structure and relationship of chords.

harp an instrument, of ancient origin, consisting of strings stretched across an open frame. It is played by plucking the strings, each of which is tuned (*see* TUNING) to a separate NOTE.

harpsichord a keyboard instrument, developed in the fourteenth and fifteenth centuries, in which the strings are plucked (not struck) by quills or tongues (PLECTRA). The tongues are connected to the KEYS by a simple lever mechanism. The harpsichord went out of favour during the late eighteenth century due to the introduction of the PIANO. However, the instrument has seen a revival in the twentieth century, and new compositions exploiting its "twangy" sound have been written for it.

Harris, Roy (1898-1979) prolific American composer who succeeded in amalgamating some of the qualities of American FOLK SONGS with modern composition methods. His works include sixteen symphonies and works for chorus and orchestra.

Harrison, George (1943–) English singer-songwriter who played lead guitar for the Beatles (1962–70). His songs with the group include "With a Little Help From My Friends" (i.e. drugs) and "Something." His work displays a fascination with Eastern religions and mysticism, for example "My Sweet Lord." He organized the "Concert for Bangladesh" of 1971, the first great rock charity show.

Hart, Lorenz [Milton] (1895–1943) American lyricist. His collaborations, around thirty in all, with the composer Richard RODGERS include *The Boys from Syracuse* (1938) and *Pal Joey* (1940).

Hauptwerk (*German*) a GREAT ORGAN, as distinct from a SWELL ORGAN etc. *See* ORGAN.

hautbois (*French*) literally "high" or "loud wood." *See* OBOE. From the Elizabethan period to the eighteenth century, the English equivalent was "hautboy."

Hawaiian guitar a style of GUITAR playing in which a steel bar is moved up and down the strings (as opposed to the more usual STOPPING of strings with the fingers) to produce a distinctive slurred sound. The guitar is usually played horizontally. Electrically amplified instruments are now frequently used.

Hawkins, Coleman (1904–69) American jazz tenor saxophonist. His recording of the ballad "Body and Soul" (1939) was regarded as a model of the SWING style by his peers.

Haydn, Franz Joseph (1732-1809) Austrian composer who, like many great musicians, started his career as a choirboy in Vienna. In 1761 he was employed by the aristocratic Esterházy family as an assistant KAPELLMEISTER, and then Kapellmeister from 1766. He stayed with the Esterházys for thirty years and, although he was committed to carrying out certain administrative duties, he was allowed time to compose. He gradually earned a reputation as an outstanding and original composer and he received many commissions, including one from the Concert de la Loge Olympique in Paris for six symphonies. By this time he was friendly with MOZART and the two composers had the highest regard for each other. When Prince Nikolaus Esterházy died in 1790,

Haydn was no longer required to live at Esterház (although his salary was maintained) and he took the opportunity to visit England, where he received more commissions, most notably from the impresario J. P. SALOMON for an opera, six symphonies and assorted other pieces of music. After a year, he returned to Vienna and bought a house (where he taught BEETHOVEN). He returned to London again in 1794 where he was fêted, and he wrote a further six symphonies for Salomon. In 1795 he rejoined the Esterházy household but his official duties were light and he concentrated on composing. Over the next six years, he completed six magnificent Masses and the great choral works *The* CREATION and *The* SEASONS. The last years of his life were uneventful and he wrote little, preferring to live quietly in Vienna.

Haydn is often called the father of the SYMPHONY because, although he did not invent it, he extended its range and expressive power, and each of his 104 symphonies is startlingly original. Later, his music was overshadowed by the works of Beethoven and Mozart and it was the mid-twentieth century before it was generally recognized how innovative and influential his compositions were. He produced a colossal amount of work and was never afraid to experiment with new ideas and techniques.

Haydn's principal works include: eighteen operas (for example *Il Mondo della Luna,* ARMIDA); 104 symphonies; eight oratorios and cantatas; eighty-four string quartets; fifty-two piano sonatas; twelve Masses; and forty-seven songs.

Haydn, Johann Michael (1737-1806) Austrian composer and the brother of Franz Joseph HAYDN. His works include twenty-four Masses, two Requiem Masses and many miscellaneous compositions for orchestra.

head voice the upper register of a VOICE (1), so called because the sound seems to vibrate in the head of the singer. *Compare* CHEST VOICE.

Hebrides Overture, The *see* **Fingal's Cave**.

Heckelphone a double-REED instrument which is effectively a baritone OBOE. It was used by Richard STRAUSS in his opera SALOME.

Heifetz, Jascha (1901-87) Russian-born violinist who became an American citizen in 1925. Noted for his technical mastery and his flamboyant and expressive interpretation, he had several works composed for him, for example by WALTON.

Heldentenor (*German*) literally, a "heroic tenor", i.e. a tenor with a strong voice suitable for WAGNER's heroic roles.

Heller, Stephen (1813-88) Hungarian virtuoso pianist and composer who travelled Europe giving recitals. He composed some 150 pieces for the piano, mainly using innovatory techniques.

Helmholtz, Hermann Ludwig Ferdinand von (1821-94) German physiologist and physicist who published highly important and influential books on sound theory. His work *On the Sensations of Tone,* which was first published in 1862, is the foundation of the modern theory of ACOUSTICS.

hemiola a RHYTHM in which two BARS in triple TIME are played as though they were three bars in DUPLE TIME.

hemiope a Greek FLUTE with three holes.

hemisemidemiquaver the sixty-fourth NOTE, i.e. a note with a value of a quarter of a SEMIQUAVER or ¹/₆₄th of a SEMIBREVE.

Hen, The the nickname given to HAYDN's Symphony No. 83 in G Minor. It is so called because in the first movement the oboes make a clucking sound.

Hendrix, Jimi [James Marshall Hendrix] (1942–70) American rock guitarist, singer and songwriter. With his trio, the Jimi Hendrix Experience, he became perhaps the most influential rock guitarist of the 1960s with his loud, exuberant style, for example in his *Purple Haze* album. He died of alcohol and drug abuse.

Henry VIII (1491-1547) the King of England from 1509-47. He is said to have been an accomplished musician, and he wrote a number of compositions, including songs and instrumental pieces, although probably not GREENSLEEVES.

Henze, Hans Werner (1926-) German composer who has never been tied down to a particular style and whose compositions are extraordinarily diverse. He was at first influenced by STRAVINSKY and SCHOENBERG, and he made a name for himself with the opera *Boulevard Solitude* in 1952. His political thinking moved dramatically to the far Left in the 1960s, and his music drama the *Raft of the Medusa* is dedicated to the South American revolutionary, Ché Guevara (1928–69). His works include operas, ballets, symphonies, concertos and choral pieces such as *Voices,* which has a text partly written by the Communist Vietnamese leader Ho Chi-Minh (*c*.1890–1969).

Herbert, Victor (1859-1924) Irish-born composer, conductor and cellist who settled in the USA. He is best known for his operettas (for example *Babes in Toyland*) but he also wrote a cello concerto, a symphonic poem and various pieces of orchestral music.

Here Comes the Bride *see* **Lohengrin**.

Heseltine, Philip *see* **Warlock, Peter**.

Hess, Dame Myra (1890–1965) an English pianist, who was a much acclaimed concert pianist and an influential teacher. Her transcriptions of BAROQUE music, particularly her version of Johan Sebastian BACH's "Jesu, Joy of Man's Desiring," were very popular.

heterophony (*Greek*) literally "difference of sounds," i.e. two or more performers playing different versions of the same MELODY simultaneously.

hexachord a SCALE of six NOTES which was used in medieval times.

Hierold, Louis Joseph Ferdinand (1791-1833) French composer of ballets and operas, for example *Zampa* and *Le Pré aux clercs*.

High Mass MASS that is sung throughout, as distinguished from Low Mass, which is said. In Latin, MISSA SOLEMNIS.

Highland fling a dance to the music of the strathspey (*see* REEL), 4/4 time, and takes its name from a peculiar kicking step or "fling".

Hindemith, Paul (1895-1963) German composer, teacher, conductor and virtuoso viola player. He was considered degenerate by the Nazis and stayed

Hindemith, Paul (1895-1963) German composer, teacher, conductor and virtuoso viola player. He was considered degenerate by the Nazis and stayed in the USA for the duration of World War II. He was ultimately revered as one of the most important and versatile musicians of his era. He was a great believer in making music that could be readily understood and he composed pieces for children and amateurs, as well as sophisticated concertos and operas. His principal works include: operas (for example, *Cardillac, News of the Day*); orchestral pieces (for example, *Symphonic Metamorphoses*); and many pieces for chamber orchestra. He also wrote several influential books on musical theory, such as the *Craft of Musical Composition*.

Hines, Earl [Kenneth] "Fatha" (1903–83) an American jazz pianist, band leader and songwriter. He became one of the most influential jazz pianists of the 1930s and 1940s, renowned for his virtuoso solos and exuberant style.

HMS Pinafore an OPERETTA by GILBERT and SULLIVAN. The story, set on board a British warship, tells of the romance between Sir Joseph Porter, First Lord of the Admiralty, and Josephine, the Captain's daughter. It was first performed in London in 1878, and its popularity was so great that a second company was soon required. In New York there were four companies performing it simultaneously at different theatres.

hocket (*French*) the breaking-up of a MELODY into very short PHRASES or single NOTES, with RESTS in between them.

Beach of Falesa), symphonies, and the oratorio *Job.*

Holbrooke, Joseph (1878-1958) English composer, pianist and conductor. His works include the trilogy of Celtic operas the *Cauldron of Annwen,* and the symphonic poem *The Raven.* He was also a controversial writer on music.

holding note a TONE sustained while others are in MOTION.

Holiday, Billie (1915-59) American jazz singer who had a remarkably sensuous and evocative voice. She became one of the most influential jazz singers of her time, with her sad, elegiac and subtle interpretations of popular songs. She sang with several bands, for example GOODMAN's and BASIE's, and appeared in several films, for example *New Orleans* (1947), which also featured ARMSTRONG. Drug addiction brought her life to a tragic end.

Holly, Buddy [Charles Hardin Holley] (1936–59) American rock singer, songwriter and guitarist. One of the most influential of all rock singers, his band, the Crickets, was the first to use the soon to be standard line-up of lead, rhythm and bas guitars, with drums. His songs include several standards, for example "That'll Be the Day," and "Peggy Sue." He died in a plane crash.

Holst, Gustav Theodore (1874-1934) English composer and teacher, of Swedish descent. He had a range of diverse interests, from English folk music to Sanskrit literature, which at various times influenced his compositions. His most famous orchestral piece is the PLANETS, but he also wrote operas (for example, *Avitri, At the Boar's Head*), choral pieces (for example, *Hymns from the Rig-Veda, The Hymn of Jesus*), and many songs.

Home, Sweet Home a song composed by BISHOP, in 1823 to words by John Howard Payne (1791–1852), and first sung in his opera *Clari, or the Maid of Milan*. The verses are not original, being a paraphrase of an earlier song by T. H Bayly (1797–1839), and Bishop had published the tune, without the refrain, three years before.

homophony a term applied to music in which the PARTS move "in step" and do not have independent RHYTHMS. *Compare* POLYPHONY.

Honegger, Arthur (1892-1955) Swiss composer who spent most of his life in France. He was a member of the group of composers called *Les* SIX and achieved fame with his orchestral piece *Pacific 231*, which is a representation of a locomotive engine. His other works include the oratorio *Le Roi David*, the operas *Antigone* and the *Eaglet*, and five symphonies.

hook the black line attached to the stem of all NOTES of less value than a CROTCHET.

hootenanny an American term for a small festival of FOLK music.

horn a BRASS INSTRUMENT consisting of a conical tube coiled into a spiral and ending in a bell. The lips are pushed into a funnel-shaped MOUTHPIECE. The modern orchestral horn is called the French horn (because that is where it was developed) and is fitted with three (sometimes four, sometimes seven) valves which open and close various lengths of tubing so that the PITCH of the NOTES can be changed. There are two common "horns," which are in fact WOODWIND instruments, the BASSET HORN (ALTO (2) CLARINET) and the English horn or COR ANGLAIS (alto OBOE).

hornpipe (1) a single-REED WIND INSTRUMENT played in Celtic countries. (2) a sixteenth-century dance in triple TIME, originally accompanied by the hornpipe and later erroneously associated with sailors.

Horowitz, Vladimir (1904-87) Russian-born pianist who settled in the USA in 1928. He achieved virtuoso status and was especially noted for his interpretation of music by CHOPIN and SCARLATTI.

Hosanna (*Hebrew*) "Save now," part of the SANCTUS in the MASS.

Hovhaness, Alan (1911-) an American composer who has often relied upon oriental subjects and instruments for inspiration. His most famous piece, *And God Created Whales,* is for a taped whale solo and orchestra, but he has also written some twenty symphonies and several operas.

Howells, Herbert (1892-1983) English composer who was much influenced by ELGAR and VAUGHAN WILLIAMS. His works include choral pieces (for example *Hymnus Paradisi*), organ and piano compositions, and chamber music.

Hummel, Johann Nepomuk (1778-1837) Austrian composer and pianist who studied under MOZART. He wrote nine operas and seven piano concertos, in addition to choral pieces.

humoresque (*French*), **Humoreske** (*German*) a word used by, for example, SCHUMANN, as the title for a short, lively piece of music.

Humperdinck, Engelbert (1854-1921) German composer of operas, incidental music and songs who was for a time an assistant to WAGNER. His best known opera is HANSEL AND GRETEL.

Hunter, Rita (1933-) English soprano with an international reputation. Her best known role is that of Brünnhilde in WAGNER's *Ring Cycle*.

hurdy-gurdy a medieval stringed instrument, shaped like a VIOL. A wooden wheel, coated in RESIN, is cranked at one end to make all the strings resonate. The strings are stopped by rods operated by KEYS. The hurdy-gurdy was often used to provide DANCE MUSIC.

hymn In the Christian Church, a poem sung to music in praise of God.

Hypoaeolian, Hypodorian *see* **mode**.

I

Ibert, Jacques François Antoine (1890-1962)
French composer who was famed for his light and
witty music. His best-known compositions in-
clude the symphonic poem the *Ballad of Reading
Jail* (after Oscar Wilde; 1856–1900), his opera *Le
Roi d'Yvetot,* and his orchestral piece *Escales*.

idée fixe (*French*) "fixed idea," i.e. a recurring
theme.

idiophone any instrument in which SOUND is produced by the VIBRATION of the instrument itself, for
example, CYMBALS, BELLS, CASTANETS etc.

Idomeneo, Rè di Creta (Idomeneo, King of
Crete) an opera by MOZART to a libretto by
Giovanni Battista Veresco, in which Idomeneo
promises Neptune that if he is saved from a
storm, he will sacrifice the first person he sees
on returning home. The victim turns out to be
his son. Neptune, however, is appeased and
Idomeneo's son takes over the throne. It was
first performed in 1781.

imitation a device in COUNTERPOINT whereby a
PHRASE is sung successively by different VOICES.

"Imperial" Symphony the nickname for HAYDN's Symphony No. 53 in D. It is so called because of the grand introduction to the first movement.

imperioso(*Italian*) "imperiously."

impetuoso (*Italian*) "impetuously."

imponente (*Italian*) "emphatic and pompous."

Impressionism a style of painting of the late nineteenth century in which forms were conveyed by dappled effects rather than by rigid outlines. By analogy, the word is also used to identify certain types of atmospheric music, such as the music of DEBUSSY and RAVEL.

impromptu a type of PIANO music that sounds as if it has been improvised, i.e. written in a free and easy style.

improvisation the art of playing or "inventing" music that has not already been composed, i.e. spontaneous composition. Some forms of music (especially JAZZ) often rely heavily on the ability of performers to improvise certain sections. It has the same meaning as extemporization.

in alt *see* **alt**.

incalzando (*Italian*) "pressing forward," i.e. working up speed and force.

incidental music music written to accompany the action in a play, but the term is also commonly applied to OVERTURES and INTERLUDES.

inciso (*Italian*) "incisive," hence an instruction that a strong RHYTHM is required.

Incoronazione di Poppea, L' (The Coronation of Poppaea) an opera by MONTEVERDI to a libretto by Giovanni Francesco Busenello. Set in ancient Rome, it tells of the ambitions of Poppaea to become Empress. It was first performed in 1642.

indeciso (*Italian*) "undecided," i.e. the pace of a piece of music can be varied according to the performer's feelings.

indeterminacy a term used by John CAGE to describe music that does not follow a rigid NOTATION but leaves certain events to chance or allows performers to make their own decisions when performing it.

Indy, Paul Marie Theodore Vincent d' (1851-1931) a French composer who also wrote music textbooks and important biographies of BEETHOVEN and FRANCK. His compositions include the operas *Fervaal, L' Etranger* and *La Légende de St Christophe,* symphonies, and pieces of chamber music.

inflected note a NOTE with an ACCIDENTAL placed before it, i.e. it is sharpened or flattened.

inner parts the PARTS of a piece of music excluding the highest and lowest; for example, in a work for SOPRANO, ALTO, TENOR and BASS, the alto and tenor roles are inner parts.

In nomine (*Latin*) (In the name of the Lord) a type of CANTUS FIRMUS used by English composers of the sixteenth century. It was first used by TAVERNER in his setting of *In nomine Domini* for one of his Masses.

instrument in music, a device on which or with which music can be played. There are five traditional categories of instrument: WOODWIND, BRASS,

PERCUSSION, KEYBOARD, and STRING. However, ELEC-
TRONIC and MECHANICAL INSTRUMENTS also exist.

instrumentation *see* **orchestration**.

interlude a title sometimes used for a short PART
of a complete composition; for example, a piece of
music performed between the acts of an opera.
See also ACT TUNE, ENTR'ACTE, INTERMEZZO (2).

intermezzo (*Italian*) (1) a short piece of piano
music. (2) a short comic opera performed between
the acts of a serious opera, especially in the
sixteenth and seventeenth centuries. *See also* ACT
TUNE, ENTR'ACTE, INTERMEZZO.

Internationale the international—and once official—Communist anthem. The words (1871) are
by Eugene Pottier and the music is by Pierre
Degeyter. The Soviet Union abandoned its use in
1944, but it is still sung at some European Communist and socialist gatherings.

interpretation the way in which a performer
plays a piece of composed music. No composer can
possibly indicate exactly how a piece should be
played and, to some degree, it is up to the performer to play it as he or she thinks fit.

interval the gap or "sound distance", expressed
numerically, between any two NOTES, i.e. the difference in PITCH between two notes. For example,
the interval between C and G is called a FIFTH
because G is the fifth note from C. *Perfect intervals* are intervals that remain the same in MAJOR
and MINOR KEYS (i.e. FOURTHS, fifths, OCTAVES.)

intonation a term used to describe the judgement
of PITCH by a performer.

intone to sing on one NOTE. A priest may intone

during a Roman Catholic or Anglican service.

introduction a section, often slow, found at the start of certain pieces of music, notably SYMPHONIES and SUITES.

Introit an ANTIPHON, usually sung in conjunction with a PSALM verse, in the Roman Catholic and Anglican LITURGIES.

invention a title used by BACH for his two-part keyboard pieces in CONTRAPUNTAL form.

inversion a term which literally means turning upside-down. It can refer to a CHORD, INTERVAL, THEME, MELODY or COUNTERPOINT. For example, an inverted interval is an interval in which one NOTE changes by an OCTAVE to the other side, as it were, of the other note.

Iolanthe (subtitled **The Peer and the Peri**) a comic opera by GILBERT and SULLIVAN. The story concerns the love of Strephon, the son of the fairy Iolanthe and the Lord Chancellor, for a maiden named Phyllis. It was first performed in 1882.

Ionian mode a MODE which, on the PIANO, uses the white NOTES (3) from C to C.

Iphigénie en Aulide (**Iphigenia in Aulis**) an opera by GLUCK to a libretto by François Louis Lebland du Roullet based on Jean Racine and Euripides. It relates the story of the sacrifice of Iphigenia, the daughter of Agamemnon and Clytemnestra, and was first performed in 1774.

Iphigénie en Tauride (**Iphigenia in Tauris**) an opera by GLUCK to a libretto by Nicolas François Guillard based on Euripides. It is the sequel to IPHIGÉNIE EN AULIDE and tells of how

Iphigenia is rescued by her brother, Orestes. It was first performed in 1779.

Ireland, John [Nicholson] (1897-1962) English composer who was greatly influenced by French music and, like DELIUS and HOLST, by English poetry, his works including several song cycles to words by Thomas Hardy, A. E. Housman, and others. His other works, which were often inspired by a mystical reverence for English landscape, include a piano concerto and the orchestral tone poem *The Forgotten Rite*.

Irish bagpipe the only BAGPIPE having a DIATONIC SCALE.

Irish harp a prototype of the Ital;ian HARP from which the modern instrument was developed.

irlandais (*French*) "in Irish style."

isorhythm a term used to describe a short RHYTHM pattern that is repeatedly applied to an existing MELODY which already has an distinct rhythm.

Italian sixth *see* **augmented sixth**.

italiano (*Italian*), **italienne** (*French*) "in Italian style."

Ivanhoe Sir Arthur SULLIVAN's three-act romantic opera, to a libretto by Julian Sturgis after the novel by Sir Walter Scott (1771–1832), was first performed on January 31, 1891, at the Royal English Opera House, London. It is Sullivan's only GRAND OPERA.

Ivan the Terrible (1) an opera by BIZET to a libretto by Leroy and Trianon, composed in 1865. (2) the English name given by the Russian ballet impresario Sergei Diaghilev (1872–1923) to RIMSKY-KORSAKOV's opera *Pskovitianka (The Maid of Pskov)*.

Ives, Charles Edward (1874-1954) an American composer who is regarded as a pioneer of twentieth-century music, although his works were largely ignored during his lifetime. He explored the possibilities of mixing apparently discordant (*see* DISCORD) sounds to create a satisfactory result; he wanted everyday sounds (such as radio transmissions) to be incorporated into compositions to make the music more readily understood. His works include five symphonies, chamber music, includng a well-known piano sonata, the *Concord Sonata*, but he is perhaps best known for his orchestral pieces, for example *General Booth enters into Heaven,* the *Unanswered Question* and *Central Park in the Dark.*

J

Jackson, Michael [Joe] (1958–) American
pop singer, the youngest of five brothers (the
others are Jackie, Jermaine, Marion and Tito) wh
as children foormed the Jackson 5, a rock soul
group popular in the late 1960s and the 1970s.
Michael became a solo performer in the late 1970s,
and in the early 1980s became very successful
with young teenagers, exploiting the development of pop videos.

Jackson, Michael [Joe] (1958–) American
pop singer, the youngest of five brothers (the
others are Jackie, Jermaine, Marion and Tito) wh
as children foormed the Jackson 5, a rock soul
group popular in the late 1960s and the 1970s.
Michael became a solo performer in the late 1970s,
and in the early 1980s became very successful
with young teenagers, exploiting the development of pop videos.

Jagger, Mick [Michael Philip Jagger] (1943–
) English singer and songwriter, and lead singer
with the Rolling Stones rock group, the original
members of which, with Jagger, were the guitarist and co-writer with Jagger of many of their
songs, **Keith Richard** (1943–), bass guitarist
Bill Wyman (1936–), drummer **Charlie Watts**
(1941–) and guitarist **Brian Jones** (1944–69).
Several of the Jagger-Richard songs, for example
the ballad "Ruby Tuesday," have become pop
standards. Jagger is also regarded as one of the
finest white rock/blues singers of his generation.

jam session a twentieth-century slang expression
for an occasion when a group of musicians join
forces to improvise (*see* IMPROVISATION) music.

It is usually only appropriate to JAZZ, BLUES and ROCK music.

Janácek, Leos (1854–1928) Czech composer, conductor and organist who was also an influential teacher. He was particularly drawn to the rhythms and constructions of FOLK SONGS and is best known for the operas that he wrote in old age, such as *The Excursions of Mr Broucek, The Cunning Little Vixen* and *From the House of the Dead.* However, he also wrote numerous other pieces, which include the SYMPHONIC POEM *Taras Bulba* and his famous *Sinfonietta*, as well as the *Glagolitic Mass.*

Janissary music the music of Turkish MILITARY BANDS which influenced European composers during the eighteenth century. It is particularly associated with CYMBALS, DRUMS and TAMBOURINES.

Jaques-Dalcroze, Emile (1865-1950) Swiss composer and teacher who developed the concept of musical teaching through EURHYTHMICS. He also composed some five operas and two noted violin concertos.

Järnefelt, (Edvard) Armas (1869-1958) Finnish composer and conductor who elected to become a Swedish national in 1910. He is best known for his orchestral, choral and piano works, such as *Berceuse.*

jazz a term used to describe a style of music that evolved in the Southern States of the USA at the turn of the century. It owes a great deal to the RHYTHMS and idioms of BLUES and SPIRITUALS, but many of the favoured instruments (for example, SAXOPHONE, TRUMPET and TROMBONE) were European in origin. Jazz traditionally relies upon a strong rhythm "section", comprising BASS and DRUMS, which provides a springboard for other instruments. Jazz developed from being a form of music played in the back streets of New Orleans to a sophisticated art form performed by small dedicated groups as well as "BIG BANDS" or "jazz orchestras".

Self-expression, and therefore IMPROVISATION, has always been a crucial aspect of jazz and this has allowed many individuals (such as Louis ARMSTRONG and Benny GOODMAN) to blossom and further its cause. *See also* BEBOP.

Jerusalem a famous choral song by Sir Hubert PARRY to words by William Blake (1757–1827), composed in 1918.

Jeune France (Young France) the name adopted by a group of French composers, including JOLIVET and MESSIAEN, who identified their common aims in 1936.

Jew's harp a simple instrument consisting of a small, heart-shaped, metal frame to which a thin strip of hardened steel is attached. The open-ended neck of the frame is held against the teeth and the strip is twanged to produce sound, which is modified by using the cavity of the mouth as a soundbox.

jig a generic term for a lively dance. *See also* GIGUE.

jingles (1) an instrument consisting of a number of small bells or rattling objects on a strap, which are shaken to produce sound. (2) In the singular, a short, catchy piece of music with

207

equally catchy LYRICS, often used to enliven the commentary of radio stations broadcasting popular music.

jingling johnny an instrument, of Turkish origin, comprising a long stick to the head of which is attached a series of small bells, formerly much used in MILITARY BANDS..

Joachim, Joseph (1831-1907) Hungarian virtuoso violinist celebrated for his performances of BACH, BEETHOVEN, MENDELSSOHN and, notably, BRAHMS, of whom he was a close friend. He was also the composer of several works for violin and orchestra.

John, Elton [originally Reginald Kenneth Dwight] (1947–) an English pop and rock musician. He was particularly popular in the 1960s and 1970s with hit songs such as "Daniel" and "Don't Go Breaking My Heart."

John Brown's Body a marching tune, of unknown authorship, which was popular with the Union forces during the American Civil War of 1861–65, and which was probably composed in about 1850, and swiftly taken up as a revivalist hymn. The doggerel words about the abolitionist John Brown were replaced in 1861 by the song "Mine eyes have seen the glory of the coming of the Lord," by Mrs Julia Wood Howe (1819–1910), a social reformer and ardent campaigner for the abolition of slavery; her version became known as "The Battle Hymn of the Republic."

Jolivet, André (1905-74) French composer and a founder member of the JEUNE FRANCE group. He was influenced by oriental music and he is best known for his opera *Dolores,* oratorio *La Verité,* and ballets.

Jones, Brian *see* **Jagger, Mick**.

jongleur a medieval MINSTREL.

Joplin, Scott (1868-1917) American RAGTIME composer and pianist. Although he wrote two operas, he is best known for his RAGS, such as *Maple Leaf Rag*, which sold over a million copies in sheet music when it was published in 1899. Longing to be accepted as the first black composer of "serious" music, Joplin grew depressed by the failure of his operas and died in a mental home.

Joshua an ORATORIO by HANDEL to a libretto by Thomas Morell. It was first performed in 1748.

Josquin des Prés *or* **Deprez** (c.1440-1521) an innovatory Flemish composer, the most celebrated of his day. He worked in both France and Italy and composed some thirty Masses and fifty motets.

jota a Spanish dance from Aragon in 3/4 TIME usually accompanied by CASTANETS; the dancers occasionally sing.

juke box an automatic, coin-operated, machine that plays records.

Jupiter Symphony the name given to MOZART's Symphony No. 41 in C. It is so called because of the stately opening to the first movement.

K

K when followed by a number, a reference to either a catalogue of MOZART's works (compiled by Ludwig von KOCHEL), or a catalogue of SCARLATTI's works (compiled by Ralph Kirkpatrick).

Kabalevsky, Dmitri Borisovich (1904-87) a Russian composer of ballets, symphonies, piano pieces and operas (for example, *Invincible* and the *Sister*).

Kapellmeister (*German*) literally "master of the chapel," i.e. director of music to a noble court or bishop.

Karajan, Herbert von (1908-89) an Austrian conductor who by the mid-1930s was regarded as a brilliant, if dictatorial, conductor of symphonies and operas and who worked with most of the world's leading orchestras, particularly the Berlin Philharmonic Orchestra. He was well known for conducting works by BEETHOVEN, BRAHMS, WAGNER, SCHUMANN and VERDI, and his recordings are held by some critics to be definitive. His membership of the Nazi party from 1933 on is claimed by his admirers to have been simply a "career move."

Karelia an overture and orchestral suite by

SIBELIUS, composed in 1893 and named after the province of Finland in which he lived.

kazoo a simple instrument consisting of a short tube with a small hole in the side which is covered with a thin membrane. When a player hums down the tube, the membrane makes a buzzing sound. It is usually considered a children's instrument although it is frequently used by folk and jazz musicians.

Kern, Jerome [David] (1885-1945) an American songwriter and composer of musical comedies, who had a huge influence on the American musical tradition with works such as *Show Boat* in 1927, in which the songs were integral parts of the dramatic action rather than merely decorative. Some of his songs, for example, "Ol' Man River" (from *Show Boat*) and "Smoke gets in your Eyes" are considered "classics."

kettledrum *see* **timpani**.

key (1) on a piano, harpsichord, organ etc., one of the finger-operated levers by which the instrument is played. (2) On woodwind instruments, one of the metal, finger-operated levers that opens or closes one or more of the soundholes. (3) a note that is considered to be the most important in a piece of music and to which all the other notes relate. Most pieces of Western music are "written in a key," i.e. all the chords in the piece are built around a particular note, say F minor. The concept of a key is alien to certain types of music, such as Indian and Chinese.

key note *see* **tonic**.

key signature the sign (or signs) placed at the

beginning of a composition to define its KEY. A key signature indicates all the notes that are to be sharpened or flattened in the piece; should a piece move temporarily into another key, the relevant notes can be identified with ACCIDENTALS.

Khachaturian, Aram Ilich (1903-78) a Russian Armenian composer who was influenced by the folk music of Armenia. He wrote music that was generally acceptable to the Soviet authorities of the time, although his second symphony was not well received. His works include symphonies, piano concertos, pieces for chorus and orchestra, and the ballet *Spartacus*.

Kindersymphonie *see* **Toy Symphony.**

Kindertotenlieder (Songs on the death of children) a cycle of five songs for voice and orchestra by MAHLER with words by F. Ruckert.

Kirbye, George (*c.*1565-1634) an inventive English composer of motets and madrigals.

kit a miniature violin which was particularly popular with dancing masters of the seventeenth and eighteenth centuries, who could carry one in the pocket and thereby provide music for lessons.

Klangfarbenmelodie (*German*) literally, "melody of tone colours"; a term used by SCHOENBERG to describe a form of composition in which the pitch does not change; "colour" is achieved by adding or taking away instruments.

klavier *see* clavier.

Klebe, Giselher (1925-) a German composer who has experimented with various musical forms and who has used electronic instruments. He has written several operas (such as *Die Rauber*) as well as orchestral and chamber music.

Kleine Nachtmusik, Eine (A Little Night Music) a popular serenade by MOZART for a small orchestra or string quartet, composed in 1787.

Klemperer, Otto (1885-1973) a German conductor and composer. By the late 1920s he was established as a great interpreter of both classical and contemporary works (for example BEETHOVEN, his friend MAHLER, and JANACEK). Being Jewish, he fled to the USA in 1933, where he became director of the Los Angeles Symphony Orchestra. After the war, he returned to Europe and dedicated himself to conducting. He was director of the Budapest Opera (1947–50) and became an Israeli citizen in 1970. He was especially famous for conducting the works of BRAHMS and BEETHOVEN. His compositions include two symphonies and a Mass.

Köchel, Ludwig Alois Friedrich, Ritter von (1800-77) an Austrian scientist who was a great admirer of MOZART and catalogued the great composer's works, giving each one a "K[öchel] number".

Kodály, Zoltán (1882-1967) a Hungarian composer and teacher who was greatly influenced by Hungarian folk songs. He wrote operas (for example, the *Spin ning* Room), choral works (for example, *Psalmus Hungaricus*), chamber music, and various pieces for orchestra.

Koechlin, Charles (1867-1950) a prolific French composer, most of whose music is rarely heard today. His works include ballets, chamber music and several symphonic poems which were inspired by Kipling's *Jungle Book*. He was also an author of textbooks and a treatise on DEBUSSY.

Königskinder (The Royal Children) an opera by HUMPERDINCK to a libretto by Ernst Rosmer, which was first performed in 1897 in Munich, and subsequently in an English version in London. While it did not achieve the instant popularity of its predecessor, HANSEL UND GRETEL, it is likewise music drama of the strictest Wagnerian type, using as its story line the fairy tale of the goose-girl who falls in love with the king's son.

Korngold, Eric Wolfgang (1897-1957) a prolific Austrian-born composer who was a child prodigy. He went to live in the USA in 1938 (becoming an American citizen in 1943) and settled in Hollywood where he wrote film music (for example, the *Adventures of Robin Hood,* the *Sea Hawks*). His other works include operas, chamber music and various pieces for orchestra.

koto a Japanese zither which has 13 silk strings stretched over a long box. The strings pass over moveable bridges and are played with plectra worn on the fingers. The instrument is placed on the ground and produces a distinctive, somewhat harsh, sound.

Kreisler, Frik (1875-1962) a celebrated Austrian violinist, for whom ELGAR wrote his violin concerto. He settled in the USA, and wrote a variety of pieces, including some which he initially attributed to seventeenth and eighteenth-century composers.

Krenek, Ernst (1900-) an American composer, conductor and pianist of Czech origin. He emigrated to the USA in 1938 and was influenced by jazz before writing TWELVE-NOTE MUSIC. He has experimented with various styles of music and has composed for electronic instruments. His works include operas (for example, *Tarquin, Dark Waters*), choral pieces, ballets (for example, *Mammon, Eight Column Line*), and compositions for orchestra and piano.

Kreutzer Sonata the nickname given to BEETHOVEN's sonata for violin and piano in A, Op. 47 (1802-3), which he dedicated to the French violinist Rudolphe Kreutzer.

Krumhorn *or* **Krummhorn** (*German*) or **crumhorn** a double-reed instrument, common in the sixteenth and early seventeenth centuries. The tube was curved at the lower end and the reed was enclosed in a cap into which the player blew. It was made in several sizes: treble, tenor and bass.

Kuhreigen *see* **Rauz des Vaches.**

Kyrie Eleison (*Greek*) "Lord have Mercy," the formal invocation at the start of the Mass and communion service.

la *or* **lah** (1) the note A. (2) In the TONIC SOL-FA, the sixth note (or SUBMEDIANT) of the major scale.

Lablache, Luigi (1794–1858) Italian bass singer, who became the most famous of his generation because of his extraordinarily powerful voice and a dramatic talent that make him equally at home in comedy or tragedy. Of Irish-French parentage, he studied violin and cello before making his debut as a singer. As a teacher, one of his pupils was Queen Victoria.

lacrimose (*Italian*) "mournfully, tearfully".

lacrimoso (*Italian*) "tearful."

Lady Henriette a ballet-pantomime by Flotow, in collaboration, which was first performed in Paris in1844. Flotow afterwards expanded it as Marta, his most successful opera.

L'Africaine *see* **Africaine, L'**.

lah *see* **la**.

la Hale *or* **la Halle, Adam de** (1230–88) French composer and priest who wrote *Le jeu de la feuillée*, first performed in Arras, France, in 1262, and *Le jeu de Robin et Marion*, first performed in Naples in 1285, which are now regarded as the earliest forms of comic opera. He also wrote chansons, and his works were republished in 1872.

lai (*French*) a thirteenth- and fourteenth-century French song usually consisting of twelve irregular stanzas sung to different musical phrases.

Lakmé an opera by DELIBES to a libretto written by E. Gondinet and P. Gille. The story is set in India, where Lakmé, the daughter of a Brahmin priest, falls in love with Gerald, a British Army officer. It was first performed in Paris in 1883. When her father discovers, he stabs Gerald, but Lakmé nurses him back to health. The sound of his regimental band recalls Gerald to his duty, and Lakmé, discovering she has been deserted, poisons herself.

Laland, Michel Richard de (1657–1726) French composer of church music, whose compositions also include works for the court theatre of Louis XIV and Louis XV, of which he ewas musical director.

Lalo, Victor Antoine Edouard (1823-92) a French composer of Spanish descent who is best known for his *Symphonie espagnole* for violin and orchestra. His other works include operas (for example, *Le Roi d'Ys*), a ballet (*Namouna*), concertos, and songs.

lambeg drum a large, double-headed bass drum from Northern Ireland.

Lambert, Constant (1905-51) an English composer, conductor and critic who was commissioned by Diaghilev to write the music for the ballet *Romeo and Juliet*. His other works include a piano sonata, choral pieces and several songs.

lament a Scottish or Irish folk tune played at a

death or some disaster, usually on the bagpipes.

"Lamentation" Symphony the nickname for HAYDN's symphony no. 26 in D minor. It is so called because some themes resemble the PLAIN-SONG melodies sung in Roman Catholic services during Holy Week.

lamentoso (*Italian*) "mournfully."

Lamond, Frederick (1868–1948) a Scottish pianist and composer who studied with von BÜLOW and LISZT. He made his debut in Vienna in 1885 and later toured Europe and America before becoming professor of piano in the Hague Conservatory. His compositions include a ymphony, the concert overture *Aus dem Schottischen Hochlande*, and a sonato for piano and cello.

Lamoureux, Charles (1834–99) a French conductor and violinist. He found the Lamoureux concerts in Paris in 1881, which premiered works by INDY, among others, and introduced WAGNER's music to France.

lampon (*French*) a drinking song.

Lancers, The a type of QUADRILLE in which 8 or 16 couples take part.

Land of my Fathers (Hen Wlad fy Nhadau) a song adopted by the Welsh as their "national" anthem. The words were written by Evan James and the tune by James James in 1860.

Landini, Landino, Francesco (*c*.1335-97) an Italian composer, organist and lute player who was blind from childhood. Among the most important musicians of his time, he composed numerous songs.

Ländler a country dance in slow 3/4 time from

Austria and Bavaria, from which the WALTZ was probably derived.

Landowska, Wanda (1877–1959) Polish harpsichordist and pianist, who frequently performed works by Johan Sebastian Bach and Handel as originally scored and then in modern piano versions.

langsam (*German*) "slow."

languido (*Italian*) "languidly."

Lanner, Joseph Franz Karl (1801-43) an Austrian composer and conductor who was a contemporary of Johann STRAUSS "the Elder," with whom he formed a quintet. He composed some 100 waltzes and many other dances.

l'apres-midi d'un faune *see* **apres-midi d'un faune, Prelude a l'**.

largamente (*Italian*) literally "broadly," meaning slowly and in a dignified manner.

larghetto (*Italian*) "slow" or "broad," but not as slow as LARGO.

largo (*Italian*) literally "broad," meaning slow and in a dignified manner.

largo assai (*Italian*) "quite slow."

"Lark" Quartet the nickname of HAYDN's string quartet Op. 6, No. 5, in D. It is so called because of the high-soaring violin notes at the beginning of the first movement.

Larsson, Lars-Erik (1908-86) a Swedish composer, conductor and critic who was influenced by BERG. His works include three symphonies, three concert overtures, a saxophone concerto and film music.

larynx the organ by which the sounds of the

human voice are produced. It is situated at the upper end of the trachea, or windpipe, with which it is continous.

Lassus, Roland de *or* **Orlando di Lasso** (1532-94) a Flemish composer who experimented with a wide range of musical forms and was one of the most prolific and versatile composers of his era. His compositions include Masses, motets, madrigals, and many other choral pieces. Four of his sons and a grandson were also musicians.

Last Post, The a bugle call of the British Army to signal the end of the day at 10 pm. It is also played at military funerals.

Last Rose of Summer, The a song by Thomas Moore that appeared in the first issue of his Irish Melodies in 1813 and sprang into instant favour. The verses were set to the tune "The Groves of Blarney," the work of an unknown composer.

Lauder, Sir Harry [originally Hugh MacLennan] (1870–1950) a Scottish music-hall comedian and singer, who wrote and composed Scottish songs, out of which he made an internation career. His songs include "Stop Your Tickling, Jock" and "Roamin' in the Gloamin'." He was knighted in 1919 for services in entertaining soldiers in France during World War I (in which he lost his only son).

Lawes, Henry (1596-1662) an English composer whose works were admired by the aristocracy; he composed the coronation anthem *Zadok the Priest* for Charles II. He wrote the music for Milton's masque *Comus,* and many songs and madrigals. His brother **William Lawes** (1602-45) was also a composer, who wrote psalms, anthems and songs, including the part-song "Gather ye rosebuds while ye may." He was killed in the English Civil War.

lay a song or ballad.

lay clerk an adult male member of an Anglican cathedral choir.

lead (1) the announcement of a subject or theme that later appears in other parts. (2) a sign giving the cue or entry of the various parts.

Leadbelly [originally Huddie Ledbetter] (1888–1949) an American blues singer, composer, 12-string guitarist and piano player. He led a violent life and was imprisoned several times, he was discovered in a Louisiana prison in 1933, where he was being held for attempted murder. He reputedly earned his name from the number of lead bullets that remained in his body. Leadbelly later recorded several songs that soon became recognized as folk-blues classics, for example "Rock Island Line" and "Goodnight, Irene."

leader (1) in Britain, the title of the principal first violin of an orchestra or the first violin of a string quartet or similar ensemble. (2) the leader of a section of an orchestra. (3) In the USA, an alternative term for conductor.

leading motif *see* **Leitmotiv**.

leading note the seventh note of the scale; it is so called because it "leads to" the TONIC, a semitone above.

lebhaft (*German*) "vivacious" or "lively."

Leclair, Jean-Marie (1697-1764) a French composer and violinist. He wrote the opera *Scylla et Glaucus,* ballets and many pieces for violin. He was murdered outside his home, perhaps by his nephew. His younger brother, who rather confusingly had exactly the same name, was also a composer and violinist.

Lecocq, Alexandre Charles (1832–1918) a French composer whose compositions included operettas, songs and a collection of sacred music for female voices. His operettas, for example *La Fille de Madame Angot* and *Giroflé Girofla*, dominated for a generation, but he failed to obtain a hearing for his more serious work.

Ledbetter, Huddy *see* **Leadbelly**.

ledger lines *see* **leger lines**.

legato (*Italian*) "smooth."

leger lines *or* **ledger lines** short lines added above or below a STAVE to indicate the pitch of notes that are too high or low to be written on the stave itself.

leggiero (*Italian*) "light."

legno (*Italian*) "wood"; *col legno* is a direction to a violinist to turn the bow over and to tap the strings with the wood.

Lehar, Franz (originally Ferencz) a Hungarian-born composer. After conducting military bands for a while, he settled in Vienna where he composed operettas, the most famous being *The* MERRY WIDOW, *The Count of Luxembourg* and *The Land of Smiles*.

Leigh, Walter (1905-42) an English composer who is best known for his operettas, for example, *The Jolly Roger*. He was killed in action during World War II.

leicht (*German*) "light," "easy."

leise (*German*) "soft" or "gentle."

leitmotif *or* **Leitmotiv** (*German*) literally a "leading theme," i.e. a recurring theme of music, commonly used in opera, that is associated with a character or idea, thus enabling the composer to tell a story in terms of music. It has been used by many composers, including MOZART and BERLIOZ, but it is particularly associated with WAGNER. In the last act of *Götterdämmerung*, for example, every leitmotif associated with Siegfried is woven into the death march.

"Leningrad" Symphony the subtitle of SHOSTAKOVICH'S symphony no. 7, which was composed during the siege of Leningrad during World War II.

Lennon, John (1940-80) an English rock guitarist, singer and songwriter who was a founder member of the group The Beatles (1961-70), the most popular rock group ever, with Paul MCCARTNEY, George HARRISON and Ringo STARR. The success of the band was based on his songwriting partnership with McCartney. After the group's split, his subsequent albums included, notably, *Imagine*, but his career was brought to a tragic close by his murder in New York.

lentamente (*Italian*) "slowly."

lento (*Italian*) "slow."

Leoncavallo, Ruggiero (1858-1919) an Italian composer who started his musical career as a café pianist. He is best known for his opera *I Pagliacci*, although he composed several others. He also wrote a ballet and the symphonic poem *Serafita*.

Leoninus *or* **Léonin** (*fl.* twelfth century) a French composer and organist of whom little is known.

Leonora overtures

He is thought to have been one of the first musicians to use time values.

Leonora overtures the title of three overtures written by BEETHOVEN for his opera FIDELIO, in which Leonore is the heroine. A fourth, definitive overture, *Fidelio*, was composed in 1814. Today, the "Three Leonoras" are invariably played as concert overtures.

Lesueur, Jean François (1760–1837) a French composer and teacher who also worked for Napoleon and Louis XVIII. As choirmaster in Notre Dame, Paris, in 1786, he used a full orhestra in an attempt to make the Mass "dramatic and descriptive." The attempt failed, the orchestra was reduced, and he left Notre Dame shortly afterwards. He wrote much church music including Masses, motets and psalms, but also wrote oratorios, operas and cantats, including *Ruth et Boaz* for Napoleon's marriage. As a professor at the Paris Conservatoire his pupils included BERLIOZ and GOUNOD.

LH an abbreviation for "left hand", commonly found in piano music.

Liadov *or* **Lyadov, Anatol Konstantinovich** (1855-1914) a Russian composer, teacher and conductor who was a pupil of RIMSKY-KORSAKOV. He helped Balakirev make a collection of Russian folksongs and taught at the St Petersburg Conservatory. His most famous works are the symphonic poems *Baba Yaga*, *The Enchanted Lake* and *Kikimora*.

liberamente (*Italian*) "freely," i.e. as the performer wishes.

libretto (*Italian*) literally "little book." It is a term used for the text of an opera or oratorio.

licenza (*Italian*) "licence" or 'freedom"; *con alcuna licenza* means "with some freedom."

Liebeslied (*German*) a love song.

Liebestod (German) "love-death," the title now given to Isolde's death scene at the end of Act 3 of WAGNER's *Tristan and Isolde*, but in fact used by Wagner himself to describe the love duet in Act 2.

Liebesverbot, Das ("The Ban on Love") an opera by Wagner to his own libretto based on Shakespeare's play Measure for Measure. It was the first of Wager's operas to be performed, in Magdeburg, Germany, in 1836.

Lied, Lieder (*German*) "song, songs." The term is now used for songs by the German romantic composers, for example BRAHMS, SCHUBERT, STRAUSS, etc.

Lied ohne Worte (*German*) "song without words") a name used for some of MENDELSSOHN's piano pieces.

Lied von der Erde, Das *see* **Song of the Earth**.

ligature (1) a twelfth-century form of notation for a group of notes. (2) a slur indicating that a group of notes must be sung to one syllable. (3) the tie used to link two notes over a bar line. (4) the metal band used to fix the reed to the mouthpiece of a clarinet, etc.

Ligeti, György (1923-) a Hungarian composer who has settled in Austria. He is renowned for composing sophisticated yet easy-to-listen-to pieces such as *Atmospheres* and *Lontano* for orchestra. He has also composed an opera, *Le Grand*

Macabre, and pieces for flute and oboe.

light a term that is used to describe music that is easy to listen to.

Lilburn, Douglas (1915-) New Zealand's most famous composer, who studied in England for a period. He has experimented with electronic instruments but is best known for his more conservative works, which include three symphonies and his *Aotearoa Overture*.

Lilliburlero a seventeenth-century dance tune, of uncertain origin, which made fun of Irish Roman Catholics. It has subsequently been adopted as an Orangemen's song with new words ("Protestant Boys").

Lind, Jenny (1820–87) a Swedish soprano who made her debut at the age of ten and went on to become one of the world's great singers. Her voice was remarkable for its power and flexibility, and gained her the nickname "The Swedish Nightingale." She retired from opera in 1849 and thereafter sang only in concerts. She settled in London but continued to tour until 1883. She was a teacher at the Royal College of Music in Lond from 1883 to 1886.

Linley, Thomas (1733-95) an English composer and teacher who wrote incidental music for plays, including Sheridan's *The Duenna* and *School for Scandal*. He also wrote madrigals, songs and cantatas. His son, Thomas Linley (1756–78), was a violinist and friend of MOZART, and also composed songs before his accidental death by drowning. His daughter, **Elizabeth Ann Linley** (1754–92), was a noted soprano who married Sheridan.

"Linz" Symphony the nickname of MOZART's symphony no. 36 in C. It is so called because it was first performed in Linz in 1783.

lira da braccio *or* **lira da gamba** an Italian stringed instruments of the fifteenth and sixteenth centuries. The *lira da braccio* had seven strings and was played like a violin; the *lira da gamba* was a bass instrument, played between the knees, and had anything up to sixteen strings.

lira organizzata a type of HURDY-GURDY that included a miniature organ.

Liszt, Ferencz *or* **Franz** (1811-86) a Hungarian composer and pianist who was a great showman as well as a formidable musician. He went to Vienna as a child prodigy in 1823 and impressed BEETHOVEN amongst others. He travelled to France and England and his reputation as a virtuoso performer became legendary. In 1835 he eloped to Switzerland with Countess d'Agoult (who adopted the pseudonym of Daniel Stern when she became a novelist) and their daughter, Cosima, who eventually married WAGNER. In 1847 he settled in Germany with his new mistress, Princess Carolyne Sayn-Wittgenstein. During this period his composing flourished and, amongst other works, he wrote his famous *Hungarian Rhapsodies* for piano. He also became deeply religious and lived in Rome for a time where he composed two oratorios.

Liszt was undoubtedly one of the greatest (and most flamboyant) virtuoso pianists of all time. He was also an accomplished composer and he greatly furthered the development of piano music. He also wrote symphonies and symphonic poems (a term which he invented) and several choral works. His principal compositions include: the FAUST and *Dante* symphonies; 12 *Etudes d'Execution Transcendante* and 20 *Hungarian Rhapsodies* for piano; several choral pieces; and 12 symphonic poems.

litany a solemn supplication or prayer in which the petition is offered by the priest and the response is made by the choir or congregation in plainsong. The Greek church was probably the first to make use of the litany, as the words KYRIE ELEISON are retained in the ritual of the Roman Catholic Church.

"Little Russian" Symphony the nickname for TCHAIKOVSKY's symphony no. 2 in C minor. It is so called because it uses Ukrainian (Little Russian) folk tunes.

"Little" Symphony the nickname for SCHUBERT's symphony no. 6 in C. It is so called to distinguish it from his Great C Major Symphony.

liturgy a term for any official, and written down, form of religious service.

Lloyd Webber, Andrew (1948–) an English composer. With the librettist Tim Rice, he composed several highly successful musicals, notably *Joseph and the Amazing Technicolour Dreamcoat*, *Jesus Christ Superstar*, and *Evita*. Successes with other collaborators were *Cats* (adapted from T. S. Eliot's *Old Possum's Book of Practical Cats*), *Starlight Express* and *Phantom of the Opera*. His brother, **Julian Lloyd Webber** (1951–) is a cellist.

Locke, Matthew (*c.*1630-77) an English composer who was employed by Charles II. His works include incidental music for Shadwell's *The Tempest,* several anthems and many pieces for the recorder.

loco (*Italian*) literally "place". It is used in music to indicate that a passage is to be played at normal pitch, after a previous, contrary instruction, i.e. the music reverts to its original "place" on the stave.

Loeffler, Charles Martin (1861-1935) an Alsatian-born composer and violinist who settled in the USA. He was influenced by DEBUSSY and is best known for the orchestral pieces *La Morte de Tintagiles, A Pagan Poem* and *The Canticle of the Sun* (with voice).

Loewe, Frederick (1904-88) an Austrian-born composer who settled in the USA in 1924 and became an American citizen. In collaboration with the lyricist Alan Jay Lerner, he created many famous musicals including *Paint Your Wagon, My Fair Lady* (from Shaw's *Pygmalion* and *Camelot.* He also wrote, with Lerner, the songs for the film Gigi.

Loewe, Johann Karl Gomried (1796-1869) a German composer, conductor, pianist and singer who was the son of a noted musician of the same name. He wrote some 500 songs, five operas, 18 oratorios and many other pieces.

Lohengrin an opera by WAGNER, who also wrote the libretto. It relates how a mysterious knight tries to protect Elsa against the machinations of the warlord, Friedrich of Telramund, and his wife Ortrud, who have unjustly accused Elsa of mur-

dering her brother Gottfried. The knight makes
Elsa agree to three conditions: that she will be his
wife and that she will never ask his name or
lineage. Elsa agrees readily, but Ortrud sows
distrust in Elsa's mind and she persuades the
knight to tell her his name, Lohengrin, and to
admit that he is a Knight of the Holy Grail and son
of Parsifal. Lohengrin tells Elsa that he is free to
remain with men so long as he is unknown and
unvulnerable to villainy so he must return to
Monsalvat, the home ot the Grail. Lohengrin
prepares to depart as he came, in a boat drawn by
a swan. He unchains the swan, which disappears
beneath the water and is replaced by Gottfried,
who had been bewitched into that form by Ortrud.
The opera contains the famous "Here Comes the
Bride" wedding march and was first performed in
Weimar in 1850 under the direction of LISZT.
Wagner was unable to be present as he was in
exile in Switzerland.

London Symphony (1) the nickname given to
HAYDN's last symphony, no. 104 in D, which was
first performed in London in 1795. (2) VAUGHAN
WILLIAM's second symphony (1914), which includes
sounds associated with London, such as street
cries and the chimes of Big Ben.

lontano (*Italian*) "distant."

Lortzing, Gustav Albert (1801-51) a German
composer, singer and conductor who is best known
for his comic operas, which he wrote to his own
libretti, for example *Zar und Zimmermann*..

lo stesso tempo (*Italian*) "the same tempo."

Louise a VERISMO opera by CHARPENTIER to his own

libretto, which was first performed in Paris in 1900. It concerns Louise, a dressmaker, who is in love with Julien, a singer, but their love story is thwarted by parental opposition.

Louis Ferdinand (1772–1806) prince of Prussia and nephew of Frederick the Great. He was a talented musician who played the piano "not like a prince, but like a pianist," according to his friend BEETHOVEN, and who also composed quintets, quarters and other chamber music. He was killed in battle.

loure a type of bagpipe played in northern France, especially Normandy.

Love of Three Oranges, The an opera by PROKOFIEV, who also wrote the libretto. It is a play within a play and concerns a prince who loves three oranges and finds his desired princess in the third. It was first performed in Chicago in 1921.

Love, the Magician *see* **Amor Brujo, El**.

Lucia di Lammermoor a tragic opera by DONIZETTI to a libretto by S. Cammarano (based on Walter Scott's *The Bride of Lammermoor*). It relates the story of Lucia, who falls in love with Edgar, her brother Enrico's greatest enemy. Enrico has promised his sister to Arturo in order to restore the family fortunes so he intervenes, with disastrous consequences, as Lucia becomes insane and kills Arturo, while Edgar commits suicide. It was first performed in Naples in 1835.

Lucio Silla an opera by MOZART to a libretto by G. de Gamera. It was first performed in Dresden in 1835. Other operas of the same name were com-

Lucrezia Borgia

posed by Anfossi and Johann Christian BACH.

Lucrezia Borgia an opera by DONIZETTI to a libretto by F. Romani based on a play by Victor Hugo. It tells of how Lucrezia, married to the Duke of Ferrara, causes the death of her own son, of whose existence the Duke is unaware, and ultimately commits suicide. It was first performed in Milan in 1834, but when it was put on in Paris in1840, Hugo forbade its performance, and was withdrawn, rewritten and renamed *La Ringata*, the action being transposed from Italy to Turkey.

Ludwig, Christa (1928–) a German mezzo-soprano who has established an international reputation. She is particularly noted for her Leonore in BEETHOVEN's *Fidelio* and as Octavian in Richard STRAUSS's *Rosenkavalier*.

Lully, Jean-Baptiste [originally Giambattista Lulli] (1632–87) a French composer of Italian origin who worked in the court of Louis XIV. He composed many comedy ballets (for example, *Le marriage force, Le Sicilien*), in which he acted and danced himself. He became immensely rich as a favourite of the king, but worked tirelessly at writing operas (some 20 in all) and helped to establish a distinctive French opera style. He died from an abscess after striking his foot with his conductor's baton. In addition to operas, his principal compositions include church music and two orchestral suites.

Lulu an unfinished opera by BERG, who also wrote the libretto (after plays by Wederkind). The story concerns Lulu, a *femme fatale*, who causes the death of her lovers, but is ultimately killed by

Jack the Ripper. It was not performed until 1979.

lunga pausa (*Italian*) a "long pause."

Lupu, Radu (1945-) a Romanian pianist, currently living in Britain, who has worldwide reputation as a virtuoso performer.

lur a primitive Scandinavian bronze instrument, similar to a bugle. Lurs came in pairs and resembled the horns of a ram.

lusingando (*Italian*) literally "flattering," i.e. in a cajoling manner.

lustig (*German*) "merry."

Lustigen Weiber von Windsor, Die see **Merry Wives of Windsor, The**.

Lustige Witwe, Die see **Merry Widow, The**.

lute a plucked stringed instrument with a body resembling that of a half-pear. It is thought to have a history dating back some three thousand years and was particularly popular during the sixteenth and seventeenth centuries; it has since been revived by twentieth-century instrument makers. It has a fretted fingerboard with a characteristic "pegbox" (a string harness) bent back at an angle to the finger-board. A lute can have anything up to 18 strings. It was traditionally used as an instrument for accompanying dances, but many solo works have also been written for it.

Lutoslawski, Witold (1913-) a Polish composer who is renowned for his AVANT-GARDE pieces, for example *Funeral Music for Strings*.

luttuoso (*Italian*) "mournfully, sadly."

Lutyens, Elisabeth (1906–83) an English composer who writes twelve-note music. Her compositions include concertos for horn and violin, film music, operas, chamber music.

Lydian mode (1) a scale used in ancient Greek music, the equivalent of the white notes on a piano from C to C. (2) From the Middle Ages onwards, the equivalent of a scale on the white notes on a piano from F to F.

lyre an instrument familiar to the ancient Greeks, Assyrians and Hebrews. It comprised a small, hollow box from which extended two horns that supported a cross bar and anything up to 12 strings, which could be plucked or strummed. It is traditionally taken to represent a token of love (Orpheus played the lyre).

lyric a short poem, or sequence of words, for a song. The term has a particular application to twentieth-century musicals and pop songs. A "lyricist" is the person who writes the words to a popular tune.

M

m *abbreviation for* MAIN, MANO, MANUAL.

m (me) In TONIC SOL-FA. the third note (or MEDIANT) of the major scale.

ma (*Italian*) "but," as *Andante ma non troppo*, "slow, but not too slow.

Macbeth (1) an opera by VERDI to a libretto by F. M. Piave. It tells the familiar Shakespeare tale of the murder of King Duncan in his pursuit of the throne of Scotland by Macbeth and his ambitious wife, Lady Macbeth. It was first performed in Florence in 1847. (2) a symphonic poem, on the same subject, by Richard STRAUSS (1890). (3) an opera by BLOCH to a libretto by E. Fleg (1910). (4) an opera by Lawrence Collingwood (1934).

McCabe, John (1939–) an English composer and pianist who has specialized in performing twentieth-century pieces and works by HAYDN. His compositions include operas (for example, *The Play of Mother Courage*), ballets (for example, *Mary, Queen of Scots*), three symphonies, and many miscellaneous pieces for orchestra and/or chorus.

McCartney, Paul (1942–) a British rock musician who was a founder member of the group The Beatles (1961–70). He is one of the most successful songwriters of the twentieth century, and many of the songs which he wrote in partnership with John LENNON are now considered "classics."

McCormack, [Count] John (1884–1943) an Irish-born tenor who became a US citizen in 1919. Trained in Milan, at first he sang in both concerts and operas but abandoned the latter in 1913 as he considered his acting ability to be poor. His sure technique and pure voice established his reputation worldwide.

MacCunn, Hamish (1868–1916) a Scottish composer and conductor whose best known work is the concert overture *Land of the Mountain and the Flood*. He also wrote operas, for example *Jeanie Deans* and *Diarmid*, a masque, *The Masque of War and Peace*, cantatas, for example *Lord Ullin's Daughter*, incidental music, overtures, songs, and dances.

MacDowell, Edward Alexander (1861–1908) an American composer who studied in Europe, where he met LISZT. He taught in Germany before returning to the USA in 1888, where he taught in Boston and New York. After his death, his widow established a summer camp for artists, musicians and writers in New Hampshire. He is remembered for his piano pieces, symphonic poems, and vocal compositions.

Macfarren, Sir George Alexander (1813–87) English composer of four oratorios, eight symphonies, two cantatas, overtures, songs, chamber music, and thirteen operas of which nine were produced. The son of the playwright George Macfarren, he also conducted, taught, becoming principal of the Royal Academy of Music in 1876, and wrote farces and melodramas. He was knighted in 1883.

Machado, Augusto (1845–1924) a Portuguese composer of piano and organ music and of a cantata, *Camoëns*, several operas, including *Lauriane*, and an operetta.

Machaut, Guillaume de (*c.*1304–77) a French composer, poet and diplomat. He composed many motets and madrigals, several using his own poems. One of his most important works is his Mass, *Messe de Notre Dame*, for four voices.

machete a small Portuguese guitar.

Madama Butterfly an opera by PUCCINI to a libretto by Giuseppe Giacosa and Luigi Illica, based on a play by David Belasco of a story by John Luther Long. It tells the tragic story of the Japanese girl, Cio-Cio-San (Madame Butterfly), who marries a Lieutenant Pinkerton of the US Navy. He deserts her to return to the USA, unknowingly leaving her pregnant with his child. Cio-Cio-San is convinced he will return to Japan "One fine day," but when he does it is with a new American wife. Overcome with grief, Cio-Cio-San stabs herself. The opera's first performance, conducted by TOSCANINI, in Feburary 1904 was a disaster. Puccini returned his fee and revised the opera, which had its second performance in May 1904, which established it as one of the most popular of all operas.

Maderna, Bruno (1920–73) an Italian composer and conductor. He composed piano, flute and oboe pieces and also favoured electronic instruments

madrigal

as in his *Musica su due dimensioni* (for flute, percussion instruments and electronic tape). As a conductor, he was a renowned interpreter of contemporary music.

madrigal a musical setting of a secular poem for two or more voices in COUNTERPOINT, usually unaccompanied. The first madrigals date back to the fourteenth century, and the first publications were made in Italy about 1501. The art of madrigal spread to every part of Europe, with the result that a ealth of polyphonic vocal music was created and reached a high art before the development of instrumental music. In the seventeenth century madrigals were superseded by cantatas.

Maelzel *or* **Mälzel, Johann Nepomuk** (1772–1828) a German-born inventor who settled in Vienna where he constructed various mechanical instruments. He is best known for patenting the first clockwork METRONOME, although it had originally been invented by WINKEL.

maestevole (*Italian*) "with majesty."

maestoso (*Italian*) "majestic" or "dignified."

maestro (*Italian*) literally "master," a term used for a master musician, particularly a conductor.

maestro del coro (*Italian*) the conductor of a chorus, a KAPELLMEISTER.

maestro di capella (*Italian*) a KAPELLMEISTER.

maestro sostitutto (*Italian*) literally "substitute conductor," an assistant conductor responsible in opera for an offstage chorus or band. Also, a RÉPÉTITEUR.

maggiore (*Italian*) "major mode."

Magic Flute, The (*Die Zauberflöte*) an opera

(with dialogue) by MOZART to a libretto by E.
Schikaneder. Set in Egypt, it tells the story of how
Prince Tamino, rescued from the toils of serpent
by three attendants of the evil Queen of the Night,
is persuaded to bring Pamina, the daughter of the
Queen of the Night, from the care of the High
Priest of Isis, Sarastro. The Queen gives him a
magic flute for his protection. When Tamino and
Pamina meet, they fall in love, and under the care
of the wise Sarastro they pass through fire and
water protected by the flute. A parallel tale concerns Papageno, a bird. catcher with a set of
magic bells, who searches for his Papagena. It
was first performed in 1791.

Magnificat (*Latin*) short for *Magnificat anima
mea Dominum* ("My soul magnifies the Lord") the
canticle of the Virgin Mary sung at Roman Catholic Vespers and Anglican Evensong. It is usually
chanted, but many composers, such as BACH, have
set it to their own music.

Mahler, Gustav (1860–1911) an influential Austrian composer and conductor, who started to
learn the piano when he was six and was giving
public recitals four years later. He studied in
Vienna and was impressed by the work of
BRUCKNER. He conducted at many of Europe's
leading opera houses before becoming the director of the Vienna State Opera in 1897. For much
of his life, he spent the summer months composing and the winter ones conducting. In 1907 he
went to the USA where he became conductor of
the New York Metropolitan Opera, but returned
to Vienna in 1911 because of his flagging health.

He died of pneumonia, aged forty-nine.

Mahler was famous in his lifetime as a conductor but many of his compositions were not well received. However, his works have subsequently been hailed as masterpieces and are perceived to form a musical link between the nineteenth and twentieth centuries. Towards the end of his short life, he became obsessed with the fear of death, which he expressed eloquently in his music. He is particularly famed for the way in which he used voices, especially with his vocal symphonies.

Mahler's principal works include: ten symphonies (the tenth was unfinished); the song cycles *Lieder eines fahrenden Gesellen* (Songs of the Wayfarer) and KINDERTOTENLIEDER; the song symphony *Das Lied von der Erde* (*The* SONG OF THE EARTH); the completion of WEBER's opera *Die Drei Pintos*, and numerous individual songs.

main (*French*) literally "hand", so *main droite* means "right hand" (particularly in piano music).

maître de chapelle (*French*) KAPELLMEISTER.

majeur (*French*) "major."

major (*Latin*) "greater," as opposed to MINOR or "lesser." Major scales are those in which a major third (INTERVAL of four semitones) occurs in ascending from the tonic; while the minor scales involve a minor third (three semitones). A major tone has the ratio 8 : 9 while a minor tone has the ratio 9 : 10.

malagueha a Spanish dance in 3/4 or 3/8 time, named after the town of Malaga. The tune is often sung as it is danced.

Malibran, Maria *see* **Garcia, Manuel**.

malinconia (*Italian*) "melancholy."

Malipiero, Gian Francesco (1882–1973) an Italian composer who is best known for his operas, for example, *Julius Caesar, Antony and Cleopatra*, oratorios, piano pieces, songs, and the ballet *La Mascarade des Princesses Captives*.

Mälzel, Johann Nepomuk *see* **Maelzel**.

mancando (*Italian*) "decreasing" or "fading away."

Manchester School the name applied to a group of British composers who studied music at the Royal Manchester College during the 1950s. They include Harrison BIRTWISTLE and Peter Maxwell DAVIES, among others.

mandolin, mandoline a stringed instrument, similar to the lute, but smaller and usually played with a plectrum. It has four pairs of strings and has occasionally been used as an orchestral instrument.

Manfred a dramatic poem by Lord Byron (1788–1824), in which the hero, Count Manfred, sells his soul to the Devil and lives in total solitude in the Alps. SCHUMANN wrote incidental music for it, and it inspired a symphony by TCHAIKOVSKY.

manica (*Italian*) "fingering."

Manners, Charles [originally Charles Mansergh] (1857–1955) an Irish bass singer who sang in many parts of the world before establishing the Moody-Manners Opera Company in 1898 with his wife, the English soprano **Fanny Moody** (1866–1945). The company toured successfully until 1916.

mano (*Italian*) "hand."

Manon an opera by MASSENET with a libretto by

Manon Lescaut

Meilhac and Gille, like MANON LESCAUT, based on Abbé Prévost's novel and first performed in 1884 in Paris. It is the story of Manon who, on her way in the care of her cousin Lescaut to be placed in a convent, meets, falls in love with, and elopes with the Chevalier des Grieux. Manon, however, wearies of des Grieux and leaves him for the wealthy Bretigny, but finds her passion revived when she learns that des Grieux is about to enter the church. She persuades him to abandon his plan and return to her. They are arrested in a police raid on a gambling party, but while des Grieux's father rescues him, Manon is sentenced to deportation and dies of exhaustion in her lover's arms while on the road to Le Havre.

Manon Lescaut an opera by PUCCINI (his third) to a libretto by a number of writers, among them Luigi Illica, based on the novel by Abbé Prévost. The story is substantially the same as that of MANON. Manon, in the charge of her brother Lescaut on the way to the convent, meets Des Grieux, who is destined for church, elopes with him but deserts him for Géronte de Ravoir. Des Grieux seeks her out, and his passion is requited, but she is arrested for immorality after being warned by Lescaut to flee and fatally delaying to gather her jewels. Des Grieux manages to get aboard the ship in which she is to be deported to America, and is with her in Louisiana when she is overcome with fever and dies. The opera was first performed in Turin in 1893. It is also the subject of several other operas and a ballet by Halévy which was first performed in Paris in 1830.

manual a keyboard on an organ or harpsichord; organs may have four manuals, named Solo, Swell, Great, and Choir.

maracas a pair of Latin-American percussion instruments made from gourds filled with seeds, pebbles or shells. Sound is produced by shaking the gourds.

Marbeck, John *see* **Merbecke, John**.

marcando (*Italian*) "marking."

marcatissimo (*Italian*) "very marked."

marcato (*Italian*) "marked" or "emphasized."

Marcello, Benedetto (1686–1739) an Italian composer, librettist and writer on music who was also a lawyer. He is known for his cantatas, psalm settings, oratorios and concertos. His brother, Alessandro Marcello, was also a composer of worth.

march a piece of music with a strict rhythm, usually 4/4 time but sometimes in 2/4, 3/4 or 6/8 time, to which soldiers can march. The pace varies with the purpose of the piece, from the extremely slow funeral or dead march to the quickstep (with about 108 steps a minute), and the Sturm Marsch or pas de charge with 120 steps a minute.

Marchand, Louis (1669–1732) French composer of organ and harpischord music who became court organist in Paris then Dresden, where he was held in high favour until Johann Sebastian BACH played there and challenged him to a contest. Marchand fled to Paris where a became a teacher.

Marchesi de Castrone, Mathilde [originally Mathilde Graumann] (1826–1913) a German mezzo-soprano who became a celebrated teacher of singing in Vienna and Cologne, and who settled in Paris where she set up her own school. MELBA was among her pupils. She also composed and published books of vocal exercises. In 1852 she married the baritone **Salvatore Marchesi**, Cavaliere de Castrone (1822–1908), son of a governor-general of Sicily, who had left Italy on the failure of the revolutionary movement in 1848. Their daughter, **Blanche Marchesi** (1863–1940), was a soprano who also became a teacher.

marche (*French*) march.

marche redoublée (*French*) double quick march.

marche triomphale (*French*) triumphal march.

Marchisio, Barbara (1834–1919) an Italian contralto and teacher. Her sister **Carlotta Marchisio** (1836–1872) was a soprano. ROSSINI wrote his *Petite Messe Solennelle* for them.

marcia (*Italian*) "march," so *alla marcia* means "in a marching style."

Marenzio, Luca (1553–99) an Italian composer who worked in Poland as well as in Rome. He is most famous for his 159 madrigals, the style of which was influential.

mariachi (*Spanish*) a Mexican folk group of variable size; it normally includes violins and guitars.

Maria di Rohan a three-act opera by Gaetano DONIZETTI, which was first performed in 1843 in Vienna.

Maria Theresa *or* **Maria Theresia** the nickname for HAYDN's symphony no. 48 in C. It is so called because it was written when Empress Maria Theresa visited Haydn's patron, Prince Esterhazy (1773).

marimba a Latin American instrument which may have originated in Africa. It is similar to a large XYLOPHONE and can be played by up to four people at the same time.

Marino Faliero a two-act opera by Gaetano DONIZETTI, which was first performed in 1853 in Paris.

Mario, Giovanni [Cavaliere di Candia] (1810–83) an Italian tenor, the son of a general, who abandoned a military career to become a singer in order to raise money to pay his debts. A handsome man, his glorious voice and acting abilities made him the leading singer of his day. He dominated the operatic stage for 25 years. He fell into poverty again after his retirement and his friends in London gave him a benefit concert.

mark a sign or word used in NOTATION to indicate the time, tone, accent or quality of a composition, or the pace at which it should be performed.

markirt (*German*) "marked."

marqué (*French*) "marked."

Marley, Bob (1945–81) Jamaican singer and songwriter. With his group, the Wailers, he became the world's leading REGGAE singer. His songs include the haunting ballad "No Woman, No Cry."

Marriage of Figaro, The (*Le Nozze di Figaro*) an opera by MOZART to a libretto by Lorenzo da Ponte based on Beaumarchais' comedy. It is the sequel to ROSSINI's opera *The* BARBER OF SEVILLE and tells how Count Almaviva, bored with his lovely Countess, plans to exercise his seigneurial rights over her maid Susanna, with whom Figaro, his manservant, is in love and whom he is about to marry.

Despite his jealousy of the page Cherubino's attentions to the Countess, he continues with his plan, but it is foiled by the Countess, Susanna and Figaro conspiring. Matters become very complicated, not least by Figaro turning out to be the son of Dr Bartolo and Marcellina, who had been planning to marry Figaro herself. All ends in happiness, however, when Almaviva begs his wife's forgiveness, and Figaro and Susanna pledge their love. It was first performed in 1786 in Vienna, and the music, which reveals Mozart at his best, has made it very popular.

Marriner, Neville (1924–) an English conductor and pianist who founded the famous Academy of St Martin-in-the-Fields in 1956.

Marsch (*German*) "march."

Marschner, Heinrich August (1795–1861) German composer who was joint kapellmeister with WEBER in Dresden and later in Hanover before dedicating himself to composing mainly vocal works. These include the operas *Heinrich IV and Aubigné* (produced in Dresden by Weber in 1820) and *Hans Heiling*, as well as songs and choruses.

Marseillaise, La the French national anthem which was composed by ROUGET DE LISLE in 1792 and is so called because it was sung by men from Marseille as they entered Paris in the same year.

Marta (Martha) an opera by FLOTOW, which he based on Lady Henrietta, the earlier ballet of which he had been joint composer. It tells the story of how Lady Henrietta, wearied of her duties at court, and her maidservant Nancy pretend to be farm servants and find themselves tied to a year's service to the two young farmers Lionel and Plunkett. Naturally, Lionel falls in love with Martha and Plunkett with Nancy. The women flee back to court, but eventually the lovers are united and all ends happily. The opera was first performed in 1847 in Vienna.

martelé (*French*) *see* **martellato**.

martellato (*Italian*) literally "hammered"; a term used mainly in music for strings to indicate that notes should be played with short, sharp strokes of the bow. The term is also occasionally used in guitar and piano music.

Martha *see* **Marta**.

Martin, Frank (1890–1974) a Swiss composer, pianist and harpsichordist who settled in Holland. In his later years, he composed TWELVE-NOTE MUSIC. He is best known for his operas *The Tempest* and *Monsieur Pourceaugnac*, ballets, orchestral pieces (for example, *Petite Symphonie Concertante*), incidental pieces, and choral works.

Martinu, Bohuslav (1890–1959) a Czech composer who at various times lived in France, the USA and Switzerland. He wrote 13 operas (for example, *Comedy on the Bridge*, *The Greek Passion*), six symphonies, choral works, ballets, sonatas and many pieces of chamber music.

Martyrs Gaetano DONIZETTI's four-act opera, to book by Scribe, was first performed April 10, 1840, at the Paris Académie, and was an adaptation of his earlier opera, "Polito."

Maryland a song written by James Ryder Randall to the tune "Lauriger Horatius," which has since become the hymn of the state of Maryland.

marziale (*Italian*) "warlike."

Masaniello an opera by Daniel AUBER with a libretto by SCRIBE and Delavigne, also known as *La Muette de Portici* or *La Muta di Portici* (The Dumb Girl of Portici). Set in the time of the Neapolitan revolt of 1647 against the foreign rule of Spain, it tells the story of Fenella, a dumb girl who has been imprisoned by Alfonso, and her brother Masaniello, who leads a revolt that is successful. Masaniello, however, is poisoned, becomes insane and dies in battle. When Fenella hears of her brother's death she plunges to her own death in the burning lava of the erupting Mount Vesuvius. It was first performed in 1828 in Paris, and its performance in Brussels in 1830 is said to have occasioned the beginning of Belgium's struggle for independence.

Mascagni, Pietro (1863–1945) an Italian composer whose outstanding early work, the opera CAVALLERIA RUSTICANA, was so successful that it overshadowed virtually everything else he wrote. His other operas include *L'Amico Fritz*, *Iris* and *Il Piccolo Marat*. He was a confirmed fascist, as his opera *Nerone* shows.

Masked Ball, A (*Un Ballo in Maschera*) the title of two operas, one by AUBER, the other by VERDI, both based on the same real event, the assassination of Gustavus III of Sweden at a masked ball in Stockholm. Gustavus and Malwina, the wife of his counsellor, Ankarström, are in love, and Gustavus ignores warnings that his death is being planned. When Ankarström discovers his wife's unfaithfulness, he turns against them both

and joins the conspiracy to kill the king. He draws
the lot to commit the deed at a masked ball, the
king's page, Oscar, telling him how he will recognize the king. At the ball Ankarström shoots the
king, who pardons him before dying. Auber's
opera was first produced in 1833, but when Verdi
first presented his version to the San Carlo Theatre in Naples in 1854, it was declined for political
reasons, it being considered unwise to portray the
assassination of a king. Verdi therefore trans-
ferred the action from Europe to America, substi-
tuting for the king Count Riccardo, governor of
Boston, Massachusetts, while Ankarström becomes Renato, and Malwina Amelia. It was first
performed in Rome in 1859.

Mason, Daniel Gregory (1873–1953) an American composer and writer on music. His works
include three symphonies (for example, *A Lincoln
Symphony*). He was the grandson of **Lowell Mason** (1792–1872), an American organist and collector of psalms, and an influential teacher, and
the nephew of **William Mason** (1829–1908), an
American concert pianist, composer and writer.

masque a spectacular court entertainment that
was especially popular during the seventeenth
century. It combined poetry and dancing with
vocal and instrumental music to tell a simple
story that invariably flattered its aristocratic
audience.

Mass (*Latin* **Missa**, *Italian* **Messa**, *French* and
German **Messe**) in musical terms, the setting to
music of the Latin Ordinary of Mass (those parts
of the Mass that do not vary). The five parts are

the KYRIE ELEISON, GLORIA, CREDO, SANCTUS with BENEDICTUS, and AGNUS DEI.

Massenet, Jules Emile Frederic (1842–1912) a French composer and teacher who was much influenced by WAGNER, but whose music is considered rather more sweet and melodious. He wrote 27 operas (for example, *Le Roi de Lahore*, MANON, *Don Quichotte*), ballets, oratorios, and some 200 songs.

Master of the Queen's Musick an honorary position (in Britain) awarded to a prominent musician of the time; it is his (or her) duty to compose anthems, etc, for royal occasions.

mastersinger *see* **Meistersinger**.

Mastersingers of Nuremberg, The *see* **Meistersinger von Nürnberg, Die**.

Mathias, William (1934–) a Welsh composer and pianist, a pupil of Lennox BERKELEY, who has written a broad variety of work, including a symphony, concertos, choral music and chamber music.

Matins the name given to the first of the "Canonical Hours" of the Roman Catholic Church. The term also refers to Morning Prayer in the Anglican Church.

Ma Vlast (My Country) a cycle of six symphonic poems by SMETANA, who was inspired by the Czechoslovakian countryside and history (1874–79).

Mazeppa (1) an opera by TCHAIKOVSKY to a libretto by V. P. Burenin. Mazeppa was a Cossack ruler who revolted against Peter the Great. It was first performed in 1884. (2) a symphonic poem by LISZT on the same subject.

mazurka a Polish folk dance of the seventeenth century for up to twelve people. The music can vary in speed and is often played on bagpipes. CHOPIN, amongst other composers, was influenced by the music and wrote some 55 "mazurkas" for piano. **me** In the TONIC SOL-FA, the third note (or MEDIANT) of the major scale.

md *abbreviation for* mano destra or maine droite, "right hand."

measure (1) a unit of rhythm or notes and rests included between two bars. (2) a stately dance of the minuet or pavanne type. (3) (US) a BAR (of music).

mechanical instruments instruments that can play complex music through the programming of their mechanism (for example, by punched paper or pins on a spindle) when supplied with power (through foot pedals, clockwork, steam power, electricity, etc).

mediant the third note in a major or minor scale above the TONIC (lowest note), for example, E in the scale of C major.

Mehta, Zubin (1936–) an Indian conductor, violinist and pianist. He is best known as a conductor and has worked with most of the world's leading orchestras, notably the New York Philharmonic Orchestra.

Meistersinger (*German*)"mastersinger," the title of highest rank in the song schools or guilds that flourished in German cities from the fourteenth century until the nineteenth century. Where the MINNESINGERS drew their members from the aristocracy, mastersingers were usually craftsmen or tradesmen who composed poems and music, and who formed themselves into powerful guilds. They were doubtless of great value as a means of extending musical culture, but in their latter days their original purpose tended to be defeated by pedantic restrictions, as satirized in WAGNER's great opera, *Die* MEISTERSINGER VON NÜRNBERG.

Meistersinger von Nürnberg, Die (The Mastersingers of Nuremberg) an opera by WAGNER, who also wrote the libretto. The story concerns Walther von Stolzing, a young Franconian knight, and his love for Eva, the daughter of Veit Pogner, a rich goldsmith who has promised his daughter's hand to the winner of the Mastersinger's contest. Walther enters the competition, his main opponent being the town clerk, Beckmesser, a man of rigid views in respect of the meistersingers' regulations. Walther has learned from David, the young apprentice of Hans SACHS, the cobbler and poet, something of the regulations of the guild. There are the tones and modes to be learned, the thirty-three canons to be observed, and when the aspirant has acquired the art of singing and composing according to the *Tablatur*, or rules, having been through the degrees of scholar and singer, he must then learn poesy, and on mastering the art of combining poetry with song, progress from poet to meistersinger. Walther tells the meistersingers that he has learned poetry from the books of Walter von der Vogelweide and music from the birds. Only Sachs is satisfied with the thoroughness of such a training, and Walter fails his first test. Helped, however, by Sachs, Walther eventually wins the challenge with his "Prize Song." The opera is a faithful if exaggerated satire of the foibles of the meistersingers, and in Hans Sachs introduces at least one historical person to the stage. It was first performed in 1866 in Munich.

Melba, Nellie [originally Helen Porter Armstrong, née Mitchell] (1859–1931) an Australian soprano who became extremely famous in Europe and the USA for her operatic roles. She chose her stage name, Melba, in tribute to the city of Melbourne. She was honoured in several ways: she was made a DBE in 1918, and the ice-cream dessert, peach Melba, and Melba toast were both named after her.

Melchior, Lauritz (1890–1973) a Danish-born American tenor who started singing as a baritone and developed a large ringing voice. He had a successful career as a HELDENTENOR, singing WAGNER roles at Bayreuth as well as the Metropolitan Opera.

melodica (*Italian*) a free-reed instrument which was developed from the harmonica. It is box-shaped and has a small keyboard; the player blows down a tube and plays notes by pressing the keys.

melodic minor scale *see* **scale**.

melodic sequence *see* **sequence**.

melodrama originally, a part of a play or opera in which words are spoken to a musical accompaniment. From this, the word has come to mean an exaggeratedly dramatic or sensational play.

melody a succession of notes, of varying pitch,

that create a distinct and identifiable musical form. Melody, HARMONY and RHYTHM are the three essential ingredients of music. The criteria of what constitutes a melody change over time.

membranophone the generic term for all instruments in which sound is produced by the vibration of a skin or membrane, for example, DRUM, KAZOO.

Mendelssohn, Felix [originally Jakob Ludwig Felix Mendelssohn-Bartholdy] (1809–47) a German composer, organist, pianist and conductor who was first taught music by his mother. He was precociously gifted. He first performed in public when he was nine years old and organized his own orchestra when he was twelve. When he was seventeen, he composed his first masterpiece, the overture to A *Midsummer Night's Dream*. In 1829 he made the first of several visits to England and Scotland, and was inspired to write his *Hebrides Overture*. Later he visited Italy and France, where he met BERLIOZ, LISZT and CHOPIN. He settled in Germany as an established conductor and, with SCHUMANN, founded the Leipzig Conservatorium. In 1846 he triumphantly conducted the first performance of his *Elijah* oratorio at the Birmingham Festival, but by now his health was failing and he died the following year.

Mendelssohn combined classical technique and romantic expressiveness. He appreciated his phenomenal gifts (he was also a better than average writer and painter). He was liked by fellow composers, as well as by the public at large, and he did much to "popularize" serious music. He pioneered the revival of Johann Sebastian BACH with a performance of the ST MATTHEW PASSION in 1829.

Mendelssohn's principal works include: five symphonies (for example, the SCOTTISH, REFORMATION, and *Italian* symphonies); overtures (for example, *The Hebrides* (FINGAL'S CAVE), *Calm Sea and Prosperous Voyage*); oratorios (for example, *St Paul*, *Elijah*, *Christus*); and numerous pieces for organ, piano and chamber orchestra.

meno (*Italian*) "less," so *meno mosso* means "slower" (less speed).

Menotti, Gian Carlo (1911–) an Italian-born composer who emigrated to the USA in 1928. He is best known for his operas, for example, *Amelia goes to the Ball*, *The Telephone*, *The Saint of Bleeker Street* and *Help, help, the Globolinks*, and especially his children's opera, *Amahl and the Night Visitors*, which received its first performance on television in 1951. He has also written ballets and various pieces for orchestra.

menuet (*French*) MINUET.

Menuhin, Sir Yehudi (1916–) an American-born violinist and conductor who settled in England after the World War II. He was a child prodigy and achieved international fame. He also has a worldwide reputation as a conductor, especially of chamber music. In 1963 he founded the Menuhin School of Music for musically gifted children. He was knighted in 1965.

Mer, La (The Sea) three symphonic sketches for orchestra by DEBUSSY, inspired by the sea (1905).

Merbecke *or* **Marbeck, John** (1510–85) an English composer and organist who was the first person to set the English (as distinct from the Latin) liturgy to music.

"Mercury" Symphony the unexplained nickname for HAYDN's symphony no. 43. in E (*c.*1771).

Merrie England a comic opera by Edward GER-MAN with a libretto by Basil Hood, which was first performed in 1902 in London.

Merry Widow, The (*Die Lustige Witwe*) an operetta by LEHAR to a libretto by V. Leon and L. Stein. The story is one of romance and diplomatic intrigue. It was first performed in 1905.

Merry Wives of Windsor, The (*Die Lustigen Weiber von Windsor*) an opera by NICOLAI to a libretto by S. H. Mosenthal (after Shakespeare). It was first performed in 1849.

Messa, Messe *see* **Mass**.

Messa di voce (Italian) a swelling and then diminishing of the voice on a held tone.

Messager, André Charles Prosper (1853–1929) a French organist, conductor and composer who was artistic director at Covent Garden (1901–1906) and became director general of the Paris Opera House in 1908. His works include the ballets *Les deux pigeons* ("The Two Pigeons") and *Scaramouche*, and the operetta *Mme Chrysanthème* (based on a novel by Pierre Loti).

Messiaen, Olivier Eugène Prosper Charles (1908–92) French composer and organist. In his formative years he was influenced by Indian music; and also by birdsong, which he wrote down in musical notation. He has subsequently used birdsong in many of his pieces. He was imprisoned in a concentration camp by the Nazis during the Second World War, when he wrote *Quartet for the End of Time.* He is one of the most influential of all modern composers and he has made use of a wide range of influences, such as ancient Greek music. His principal works include: *Nativite du Seigneur, L'Ascension* (for organ); *Turangall-lasymphonie* (for orchestra); *La Transfiguration de Notre Seigneur Jésus Christ* (for solo instruments, chorus and orchestra); *Visions de l'Amen* (for piano); and many pieces for miscellaneous instruments.

Messiah an oratorio by HANDEL to text taken from the Bible. It includes the famous HALLELUJAH CHORUS. It was composed within a month and was first performed in 1742 in Dublin.

mesto, mestoso (*Italian*) "sad."

metallo (*Italian*) "metal," *so bel metallo di voce,* "ringing quality of voice."

metallophone an instrument that is similar to a XYLOPHONE but has metal bars (usually bronze).

Metastasio, Pietro (1698–1782) an Italian poet who wrote libretti used by GLUCK, MEYERBEER, and many others. MOZART used his libretto for *La Clemenza di Tito,* which had previously been set by six other composers. He became poet laureate to the Holy Roman emperor Charles VI, and also wrote dramatic works.

metronome an instrument that produces regular beats and can therefore be used to indicate the pace at which a piece of music should be played. The first clockwork metronome was invented by WINKEL but patented by MAELZEL in 1816 and had a metal rod that swung backwards and forwards on a stand. The speed of ticking could be altered by sliding a weight up or down the rod. Electronic metronomes are also manufactured today.

Metropolitan Opera House, New York, the home of the prestigious Metropolitan Opera Company which was formed in 1883. The opera house is part of the Lincoln Center for the Performing Arts and is affectionately called "The Met."

Meyerbeer, Giacomo (1791–1864) a German-born composer who visited Italy and wrote operas in the style of ROSSINI. His best known works, written for the Paris Opera, include *Robert le Diable*, *Les Huguenots* and *L'*AFRICAINE.

mezzo (*Italian*) literally "half," so *mezzo-soprano* means a voice between soprano and contralto.

mf abbreviation for *mezzo forte*, (*Italian*) meaning moderately loud.

mg abbreviation for *main gauche*, (*French*) meaning "left hand".

microtones INTERVALS that are smaller than a SEMITONE in length, for example, the quarter-tone.

middle C the note C which occupies the first ledger line below the treble staff, the first ledger line above the bass staff, and is indicated by the C clef.

Midsummer Marriage, The an opera by TIPPETT, who also wrote the libretto. Like *The* MAGIC FLUTE of MOZART, the opera tells two parallel stories concerning two pairs of lovers (Mark and Jenifer, Bell and Jack), who have to undergo trials before they can be finally united. It contains the well-known *Ritual Dances*, and was first performed in 1955.

Midsummer Night's Dream, A (1) an overture to
Shakespeare's play by MENDELSSOHN (1826), to
which he later added incidental music. (2) Incidental music to Shakespeare's play by ORFF (1939).
(3) an opera by BRITTEN which uses text from
Shakespeare's play (1960).

Mikado, The an operetta by GILBERT and SULLIVAN.
It is set in Japan and is subtitled *The town of
Titipu*. It is probably the most famous of the
"Savoy operas" and it played for 672 nights after
its first performance in 1885. It is Japanese in
name only, but its performance was forbidden in
1907 in the UK on the ground that it might wound
the sensibilities of the Japanese people.

Mikrokomos a collection of 153 short piano pieces
by BARTOK, providing graded pieces for the teaching of technique. It is rich in invention.

Milhaud, Darius (1892–1974) a French composer
and pianist, of Jewish ancestry, who became a
member of the group known as "*Les* SIX". He was
an extremely prolific composer and experimented
with many different types of music from jazz to
Latin-American and electronic. His work includes
the ballets *The Creation of the World* and *The Ox
on the Roof*, the operas *Cristophe Colomb* and
David, and the orchestral piece *Saudades do
Brasil*.

military band a band in the armed forces that
plays military music, usually for marching. There
are many different types of military band, and the
number of players can vary. Most bands comprise
a mixture of brass, woodwind and percussion
instruments.

"Military" Symphony HAYDN's symphony no.100 in G (1794). It is so called because it employs "military" instruments (such as cymbals and bass drum, which were not used in the orchestra of the time) and has a solo trumpet call in the second movement.

Miller, Glenn (1904–44) American composer, band leader and trombonist. His dance band became one of the most popular in the world, with tunes such as "Moonlight Serenade" and "In the Mood." The plane carrying Miller and his band to play for the troops disappeared over the English Channel in 1944.

minim a note, formerly the shortest in time-value, with half the value of a SEMIBREVE; the equivalent of a half-note in in US terminology.

Minnesingers the poet-musicians of Germany in the twelfth and thirteenth centuries, who were of noble birth, like the TROUBADOURS of France, and who produced *minnelieder*, or love songs. WAGNER's *Tannhäuser* is a minnesinger. They were succeeded by the MEISTERSINGERS.

minor (*Latin*) "less" or "smaller." Minor intervals contain one semitone less than MAJOR. The minor third is characteristic of scales in the minor mode.

minor canon a priest skilled in music who supervises services in collegiate and cathedral churches.

minstrel a professional entertainer or musician of the medieval times. Such people were often employed by a royal court or aristocratic family.

minuet a French rural dance in 3/4 time that was popular during the seventeenth and eighteenth centuries. It remained popular and was incorporated into classical sonatas and symphonies as a regular movement.

"Minute" Waltz the nickname of CHOPIN's waltz in D flat (1847) which, if played very fast, should last only a minute.

miracle play *see* **mystery play**.

Mireille an opera by Gounod with a libretto by Carré based on a poem by Mistral, which was first performed in Paris in 1864. Set in Arles in Provence, it is the love story of Vincent and Mireille in opposition to Mireille's father.

mirliton (*French*) any wind instrument in which a thin membrane is made to vibrate and make a noise when the player blows, hums or sings into it. It is now known as the KAZOO.

mirror music any piece of music that sounds the same when played backwards.

Miserere (*Latin*) short for *Miserere mei Deus* ("Have mercy upon me, O God"), the first line of the 51st Psalm. It has been set to music by several composers, including VERDI.

Missa (*Latin*) "Mass," so *Missa brevis* means "short mass"; *Missa cantata* means "sung mass"; *Missa pro defunctis* is mass for the dead, or requiem; and *Missa solemnis* is solemn or high mass.

misterioso (*Italian*) "mysteriously."

misura (*Italian*) "measure"; equivalent to a BAR.

Mitridate, Re di Ponte an opera seria by MOZART to a libretto by V. A. Cigna-Santi (after Racine). Mozart wrote it when he was fourteen, and it was first performed in 1770.

Mixolydian mode (1) the set of notes, in ancient Greek music, which are the equivalent of the white notes on a piano from B to B. (2) in church music of the Middle Ages onwards, the equivalent of the white notes on a piano from G to G.

mixture an organ stop that brings into play a number of pipes that produce HARMONICS above the pitch corresponding to the actual key which is played.

MM abbreviation for MAELZEL's metronome.

moderatissimo (*Italian*) "very moderate."

moderato (*Italian*) "moderate" (in terms of speed).

modes the various sets of notes or SCALES, which were used by musicians until the concept of the KEY was accepted (*c*.1650). Modes were originally used by the ancient Greeks and were adapted by medieval composers, especially for church music. Modes were based on what are now the white notes of the piano.

modulation the gradual changing of key during the course of a part of a composition by means of a series of harmonic progressions. Modulation is *diatonic* when it is accomplished by the use of chords from relative keys; *chromatic* when by means of non-relative keys; *enharmonic* when effected by the alteration of notation; *final*, or complete, when a new tonality is established; and *partial*, or passing, when the change of key is only transient.

Moeran, Ernest John (1894–1950) an English composer of Irish ancestry. His compositions include a symphony, violin and cello concertos, miscellaneous orchestral pieces, songs, and works for chamber orchestra.

moll (*German*) "minor" (as opposed to major, *dur*).

molto (*Italian*) "very", so *allegro molto* means "very fast."

Moments Musicaux a set of six short piano pieces by Schubert. The same title has also been used by many lesser composers for piano works.

Monk, Thelonius (1920–82) an American jazz pianist and composer. He became a member of Dizzy Gillespie's band in 1946 and formed his own band in 1947, which later included many talented saxophonists, for example Coltrane. His compositions include "Round Midnight."

monodrama dramatic work for a single performer.

monody a type of accompanied solo song which was developed during the late sixteenth and early seventeenth centuries. It contained dramatic and expressive embellishments and devices, and consequently had an influence on opera.

monothematic a piece of music that is developed from a single musical idea.

monotone declamation of words on a single tone.

Monsigny, Pierre Alexandre (1729–1817) French violinist and composer of operas for the Opéra Comique in Paris, including *Félix, ou l'enfant trouvé* ("Felix, or the discovered child").

Monteux, Pierre (1875–1964) French conductor who conducted the Boston Symphony Orchestra for five years from 1919, giving first performances of works by Stravinsky, Debussy and Ravel as well as those of American composers, before going to the Metropolitan, New York.

Monteverdi (Monteverde), Claudio Giovanni Antonio (1567–1643) an Italian composer from Cremona working in Mantua and Venice, who was ordained a priest in 1632. He composed many religious works (for example, Masses, Vespers, Magnificats) but also numerous secular works, especially madrigals, operas and ballets. Unfortunately, only three of his 12 operas survive in their complete state (ORFEO, *Il ritorno d'Ulisse in patria* and L'INCORONAZONE DE POPPEA). Monteverdi's role in the development of music has been to compared to Shakespeare's in literature; he injected a new imagination into every form of music he worked with.

Moody, Dwight Lyman *see* **Sankey, Ira David**.

Moody, Fanny *see* **Manners, Charles**.

Moonlight Sonata a nickname for BEETHOVEN's sonata for harpsichord or piano, Op 27, which was published in 1802, with a dedication to ther Contessa Giulietta Guicciardi. Beethoven styled it "Sonata quasi una fantasia" and did not class it with his best work. The name comes from a criticism describing the first movement as resembling a boat on Lake Geneva in moonlight.

Moore, Douglas Stuart (1893–1969) an American composer and teacher. His works include operas (for example, *The Devil and Daniel Webster*, *The Ballad of Baby Doe*), and orchestral and choral pieces.

Moore, Thomas (1779–1852) Irish poet and musician who wrote 125 songs, including "The Last Rose of Summer" and "The Harp that Once through Tara's Halls," published as *Irish Melodies*. His poem "Lalla Rookh" has been the subject of many operas.

Morales, Melesio (1838–1908) a Mexican composer who was prolific in all forms, but is better known as the founder of the Conservatory of Music in Mexico City.

morbidezza (*Italian*) literally "gentleness" or "delicacy."

morbido (*Italian*) "soft" or "gentle."

morceau (*French*) a "piece" (of music).

mordent a musical ornament whereby one note rapidly alternates with another one degree below it; this is indicated by a sign over the note.

morendo (*Italian*) "dying," i.e. decreasing in volume.

moresca (*Italian*) a sword dance dating from the fifteenth and sixteenth centuries, which represents battles between the Moors and the Christians. It was the origin of the English morris dance. It has been included in operas, often to a marching rhythm.

morisco (*Italian*) "in Moorish style."

Morley, Thomas (1557–*c*.1602) an English composer who was given the patent to print songbooks by Elizabeth I. As well as publishing his own works, he also published works of his contemporaries and educational booklets. He is considered to be the father of the English madrigal and he also wrote ballets and pieces for the lute.

mormorando, mormorosa (Italian) "murmuring" or "whispering."

Mornington, Earl of (1735–81), Irish musician and teacher at Dublin University, who wrote church music and madrigals. His practice of openly carrying his violin case in the London streets despite the jeers of the crowd was commented on by SCHOLES: "There was courage in this family, for one of his sons was the famous Duke of Wellington.

morris dance a style of English dance, the music for which is provided by pipe and tabor. It was orginally a costume dance, the characters often being those from the Robin Hood ballads. Of Moorish or Spanish origin, the dance later became associated with many tunes, some in 4/4, others in 3/4 time.

Morrison, Jim (1943–71) an American rock singer and songwriter. His band, The Doors, with sombre doom-laden songs such as "The End," became a huge cult after his death (from alcohol and drug abuse).

Morton, Ferdinand ("Jelly Roll") (1885–1941) an American jazz pianist, singer, band leader and composer. Regarded as one of the founders of jazz as a genuine art form, his band, the Red Hot Peppers, became one of the most popular jazz bands of the mid-1920s, between the RAGTIME and SWING eras.

Mosè in Egitto (Moses in Egypt) an oratorio or opera (it has been sung as both) by ROSSINI with a libretto by Tottala, which was first performed in 1818 in Naples. It portrays the Biblical story of the flight of the Hebrews from Egypt by the parting of the Red Sea.

Moses und Aron (Moses and Aaron) an opera by SCHOENBERG, who also wrote the libretto, which is based on the Biblical story of Moses and Aaron. It was first performed in Zurich in 1957.

mosso (*Italian*) "moved," so *piu mosso* means "more

moved," i.e. quicker, and *meno mosso* "less speed."

motet a musical setting of sacred words for solo voices or choir, with or without accompaniment. The first motets were composed in the thirteenth century.

Mother Goose (*Ma mère l'oye*) a suite of five pieces for piano duet by RAVEL. It was based on fairy stories and was later produced as a ballet (1912).

motif *or* **motive** a small group of notes which create a melody or rhythm, for example the first four notes of BEETHOVEN's 5th symphony form a motif.

motion the upward or downward progress of a melody. It is said to be *conjunct* when the degrees of the scale succeed each other; *disjunct* where the melody proceeds in skips; *contrary* where two parts move in opposite directions; *oblique* when one part moves while the other remains stationary; and *similar*, or direct, when the parts move in the same direction.

moto (*Italian*) "motion," so *con moto* means "with motion" or quickly.

motto theme a short theme that recurs during the course of a composition. In this way, it dominates the poem of the supposed fatal poisoning of MOZART by SALIERI. It was first performed in 1898.

Mount of Olives an English name for BEETHOVEN's oratorio *Christus am Oelberg*.

"Mourning" Symphony the nickname for HAYDN's symphony no. 44 in E minor (1771). It is so called because Haydn requested the slow movement to be played at his own funeral.

Moussorgsky

Moussorgsky, Modeste Petrovich *see* **Mussorgsky, Modeste Petrovich**.

mouth the part of an organ pipe from which the sound comes, as opposed to the foot, where the wind enters.

mouth organ *see* **harmonica**.

mouthpiece the cup or beak-shaped end of the tube of a wind instrument to which the lips are applied.

movement a self-contained section of a larger instrumental composition, such as a symphony or sonata.

Mozart, Wolfgang Amadeus (1756–91) an Austrian composer, keyboard player, violinist, violist and conductor. He was born in Salzburg and was taught music by his father, **Leopold Mozart** (1719–1787), who was a violinist, composer and writer himself. The young Mozart was an infant prodigy and composed his first pieces for harpsichord when he was five. In 1762 Leopold took his son and daughter, **Maria Anna** (1751–1829), on a tour of Munich, Vienna and Pressburg where the children gave virtuoso harpsichord performances. By this time, Wolfgang could also play the violin, although he had received no formal instruction. The following year, Mozart went on an extended European tour, which took in Paris and London, which is where he met Johann Christian BACH and wrote his first three symphonies. In 1768 he composed his first operas, *La finta semplice* and *Bastien und Bastienne*. In Vienna, Mozart met HAYDN, who was one of the few of his contemporaries with a true appreciation of his

genius, for, despite his precocious gifts, he found
it difficult to achieve patronage. Between 1773
and 1777 he spent most of his time in Salzburg
with occasional visits to Vienna, Munich and
Paris. For a time, he entered the service of the
Archbishop of Salzburg, but this was not a success, and in 1781, after a sojourn in Paris, he
moved to Vienna where he married the singer,
Constanze Weber (d.1842). In Vienna, Mozart
earned a living as a freelance composer, teacher
and performer, but he was perpetually in financial difficulties. However, it was during his last
years in Vienna that he composed many of his
greatest pieces, including the symphonies that
have been nicknamed HAFFNER, LINZ and JUPITER,
and the operas COSÌ FAN TUTTE, *The* MARRIAGE OF
FIGARO, and *The* MAGIC FLUTE (which was influenced by his interest in Freemasonry). He never
finished his last work *The* REQUIEM, and died,
most probably of typhoid, in 1791. The theory that
he was poisoned by his rival SALIERI has never
been proved.

Mozart was influenced by the works of Johann
Christian and Charles Philip Emmanuel BACH,
HANDEL, HAYDN and GLUCK, amongst others, but
his own contribution to nearly all musical forms
was colossal. He helped to establish the classical
style of composition, especially with his operas,
symphonies and piano concertos, which are considered to be among the greatest ever written. His
work could be dramatic, witty, light-hearted or
profound, and his influence on other composers is
incalculable.

Mozart and Salieri

His principal compositions include: the operas, IDOMENEO, *The Marriage of Figaro*, DON GIOVANNI, *Cosi fan tutte* and *The Magic Flute*; 41 symphonies; 27 piano concertos; 23 string quartets; 17 piano sonatas; and 18 Masses.

Mozart and Salieri an opera by RIMSKY-KORSAKOV which is essentially a setting of Pushkin's dramatic poem of the supposed fatal poisoning of MOZART by SALIERI. It was first performed in 1898.

mp abbreviation for *mezzo piano* (*Italian*), meaning "half-soft".

MS, ms abbreviation for *mano sinistra* (*Italian*), meaning "left hand".

Much Ado About Nothing an opera by Stanford with a libretto by Sturgis, based on Shakespeare's play, which was first performed in 1990 in London. The play was also the basis for BERLIOZ's opera *Béatrice et Bénédict*.

Muette de Portici, La *see* **Masaniello**.

muffled drum a drum with a piece of cloth or towelling draped over the vibrating surfaces. It produces a sombre tone when struck, and is usually associated with funeral music.

Mundy, John (*c.*1566–1630) an English organist and composer who was taught by his composer father, William (d.1591). His works include madrigals and pieces for viols.

musette (*French*) (1) a type of small bagpipe popular at the French court in the seventeenth and eighteenth centuries. (2) an air in 2/4, 3/4 or 6/8 time that imitates drone of the bagpipe. (3) a dance tune suitable for a bagpipe. (4) an organ reed stop.

Musgrave, Thea (1928–) a Scottish composer who is best known for her operas (for example, *The Decision, The Voice of Ariadne*), and her ballets *Beauty and the Beast* and *A Tale for Thieves*. She has also written choral and orchestral works.

musica (*Italian*) "music," so *musica di camera* means chamber music; *musica di chiesa* means church music; *musica da teatro* theatrical music or opera.

musica ficta *or* **cantus fictus** (*Latin*) literally "feigned music" or "feigned song"; it is a term for ACCIDENTALS used in MODE music.

musical a type of play or film in which music plays an important part and the actors occasionally sing, for example, *My Fair Lady, West Side Story*.

musical box a clockwork MECHANICAL INSTRUMENT in which a drum studded with small pins plays a tune by plucking the teeth of a metal comb.

musical comedy a term used between 1890 and 1930 to describe a humorous play with light music and singing in it.

Musical Joke, A *see* **Musikalischer Spass, Ein**.

music drama a term first used to describe the operas of Wagner, where the action and music are completely interlocked, with, for example, no pauses to allow applause after an aria, or repetition within a piece.

musicology the scientific study of music.

Musikalischer Spass, Ein (A Musical Joke) a miniature symphony in F by MOZART for two horns and strings. It is a satire on popular music of the time.

musique concrète a term coined by the French composer Pierre Schaffer in 1948 to describe a type of music in which taped sounds are distorted or manipulated by the composer. The term ELECTRONIC MUSIC is now more generally used.

Mussorgsky *or* **Moussorgsky), Modeste Petrovich** (1839–81) a Russian composer who gave up a military career to write music. Although he came from a wealthy family, he regularly lived in a state of poverty, largely on account of his chronic alcoholism. Because of this affliction,.he left much of his music unfinished but has nevertheless been hailed as a composer of genius. Ironically, many of his pieces were tampered with after his death by composers who could not, or did not, recognize his talent for invention. For example, RIMSKY-KORSAKOV revised his opera *Boris Godunov*. He was a member of "The FIVE," and his best-known works include the operas BORIS GODUNOV and *Sorochintsy Fair* (unfinished), the piano piece PICTURES AT AN EXHIBITION, and many songs.

muta (*Italian*) "change," a musical direction: (1) that the key be changed in horn or drum music; (2) that the MUTE be used.

Muta di Portici, La *see* **Masaniello**.

mutation stops organ stops that produce sound, usually a HARMONIC—which is different from the normal or octave pitch corresponding to the key that is depressed.

mute any device used to soften to reduce the normal volume, or alter the tone, of an instrument. With bowed instruments, a small clamp is slotted onto the bridge; in brass instruments a hand or bung is pushed into the bell; in the piano the soft (left) piano is pressed; and with drums, cloths are placed over the skins, or sponge-headed drumsticks are used.

Muti, Riccardo (1941–) an Italian conductor with an international reputation.

mv abbreviation for mezzo voce.

My Country *see* **Ma Vlast**.

My Country 'tis of Thee *or* **America** a patriotic song written by the Baptist minister Samuel Francis Smith and set to the tune of GOD SAVE THE QUEEN. It was first performed in Boston in 1832 and has become an unofficial national anthem.

mystery play *or* **miracle play** a form of dramatic entertainment based on sacred subjects and given under church auspices which was used before the development of either opera or oratorio.

N

Nabucco *or* **Nabucodonosor** an opera by Verdi with a libretto by Solera. It tells the Biblical story of Nebuchadnezzar, the king of Babylon, who holds the Hebrews captive, goes mad but recovers and is converted to Judaism. The opera was first performed in 1842, at La Scala, Milan. A later production was given in London under the title *Nino*.

nachdruck (*German*) "ACCENT" or "emphasis."

Nachschlag (*German*) literally "after beat," a grace or ORNAMENT, like a short APPOGGIATURA, but occurring at the end instead of at the beginning of a NOTE.

nachspiel (*German*) a POSTLUDE.

Nachtmusik (*German*) literally "night music," that is, music suitable for performing in the evening, or suggestive of night.

Nachtstücke (Night Pieces) a name given by Robert Schumann to his four piano solos, Op. 23.

naenia a Roman funeral SONG.

nafiri an Indian trumpet.

nagaret an Abyssinian KETTLEDRUM.

naguar an Indian DRUM.

naker the medieval English name for a small

KETTLEDRUM (often with snares, *see* SIDE DRUM) of Arabic origin, from which TIMPANI developed. Nakers were always used in pairs.

Nardini, Pietro (1722-93) Italian violinist and composer. He was admired as one of the greatest violinists of his day. His works include six string quartets as well as sonatas for violin and piano.

Nares, James (1715-83) English organist and composer, who is best known for his church music and songs.

national anthem a SONG or HYMN that is formally adopted by a country and sung or played at official occasions.

nationalism a late nineteenth-century and early twentieth-century movement in which a number of composers (notably The FIVE in Russia, and SMETANA, GRIEG, ELGAR and SIBELIUS) set out to write work which would express their national identity, often by reference to FOLK music and by evocation of landscape. It was in part a reaction to the dominance of German music.

natural a NOTE that is neither sharpened nor flattened. (*See* Appendix for symbol.)

natural key KEY of C major.

natural modulation DIATONIC MODULATION.

natural tones those produced by WIND INSTRUMENTS, without overblowing or the use of VALVES or KEYS.

Navarraise, La (The Girl from Navarre) an opera by MASSENET to a libretto by J. Claretie and H. Cain. It is the story of Anita, who is betrothed to Araquil, a sergeant in the Spanish royalist army, which is at war with Carlist forces (i.e. supporters of the Spanish pretender Don Carlos [1788–1855]). Araquil's father will not allow the marriage unless she can provide a dowry, and to obtain this she kills Zuccaraga, the Carlist leader, for which there is a reward. When Araquil, badly wounded in battle, learns of this, he dies, and Anita goes mad. It was first performed in London in 1894.

neck the narrow projecting part of a stringed instrument that supports the FINGERBOARD; at the end of the neck lies the PEG-BOX, which secures the strings and enables them to be tuned.

nel battere (*Italian*) on the BEAT or down stroke (DOWN-BEAT).

neo-classicism a twentieth-century musical movement that reacted against the overtly ROMANTIC forms of the late nineteenth century. Composers who adhered to the philosophy (in particular STRAVINSKY, HINDEMITH, POULENC and PROKOFIEV) attempted to create new works with the balance and restraint found in the work of eighteenth-century composers, especially Johann Sebastian BACH.

nero (*Italian*) literally "black," a CROTCHET or quarter note.

netto, nettamente (*Italian*) "with precision" or "neatly."

Neukomm, Sigismund von (1778–1858) Austrian-born composer who was a pupil of Michael and Joseph HAYDN and a friend of MENDELSSOHN. He wrote some 1,000 works including eight oratorios, a setting for Schiller's *Braut von Messina*, a symphony, and many songs.

neume a sign used in musical NOTATION from the

seventh to fourteenth centuries before the invention of the STAVE. It gave an indication of PITCH.

Newman, Ernest (1868–1959) English music critic and writer of many books on music. His great love was opera, particularly the operas of WAGNER, many of which he translated. He wrote a massive biography of Wagner, as well as several other books on that composer and his work.

New World Symphony *see* **From the New World**.

Nibelung's Ring, The *see* **Ring of the Nibelung, The**.

Nicolai, Carl Otto Ehrenfried (1810-49) German composer and conductor whose most famous work is the comic opera *The* MERRY WIVES OF WINDSOR. He also wrote other operas, two symphonies, a requiem and other church music, as well as songs. He founded the Vienna Philharmonic Society in 1842.

Nielsen, Carl August (1865-1931) Danish composer, violinist and conductor who produced works of a strong individuality. For many years his music was not appreciated outside Denmark, but after the World War II he was widely recognized as being inventive and original. His works include the opera *Saul and David*, six symphonies, many choral pieces, and music for chamber orchestra, piano and organ.

niente (*Italian*) "nothing"; used in *quasi niente* "almost nothing," indicating a very soft tone.

Nietzsche, Friedrich (1844–1900) German philosopher and poet who at first greatly admired WAGNER and wrote in his praise, as in *Richard*

Wagner in Bayreuth, but then turned against him and all German music, writing pamphlets such as *Nietzsche contra Wagner*. He also wrote the philosophical work *Also Sprach Zarathustra*, to which title Richard STRAUSS composed a symphonic poem.

Nightingale, The an opera by STRAVINSKY, who also wrote the libretto in conjunction with Stepan Mitusov (after the fairytale by Hans Andersen). It was first performed in 1914. Stravinsky based his symphonic poem *The Song of the Nightingale* on the opera; this piece was also used as ballet music.

Night Pieces *see* **Nachtstücke**.

Nights in the Gardens of Spain (*Noches en los Jardines de España*) three symphonic impressions for piano and orchestra (1909—15) by FALLA.

Nikisch, Arthur (1855–1922) Hungarian conductor and pianist who also composed. He established a worldwide reputation as a conductor, working with, among others, the Boston Symphony Orchestra, the Budapest Opera, the Gewandhaus, Leipzig, and the Berlin Philharmonic Orchestra. His works include a symphony, a violin concerto, and cantatas and songs.

Nilsson, Birgit (1918-) Swedish soprano of international repute who is particularly famous for her role as Brünnhilde in WAGNER's operatic cycle *Der* RING DES NIBELUNGEN.

ninth an INTERVAL of nine NOTES, in which both the first and last notes are counted.

nobile, nobilmente (*Italian*) "noble, nobly."

Noches en los Jardines de España *see* **Nights in the Gardens of Spain**.

nocturne literally a "night piece," i.e. a piece of music, often meditative in character and suggesting the quietness of night. The form was invented by John FIELD and later perfected by CHOPIN.

Nocturnes the titles of certain pieces of music by FIELD and CHOPIN, and also the title of three orchestral pieces by DEBUSSY.

Noël (*French*) Christmas or Christmas CAROL.

noire (*French*) literally "black," a CROTCHET or quarter note.

nomenclature *see* **notation**.

nona (*Italian*) a NINTH.

nonet a group of nine instruments, or a piece of music for such a group.

Nono, Luigi (1924-) Italian composer who was influenced by WEBERN and is considered a champion of "Modern" music. He has devout left-wing opinions which have influenced his output. His most influential works include the opera *Intolleranza 1960* (with live and taped music, and live and filmed action), and *On the Bridge of Hiroshima*, a piece for voices and orchestra.

Norma an opera by BELLINI with a libretto by Felice Romani. It is set in Gaul shortly after the Roman conquest and is the story of Norma, the high priestess of the Druids, who advocates peace with the Romans rather than the rebellion that is being planned. Norma has secretly married Pollione, the Roman proconsul, by whom she has had two children. Pollione has been unfaithful and plans to elope to Rome with Adalgisa, one of the temple virgins. When Adalgisa seeks release from her vows from Norma so that she may go away with her lover, Norma grants her prayer, but when Norma learns who the lover is, she is filled with wrath. Adalgisa then learns that Pollione is married and joins in denouncing him. Norma determines to kill her herself, and summons the Druids to declare war on the Romans. Pollione is captured before he can leave. Norma offers him escape if he will renounce Adalgisa. He refuses, and she threatens to denounce Adalgisa, but, overcome by pity, confesses her own guilt to the Druids. Her heroism arouses Pollione's earlier passion, and he ascends the funeral pyre with her. First performed in Milan in 1831, it is still popular in opera houses around the world.

normal pitch standard PITCH.

Norman, Jessye (1945-) American opera singer who is one of the most impressive sopranos of the post-World War II era. With her magnificent voice and sensitivity of interpretation, she has been outstanding in many diverse roles.

nota (*Latin, Italian*) "NOTE," so *nota bianca* means "white note" or half-note; *nota buona* is an accented note; *nota cambita* or *cambiata* is a CHANGING NOTE; *nota caratteristica* is a LEADING NOTE; *nota cattiva* is an unaccented note; *nota contra notam* is COUNTERPOINT; *nota coronata* is a HOLDING NOTE; *nota d'abbellimento* is a GRACE NOTE; *nota di passagio* is a PASSING NOTE; *nota di piacere* is an optional grace note; *nota quadrata* is a PLAINSONG note; *nota scolta* is a STACCATO note; *nota sensibilis* is a leading note; and *nota sostenuta* is a sustained note.

notation *or* **nomenclature** the symbols used in

written music to indicate the PITCH and RHYTHM of NOTES, the combination and duration of TONES, as well as the graces and shades of expression without which music can become mechanical.

note (1) a SOUND that has a defined PITCH and duration. (2) a symbol for such a sound. (3) the KEY of a PIANO or other keyboard instrument.

Noveletten (*German*) literally "short stories"; it was a title used by SCHUMANN for a set of piano pieces that "told a story,"

Novello, Ivor (1893-1951) British composer, playwright and actor, descended from Vincent NOVELLO, who was particularly celebrated for his revues and musicals. He wrote the music for the famous World War I song "Keep the Home Fires Burning" (properly called "Till the Boys Come Home," which has words by an American woman, Lena Guilbert Ford, who died one of the rare victims, in that war, of a German air raid.

Novello, Vincent (1781-1861) a London-based editor, organist and composer who founded the firm of Novello, which published works by MOZART, HAYDN, BEETHOVEN and PURCELL, and therefore helped to publicize serious music in England. His son, **Joseph Alfred Novello** (1810–96), continued in his father's footsteps, and his daughter, **Clara Anastasia Novello** (1818–1908), became a celebrated soprano.

nowell the Old English version of NOËL.

Nozze di Figaro, Le *see* **Marriage of Figaro, The**.

nuance a subtle change of speed, TONE, etc.

number (1) an integral portion of a musical composition, particularly in opera where it can mean an ARIA, DUET, etc. (2) one of the works on a programme.

Nunc Dimittis (*Latin*) the Song of Simeon, "Lord, now lettest Thou Thy servant depart in peace," which is sung at both Roman Catholic and Anglican evening services. It has been set to music by numerous composers.

nut (1) the part of the BOW of a stringed instrument that holds the horsehair and that incorporates a screw that tightens the tension of the hairs. (2) the hardwood ridge at the PEG-BOX end of a stringed instrument's FINGERBOARD that raises the strings above the level of the FINGERBOARD.

Nutcracker, The a ballet by TCHAIKOVSKY based on a tale by E. T. A. Hoffmann (1776–1822). It relates the story of Klara, who is given a nutcracker one Christmas; when she sleeps that night, she is taken on a magical tour of the Kingdom of Sweets by a prince. It was first performed in 1892.

O

o when placed over a NOTE in a musical SCORE for strings, indicates that the note must be played on an open string or as a harmonic.

ob abbreviation for OBOE and OBBLIGATO.

obbligato (*Italian*) "obligatory"; a term that refers to a PART that cannot be dispensed with in a performance (some parts can be optional). However, some nineteenth-century composers used the word to mean the exact opposite, i.e. a part that was optional.

ober (*German*) "over," "upper," as OBERWERK.

Oberon an opera by WEBER to a libretto written by J. R. Planché based on a German version of a thirteenth-century French poem. It is subtitled *The Elf-King's Oath* and relates a story in which the king of fairies, Oberon, vows never to be reconciled with his wife, Titania, until he has found a pair of perfect lovers. This he does by testing the fidelity of Huon, a knight of Charlemagne, and Reiza. They withstand the trials Oberon sets, and he can return to Titania. The opera was first performed in London in 1826, supplanting an earlier version by WRANITZKY.

Oberwerk (*German*) a swell organ. *See* ORGAN.

oblique motion two parallel MELODY lines, or PARTS: one moves up or down the SCALE while the other stays on a consistent NOTE.

oblique piano a small PIANO with strings set diagonally in an upright case, invented in London in 1811.

oboe a WOODWIND instrument with a conical bore and a double REED. The instrument has a history dating back to ancient Egyptian times. SHAWMS evolved from these Egyptian predecessors and became known as "HAUTBOIS" (high-wood) instruments in the seventeenth and eighteenth centuries. The modern oboe (the word is a corruption of "hautbois") dates from the eighteenth century. The established variations of the instrument are: the oboe (TREBLE), the COR ANGLAIS (ALTO), or the BASSOON (tenor), and the double bassoon (BASS).

oboe d'amore (*Italian* "OBOE of love") an oboe in A with a COMPASS a MINOR third below that of the ordinary oboe, and a veiled TONE due to its hollow globular bell.

oboe di caccia (*Italian* "hunting OBOE") an oboe standing in F or E flat, for which music was written on the ALTO CLEF.

Obrecht *or* **Hobrecht, Jacob** (1450-1505) Flemish composer who travelled extensively in Europe and was one of the foremost musicians of his era. He was Kapellmeister in Antwerp from 1491. He is remembered for writing twenty-four Masses, twenty-two motets, and many songs.

Oca del Cairo, L' (The Goose of Cairo) a two-act OPERA BUFFA by MOZART with a libretto by Gianbattista Varesco. Mozart left it unfinished because of his dissatisfaction with the plot. It was patched up with other of Mozart's compositions and was first performed in Paris in 1867.

ocarina a small, egg-shaped WIND INSTRUMENT, often made of clay, which is played in a way similar to a RECORDER. It was invented in the mid-nineteenth century and is still made, mainly as a toy.

Occasional Oratorio a work by HANDEL, written to celebrate the defeat of the Jacobite Rising of 1745–46. It consists of an overture and three parts setting selections from poems by John Milton (1608–74), with additions, including a part of RULE BRITANNIA! It was first performed in 1746.

Ockeghem *or* **Okeghem** *or* **Ockenheim, Johannes** *or* **Jan** (*c.*1430–*c.*1495) Flemish composer of considerable originality, who achieved fame with his motets, including one for thirty-six voices, Masses and songs. He was also an eminent teacher, his pupils including JOSQUIN DES PRÉS.

octave an INTERVAL of eight NOTES, inclusive of the top and bottom notes, e.g. C to C.

octet a group of eight instruments or VOICES, or a piece for such a group.

octobass a huge kind of three-stringed DOUBLE BASS, some four metres in height, which incorporated hand- and pedal-operated levers to stop (*see* STOPPING) the immensely thick strings. It was invented by J.B. Vuillaume in Paris in 1849, but proved impractical.

Ode for St Cecilia's Day (1) the title of four choral works by PURCELL. (2) the title of a choral setting by HANDEL of the poem by John Dryden (1631–1700).

Odington, Walter de (d. after 1330) English Benedictine monk and musical theorist. He wrote *De Speculatione Musicae*, which gives important information about the rhythms of the thirteenth century.

Odo of Cluny (879–942) French Benedictine monk, composer and musical theorist. He took orders at nineteen and had his musical training in Paris. He was Abbot of Cluny from 927 until his death. He wrote religious music, including hymns and antiphons, and his written works include *Dialogus de Musica*.

Oedipus incidental music by MENDELSSOHN for Sophocles's trilogy of plays, *Antigone*, *Oedipus Tyrannus*, and *Oedipus at Colonos*, composed by order of the king of Prussia. The music for the first and last works were first performed in 1841 and 1845, but the music for *Oedipus Tyrannus*, "completely sketched" in 1845, has been lost. Sir Charles STANFORD wrote incidental music for *Oedipus Tyrannus*, which was first performed in Cambridge in 1887.

Oedipus Rex an "opera-oratorio" by STRAVINSKY to a Latin text by Jean Daniélou (a translation of Cocteau's play after Sophocles). It was first performed in 1927.

oeuvre (*French*) a "work" (OPUS).

offen (*German*) "open."

Offenbach, Jacques [originally Jakob Eberst] (1819-80) a German-French composer, conductor and cellist. The son of a Jewish CANTOR in Offenbach-am-Main in Germany, he studied at the Paris Conservatoire and joined the orchestra of the OPÉRA COMIQUE and later was conductor at the Théâtre Française. He was a theatrical producer before devoting himself full-time to composition. He wrote outstandingly tuneful light music. Of his ninety operettas, ORPHEUS IN THE UNDERWORLD and *Les Contes d'Hoffman* (*The* TALES OF HOFFMANN) are the most famous. The latter was his own personal favourite but was not performed until after his death.

offertory an ANTIPHON sung (or music played on the ORGAN) while the priest prepares the bread and wine at a communion service.

Ogdon, John (1937-89) English pianist and composer who was a member of the "MANCHESTER SCHOOL." He was joint winner, with ASHKENAZY, of the 1962 Tchaikovsky Piano Competition in Moscow, and developed a formidable repertoire as a pianist. He also composed many pieces for the instrument.

ohne (*German*) "without," hence *ohne worte*, "without words."

Oireachtas (*Gaelic*) an annual festival of Irish music and poetry, established by the Gaelic League in 1897.

Oistrakh, David (1908–74) Russian violinist who only gained international recognition after World War II. His son **Igor Oistrakh** (1931–) is also a celebrated violinist and a conductor.

Okeghem, Johannes *see* **Ockeghem, Johannes**.

Old Hundred (US), **Old Hundredth** (English) a hymn tune, the first known version of which appeared as the melody to PSALM 134 in an edition of the Genevan Psalter, 1554.

Olsen, Ole (1850–1927) Norwegian composer, conductor, critic and teacher. He studied in Germany and was director of military music for the Swedish government. His musical works include a symphony, symphonic poems, operas, the oratorio *Nideros*, and four cantatas. His best-known work is the children's opera *Svein Urad*.

Olympians, The an opera by BLISS to a libretto by the novelist and playwright J. B. Priestley (1894–1984). The story concerns the adventures of the gods of Mount Olympus, the gods of Greek mythology, in their modern form as a band of travelling players who, once a year, can revert to their original form. It was first performed in London in 1949.

ondeggiante (*Italian*) "undulating."

Ondes Martenot *or* **Ondes Musicales** an ELECTRONIC musical instrument patented in 1922 by Maurice Martenot (1898–). It was used by such composers as MESSIAEN.

ondulé (*French*) "undulating."

ongarese (*Italian*) "Hungarian."

On Hearing the First Cuckoo in Spring an orchestral piece by DELIUS, first performed in 1913.

Onslow, George (1784–1853) Anglo-French composer whose works include comic operas, thirty-four quintets, thirty-six quartets and three symphonies.

On Wenlock Edge a cycle of six settings by VAUGHAN WILLIAMS of poems from "A Shropshire Lad" A. E. Housman (1859–1936).

op abbreviation for OPUS.

open harmony *see* **harmony**.

open note (1) in stringed instruments, an OPEN STRING. (2) in BRASS or WOODWIND instruments, a NOTE produced without using VALVES, CROOKS, or KEYS.

open string any string on an instrument that is allowed to vibrate along its entire length without being stopped (*see* STOPPING).

Oper (*German*) "opera."

opera a dramatic work in which all, or most of, the text is sung to orchestral ACCOMPANIMENT. Opera is a formidable musical form, and has a history dating back to Italy in the sixteenth century. During the Italian Renaissance, when scholars and nobles tried to revive the beautiful in art, Vincenzo Galilei (*c*.1520–91), father of the astronomer Galileo Galilei, PERI, CACCINI, and other musicians, would meet at the home of the Conte di Vernio in Florence. The group became known as the *Camerata*, and they resolved to restore the declamatory style of drama of the Greeks, which they mistakenly believed to have had a continuous musical accompaniment. Peri's *Dafne*, privately performed at the Corsi Palace in 1597, was among the first efforts in this direction, and three years later, at the marriage of Henri IV of France to Maria de Medici, his *Euridice* was performed in public. These were tragic operas. As early as 1262 a comic opera by Adam de LA HALE had been performed at Arras in France, and in 1285 his *Jeu de Robin et Marion* had been received with delight by the French court at Naples. In its MYSTERY PLAYS, the Church had fostered dramatic performances with more or less musical accompaniment.

But the *Camerata* had begun their creative work at the right psychological moment, and their *dramma per la musica* ("music drama") or *opera in musica* ("musical work"), sung in a new style, not unlike what WAGNER was to call "aria that is recitative and recitative that is aria," which they termed *musica parlante* ("speaking music"), became the fashion, reaching its culmination in the operas of MONTEVERDI, in particular his ORFEO.

Then came the growth of the science of HARMONY and the development of the modern ORCHESTRA. As the Church retained its preference for the older music, composers of the new school found the best outlet for their genius in opera. Composers and singers travelled throughout Italy, then to France, to Germany, to England, taking with them operas that excited the interest of musicians and inspired them to attempt the same. Eventually there grew up in France the OPÉRA COMIQUE, in Austria and Germany the SINGSPIEL, and in Italy the *commedia dell' arte*, in which ordinary people could find their thoughts and aspirations reflected, but in court circles Italian opera continued to reign supreme.

A revolt against this was headed by GLUCK, a thorough musician, by birth a German trained in the arts of Italy, but a reformer, and, after LULLY, the foremost of early composers of French opera. Gluck aimed to purify opera, to prune out the excrescences that had grown up in Italian opera. What Gluck did for France, first MOZART did for Austria and later WEBER was to do for Germany, and what Weber left undone was attempted by

WAGNER, who dominated German music after him, giving a new impetus to operatic composition. In Italy, the tendency was to look upon the opera LIBRETTO merely as a necessary peg on which to hang a glorious texture of music. The later German ideal assumed that music that detracted from interest in the progress of the drama itself was bad music, and that the purpose of music, as of architecture, of lighting, of costume, and of acting, was merely to enforce the damatic interest of the text.

Opera demands a libretto, an orchestra, singers, an ample stage, and, only too often, considerable funds to produce. It also requires a suspension of disbelief, for opera is the convention of unreality, but in that unreality lies its ability to work magic.

opéra-bouffe (*French*) OPERA BUFFA.

opera buffa (*Italian*) similar to OPÉRA COMIQUE but with the dialogue sung throughout and spoken only occasionally in *opera buffa* modelled on the French style.

opéra comique (*French*) literally "a comic OPERA," but in fact an opera consisting of dramatic pieces with music and dancing and instrumental ACCOMPANIMENT, often along tragic rather than comic lines. Like the German SPINGSPIEL, all or nearly all the dialogue is spoken.

Opéra-Comique the institution set up in Paris in 1715 with the agreement of the ACADÉMIE DE MUSIQUE Royale for the performance of OPÉRA COMIQUE. It found a permanent home in a specially built theatre in 1898.

opera seria (*Italian*) "serious OPERA," as usually

applied to work of the seventeenth and eighteenth centuries.

operetta a short OPERA or, more usually, a term taken to mean an opera with some spoken dialogue, and a romantic plot with a happy ending.

ophicleide the largest member of the now redundant key-bugle family (BUGLES with KEYS).

opus (*Latin*) "work"; a term used by composers (or their cataloguers) to indicate the chronological order of their works. It is usually abbreviated to Op. and is followed by the catalogued number of the work.

oratorio the musical setting of a religious or epic LIBRETTO for soloists, CHORUS and ORCHESTRA, performed without the theatrical effects of stage and costumes, etc. Oratorio had its beginnings in the MYSTERY PLAYS of the Middle Ages, and acquired its name from the efforts of St Philip of Neri (1515–95) to attract young people to divine services held in his Oratory by performances of sacred music, composed expressly for his use by the best musicians of his generation. These compositions, known at first as *laudi spirituali*, were in MADRIGAL style, and became popular throughout Italy. From Italy, where it was soon overshadowed by OPERA, the oratorio spread to the rest of Europe. The church CANTATAS of Johann Sebastian BACH and his PASSIONS OF ST MATTHEW and ST JOHN, can be regarded as its highest expression in northern Germany. In England the oratorio was HANDEL's recourse when opera was no longer profitable or was forbidden. His MESSIAH and HAYDN's CREATION and *The* SEASONS were the culmination of the form, but later

composers also wrote oratorios, for example MEN-
DELSSOHN's *Elijah*, and ELGAR's DREAM OF GERON-
TIUS.

orchestra a group of instruments and their players. The word comes from Greek and means
"dancing place." This was a space in front of the
stage, in which a raised platform was built for the
accommodation of the CHORUS. The early composers of OPERA applied the name to the place allotted
to their musicians, and it is now used to designate
the place, the musicians or the instruments. Orchestras have grown over the centuries in response to larger auditoriums. A standard, modern orchestra contains four families of instruments: STRINGS, WOODWIND, BRASS and PERCUSSION.
The exact number of players within each section
can vary, and extra instruments can be called for
by a particular SCORE.

orchestration the art of writing and arranging
music for an ORCHESTRA.

Orfeo, L' (full title: *La Favola d'Orfeo* The Story of
ORPHEUS) an opera by MONTEVERDI to a libretto by
Alessandro Striggio, the first "proper" opera as
we would understand it. The plot tells the familiar story of Orpheus, who ventures into the underworld to retrieve his love, Euridice. It was first
performed in 1607.

Orff, Carl (1895-1982) German composer and
teacher. He was passionately involved in education and wrote many pieces especially for children
(for example *Schulwerk*). One of Hitler's favurite
composers, his most famous piece is CARMINA
BURANA, which he based on thirteenth-century

texts that he later destroyed and which he wrote as a "scenic-cantata" to be performed on the stage with dancers, etc. However, it is now usually performed as a traditional concert work. His other works include the operas *The Moon*, *The Clever Girl*, *Antigone* and *Oedipus the Tyrant*..

organ a keyboard wind instrument, played with the hands and feet, in which pressurized air is forced through PIPES to sound NOTES. PITCH is determined by the length of the pipe. There are essentially two types of pipe; FLUE PIPES, which are blown like a WHISTLE, and REED PIPES in which air is blown over vibrating strips of metal. Flue pipes can be "stopped" (blocked off at one end) to produce a sound an OCTAVE lower than when open. There are a number of keyboards on an organ, one of which is operated by the feet (PEDAL board). Those operated by the hands are called MANUALS, and there are four common categories: the solo (used for playing SOLO MELODIES), the swell (on which notes can be made to sound louder or softer, *see also* SWELL ORGAN), the great (the manual that opens up all the most powerful pipes), and the choir (which operates the softer sounding pipes, *see also* CHOIR ORGAN). In addition there are a number of "STOPS" (buttons or levers) that can alter the pitch or TONE of specific pipes. The organ dates back to before the time of Christ and has gone through many stages of evolution. ELECTRONIC organs (*see* HAMMOND ORGAN) have been invented and these tend to produce sounds rather different from those in which pumped air is actually used.

organistrum *see* **hurdy-gurdy**.

organum (1) (*Latin*) "ORGAN." (2) measured music, as opposed to unmeasured PLAINSONG, an early form of POLYPHONY.

Orgel (*German*) an ORGAN.

orgue (*French*) an ORGAN.

Orlando di Lasso *see* **Lassus, Roland de**.

Ormandy, Eugene (1899-1985) Hungarian-born conductor who was a child prodigy on the violin. He moved to the USA in 1921, where he was with the Minneapolis and Philadelphia Orchestras. He also conducted many of the world's other leading orchestras.

ornaments and graces embellishments to the NOTES of a MELODY, indicated by symbols or small notes. They were used frequently in the seventeenth and eighteenth centuries.

Ornstein, Leo (1895–) Russian-born pianist and composer who became an American citizen. He specialized in modern music and made numerous tours. His works include the symphonic poem *The Fog*, an orchestral suite, *The Life of Man*, a piano concerto and quintet.

Orphée aux enfers (Orpheus in the Underworld) an OPERETTA by OFFENBACH to a libretto by H. Cremieux and L. Halévy. The classic story of ORPHEUS is used to satirize nineteenth-century society. It was first performed in 1858 and was enormously popular from the first.

Orphée et Euridice (Orpheus and Eurydice, usually given as *Orphée*, the revised version of what was originally called *Orfeo ed Euridice*) an opera by GLUCK based on the ORPHEUS myth. The story

Orpheus

differs from the legend in having a happy ending,
Love restoring Eurydice to life, and the lovers
embracing. It was first performed in 1762.

Orpheus the legendary poet and musician of Greek
mythology whose name has been adopted by numerous musical societies, etc, including the sev-
enty-strong Glasgow Orpheus Choir, conducted
by Sir Hugh Roberton (1874–1952), which became one of Britain's premier choir from the
1920s to the 1940s. The name Orpheus has also
been used as the title of several collections of
vocal music, including *Orpheus Britannicus*
(1702), the first of the works of PURCELL.

The story tells how when his wife Eurydice dies,
Orpheus is overcome with such grief that the gods
of Olympus are moved to compassion, and Jupiter
ordains that Orpheus may descend into Hades
and bring Eurydice back to the world, provided he
can refrain from looking at her until their return
to earth. Using his musical skills, Orpheus gains
entry to Hades and finds his wife, and they begin
their journey back to the world. Eurydice, however, amazed that Orpheus has not caressed nor
even looked at her, reproaches him for loving her
no longer. At last, overcome with love and sorrow,
Orpheus turns and looks at her. He has violated
his pledge to the gods; Eurydice is snatched back
to Hades, and Orpheus becomes deranged and is
killed by the enraged women of Thrace in one of
their Bacchanalian orgies.

The myth has been the subject of innumerable
operas, including the earliest opera to survive,
Euridice by PERI (1600), but most memorably in

the serious operas *L'*ORFEO by MONTEVERDI and
ORPHÉE ET EURIDICE by GLUCK, and in ORPHÉE AUX
ENFERS, an operetta by OFFENBACH. It has also been
the subjet of a SYMPHONIC POEM by LISZT (1854), and
a ballet by STRAVINSKY, first performed in 1948.

Orpheus in the Underworld *see* **Orphée aux
enfers**.

Ortiz, Diego (1530–c.1565) Spanish composer of
religious music who also wrote on musical theory.

oscillator an ELECTRONIC INSTRUMENT that converts
electrical energy into audible sound.

ossia (*Italian*) "or," "otherwise," "else"; used to
indicate an alternative PASSAGE of music.

ostinato (*Italian*) "obstinate"; a short PHRASE or
other pattern that is repeated over and over again
during the course of a composition.

Otello (Othello) (1) an opera by VERDI to a libretto
by Arrigo Boito based on the play by Shakespeare,
but omitting the first act, the opera beginning
with the arrival of Otello in Cyprus. It was first
performed in Milan in 1887 and has become
established as perhaps the greatest opera of nineteenth-century Romanticism (*see* ROMANTIC MU-
SIC). (2) an opera by ROSSINI to a libretto by Francesco Berio di Salsa (after Shakespeare). First
performed in 1816 in Naples, it never achieved
wide popularity.

ottava (*Italian*) OCTAVE.

ottavino flauto (*Italian*) the piccolo flute.

ottetto (*Italian*) an octet.

Ours, L' (The Bear) a name given to HAYDN's
symphony no. 82 in C major, which ends with a
bear dance.

Ouseley, the Rev. Sir Frederick Arthur Gore
(1825–89) English composer and teacher whose
works include the oratorio *Hagar* (1873), many
anthems, preludes, fugues, sonatas for organ,
and two string quartets. From 1855 he was Professor of Music at Oxford University and wrote
books on HARMONY, COUNTERPOINT, FUGUE and general composition.

ouverture (*French*) OVERTURE.

overblow to increase the wind pressure in a WOOD-
WIND instrument to force an upper PARTIAL note
instead of its fundamental note, thus producing a
harmonic.

overstringing a method of arranging the lower
BASS strings of the PIANO by which they overlay
other strings diagonally.

overtones *see* **harmonics**.

overture a piece of music that introduces an an
OPERA, ORATORIO, BALLET or other major work. Overtures may be built out of the principal THEMES of
the work that is to follow, or may be quite independent of them. BEETHOVEN composed no fewer
than four overtures to his only opera, FIDELIO, and
VERDI'S OTELLO and many other operas have no
overture whatever. Overtures are nearly always
in the SONATA FORM, being, in fact, similar to the
first MOVEMENT of a SYMPHONY, on a somewhat
larger scale. The CONCERT OVERTURE is often an
independent piece, written for performance in a
concert hall.

P

p (1) abbreviation for PIANO (*Italian*), meaning "soft." (2) abbreviation for "PEDAL" (ORGAN).

Pachelbel, Johann (1653-1706) German organist and composer who wrote motets, concertos and cantatas, and is now mainly known for his Canon and Gigue in D major. His son, **Wilhelm Hieronymus Pachelbel** (1685–*c*.1764), was also an organist and composer, who succeeded his father as organist at the Nuremberg Sebalduskirche and who also composed preludes and fugues, as well as variations for the organ or harpsichord.

Pacini, Giovanni (1796–1867) Italian composer and music theorist. His compositions include ninety operas, a quartet, and a cantata in celebration of Dante Alighieri (1265–1321). His brother, **Emilio Pacini** (1810–98), was a librettist.

Paderewski, Ignace Jan (1860-1941) Polish pianist, composer and statesman. He trained in Warsaw and Vienna, and became perhaps the most fêted pianist of his era, renowned particularly for his playing of CHOPIN. At the beginning of World War I he practically abandoned music to devote himself to the establishment of Poland as a republic (achieved at the end of that war), and he was prime minister for ten months in 1919. He returned to the concert stage in 1922, but became president of the Polish government in exile in 1940. He composed the opera *Manru*, which was first performed in 1901 to critical but not popular acclaim, a piano concerto, a symphony and many songs.

Paër, Ferdinando (1771–1839) Italian-born composer who settled in France. He was KAPELLMEISTER to Napoleon (1807–12) and became director of the king's chamber music in 1832. He wrote many operas, including, in 1803, *L'amore conjugale*, which had the same subject as FIDELIO.

Paganini, Niccolò (1782-1840) Italian violinist and composer. He learned to play the violin from his father and went on to become the most famous virtuoso violinist of all time. He delighted in composing complicated and difficult pieces for himself, and he may have refused to play some other composers' works because they offered no challenge to his virtuosity. In addition to being an extrovert performer, he was also a capable composer, writing five violin concertos and several pieces for the guitar.

Pagliacci, I (The Clowns) an opera by LEONCAVALLO to his own libretto, which was based on a real incident of the murder of his wife by an actor. Leoncavallo's father was a judge at the trial. The opera was first performed in 1892 and has become popular throughout the world. One of the first VERISMO operas, it is often performed with MASCAGNI'S CAVALLERIA RUSTICANA. It tells the story of the Pagliacci, a group of travelling clowns who are preparing to perform the Harlequin story in an Italian village. Instead of an overture, the opera has an introductory aria by Tonio, telling the audience that what they will see is a real play about real people. Canio (who plays the role of Punchinello) is told by Tonio (the clown) that his wife, Nedda (Columbine), has a lover, Silvio, a young villager. Canio surprises the illicit lovers. Silvio escapes, and Beppe (Harlequin) prevents Canio from killing Nedda. As they continue preparations for the evening's performance Canio sings the famous aria *"Vesti la giubba,"* telling how he must act the clown while his heart is breaking. In the play, Columbine entertains her lover Harlequin. Canio, as her husband, Punchinello, no longer acting but living the tragedy of his own life, breaks down with emotion, and the audience applauds the reality of the scene. Columbine realizes what is happening and calls for help. Silvio, who is in the audience, rushes toward the stage, but before he can reach it, Punchinello has plunged his dagger into Columbine, and a moment later stabs Silvio. The final words addressed to the horrified spectators are *"La commedia è finita"* ("The comedy is finished").

Paine, John Knowles (1839–1906) American composer and teacher who obtained the first recognition of music as a course in an American college and who became Professor of Music at Harvard University in 1875, the first American to hold such an office. His works include two symphonies, symphonic poems, cantatas, and incidental music.

Paisiello, Giovanni (1741–1816) Italian composer who wrote a BARBER OF SEVILLE that the Roman public preferred to that of ROSSINI. He was the favourite composer of Napoleon I, who made him his director of music in 1797, and, on his retirement permitted him to name LESUEUR as his successor. He also worked for Empress Catherine of Russia from 1776 to 1784, and from 1784 to 1792 was KAPELLMEISTER to King Ferdinand IV of Naples. He wrote about a hundred operas, including *Nina*, *I Zingara in Fiera*, and *La Molinara*, an oratorio, thirty Masses, forty motets, and a Requiem.

Paladilhe, Emile (1844–1926) a French composer who was a pupil of HALÉVY at the Paris Conservatoire, where he won the first piano prize in 1857. He also won the PRIX DE ROME in 1860 with his cantata *Le czar Ivan IV*. He also wrote operas for the OPÉRA-COMIQUE and wrote two Masses and two symphonies.

Palestrina, Giovanni Pierluigi da (*c.*1525-94) Italian polyphonic composer (*see* POLYPHONY) who wrote noted Masses (for example, *Missa Papae Marcelli*), motets, and other religious works, notably a great Stabat Mater. Considered the supreme master of polyphonic music, his work ensured that the Council of Trent did not discontinue the use of music in churches. He reformed the liturgical music of Rome, and held various posts as choirmaster.

Palmgren, Selim (1878–1951) Finnish pianist, composer and conductor. His works include the operas *Daniel Hjort* and *Peter Schlemihl*, orchestral suites, much music for the piano including concertos, the symphonic poem *Floden*, and orchestral suites.

pambe a small Indian DRUM.

pandora a plucked stringed instrument of the CITTERN family. It was particularly popular in England during the sixteenth century.

Panormo, Vincenzo Trusaino (1734–1813) Italian-born instrument maker who worked in London and Paris and made violins on the large STRADIVARIUS model. One of his sons, **George Lewis Panormo** (1774–1842), made guitars, violins, and bows in London, while another, **Joseph Panormo** (1773–1825), made cellos and violins.

panpipes a set of graduated PIPES, stopped at the lower end, which are bound together by thongs. Each pipe makes a single NOTE, and sound is produced by blowing across the open end. They are popular instruments in South America and parts of Eastern Europe.

pantaleon a large DULCIMER with distinct sets of metal and gut strings, so named by Louis XIV of France after its inventor, Pantaleon Hebenstreit (1667–1750).

pantomime a combination of dancing and gesticulation by which a drama may be represented without words, although accompanied by music. In Britain, the term is now applied to a musical show with dialogue, traditionally based on a fairy tale and performed at Christmas time.

pantonality *see* **atonal**.

Panufnik, Andrzej (1914-) Polish composer and conductor who settled in England in 1954. He became a conductor of international repute and composed several noted pieces, including the ballet *Miss Julie,* and the orchestral pieces *Sinfonia rustica* and *Sinfonia sacra.*

Papillons (Butterflies) the name given by SCHU-MANN to his twelve short piano pieces, Op. 2 (1832).

Paradies und die Peri, Das (Paradise and the Peri) a cantata by SCHUMANN to his own adaptation of *Lalla Rookh* by MOORE, which was first performed in Leipzig in 1843. It consists of twenty-six NUMBERS scored for soloists, CHORUS and OR-CHESTRA.

paradis (*French*) "paradise," the name by which the highest tier of boxes in a French theatre is known.

Paradis, Marie Thérèse von (1759–1824) Austrian pianist and composer. Blinded in childhood, she trained with SALIERI, among others, and toured as a virtuoso. MOZART's piano concerto in B flat (K 456) was written for her. Her compositions include a music drama, *Ariadne and Bacchus*.

Paradise and the Peri (1) *see* PARADIES UND DIE PERI. (2) a FANTASIA OVERTURE by Sterndale BENNETT based on MOORE's poem *Lalla Rookh*, first performed in 1862. (3) a CANTATA by John Francis BARNETT for soloists, CHORUS, ORCHESTRA and OR-GAN, which was first performed in 1870.

parallel motion a PROGRESSION of two or more PARTS at fixed INTERVALS, such as thirds or sixths.

parameter a twentieth-century term used to describe aspects of SOUND that can be varied but which nevertheless impose a limit. It is particularly applied to ELECTRONIC MUSIC with regard to volume, etc.

Paray, Paul (1886–1979) French conductor and composer. He studied at the Paris Conservatoire where he won the PRIX DE ROME in 1911. He became principal conductor of the LAMOUREUX Concerts in Paris in 1923 and conducted the Detroit Symphony Orchestra from 1952 to 1964.

Paris Opéra the most important opera house in France, usually just referred to as the "Opéra"; its official title is the "Académie de Musique." It was opened in 1671.

Paris Symphonies a set of six symphonies (nos. 82–87) by HAYDN, which were commissioned by the "Concert de la Loge Olympique," a Masonic concert society based in Paris.

Paris Symphony a name given to MOZART's symphony no. 31 in D. It was composed while Mozart was in Paris (1778).

Parker, Charlie ("**Bird**") (1920-55) an American JAZZ saxophonist and composer. He helped to create the jazz style of BEBOP and gained his nickname because he was a frequent performer at the Birdland Jazz Club in New York. He is reckoned to have been one of the most creative of all saxophonists. Drug addiction caused his early death.

Parker, Horatio, William (1863-1919) American organist and composer. He wrote several oratorios (such as *Hora Novissima*), two operas, choral works, and pieces for piano and organ.

parlando (*Italian*) in declamatory or RECITATIVE style.

parlante (*Italian*) "speaking." RECITATIVE style, or played in the style of declamation.

Parry, Sir [Charles] Hubert [Hastings] (1848-1918) an English composer, teacher and musical historian who is remembered for his choral works (for example, *Blest Pair of Sirens*, *Ode on St Cecilia's Day*), motets (such as *Songs of Farewell*), and many orchestral works. However, his most famous piece of all was his setting of the poem "Jerusalem" by William Blake (1757–1827). Parry was an eminent teacher, being at various times a director of the Royal College of Music and a professor of music at Oxford University. He did much to revive the musical life of late nineteenth-century England. He was knighted in 1898 and made a baronet in 1903.

Parry, Joseph (1841–1903) a Welsh composer and teacher. His family emigrated to the United States, and he spent his early career as a popular singer and composer there before training at the Royal Academy of Music in London. His works include oratorios, operas, and chamber music. His son, **Joseph Haydn Parry** (1864–94), taught at the Guildhall School of Music, and wrote a piano sonata, a cantata, and two operettas.

Parsifal an opera by WAGNER, who also wrote the libretto. Wagner termed it a *Bühnenweihfestspiel* ("sacred festival play"), and it was his last work for the stage. It differs from *Der* RING DES NIBELUN-GEN in having rhymed instead of alliterative verses, but the music is on the same plan with ingeniously recurring LEITMOTIFS. Like his earlier LO-HENGRIN, it was based upon legends of the Holy

Grail, the character of Lohengrin being in fact the son of Parsifal. The story concerns Parsifal, who wins back from the evil magician, Klingsor, the magic spear that can heal the wounds of Amfortas, ruler of the knights of the Holy Grail at Montsalvat in the kingdom of the Grail. The opera was first performed in 1882 in BAYREUTH, and by the terms of Wagner's will its performance was to be restricted to the Festspielhaus in Bayreuth until 1913. Concert performances of the work were given in London and New York, without action or costumes, then in December 1903 a full production was mounted by the METROPOLITAN OPERA, New York. The Wagner family bitterly opposed the production in court, with the result that it became the best-advertised theatrical production there had ever been in the United States. American interest in *Parsifal* evaporated, and it was not performed again there until 1922.

part a VOICE or instrument in a group of performers, or a piece of music for it.

part book music for any one of several VOICES or instruments in a concerted number. In the Middle Ages music was so printed that when the books were laid open upon a table performers at either side had their parts before them. It was superseded by the SCORE.

Partch, Harry (1901-1974) self-taught American composer who experimented with musical ideas and invented his own instruments. Many of his instruments were virtual sculptures and he became a famous, if somewhat eccentric, performer of highly individualistic music.

parte (*Italian*) "PART," so *colla parte* means "with the part."

partial tones harmonic TONES that are produced in combination with nearly every prime tone or ordinary musical SOUND, and that give each instrument and VOICE its TIMBRE.

partition (*French*), **Partitur** (*German*), **partizione** (*Italian*) a SCORE.

part music music for more than one VOICE or instrument.

part-song a composition for unaccompanied VOICES in which the highest part usually sings the MELODY while the lower parts sing accompanying HARMONIES.

pas (*French*) "step."

Pasquini, Bernardo (1637–1710) Italian composer, organist and teacher, who was organist at the church of Maria Maggiore in Rome and who wrote seven operas, five oratorios, and harpsichord sonatas.

passacaglia (*Italian*) a type of slow and stately dance originating in Spain, for which keyboard music was written in the seventeenth century. It has come to mean a work in which such a THEME recurs again and again.

passage a FIGURE or PHRASE of music; a RUN.

passage work a piece of music that provides an opportunity for VIRTUOSO playing.

passamezzo (*Italian*) "half-step"; a quick Italian dance in DUPLE TIME that became popular throughout Europe in the late sixteenth century.

passecaille (*French*) a PASSACAGLIA.

passepied (*Italian*) a French dance in triple TIME,

like a quick MINUET, that is thought to have originated in Brittany. It was incorporated into French ballets of the mid-seventeenth century.

passing note a NOTE that is dissonant with the prevailing HARMONY but that is nevertheless useful in making the TRANSITION from one CHORD or KEY to another.

Passion music the setting to music of the story of Christ's Passion (the story of the crucifixion taken from the gospels). The first dramatic representation of the Passion is said to have been made in the fourth century by St Gregory Nazianzen (329–89), bishop of Antioch. It was sung throughout. From the thirteenth century, the Passion was changed to PLAINSONG melodies by priests in churches during Holy Week. The most celebrated of later Passions are those of Johann Sebastian BACH, the ST JOHN PASSION and the ST MATTHEW PASSION.

pasticchio (*Italian*) literally "pie," a dramatic entertainment that contains a selection of pieces from various composers' works.

pastorale (1) a vocal or instrumental MOVEMENT or composition in COMPOUND triple TIME, which suggests a rural subject; it usually has long BASS notes that imitate the sounds of the BAGPIPE drone. (2) a stage entertainment based on a pastoral (idealized rural) subject.

Pastorale Sonata a name given to Beethoven's piano sonata in D (Op. 28), probably given to it by his publisher but without the composer's consent.

Pastoral Symphony (1) BEETHOVEN's symphony no. 6 in F (1808), the most famous of his occasional incursions into the realm of PROGRAMME MUSIC. It is so called because it incorporates country sounds (such as a cuckoo, nightingale) and each of the five movements has an evocative title: "1. *Allegro ma non molto*, The pleasant feelings aroused in the heart on arriving in the country; 2. *Andante con moto*, Scene at the brook; 3. *Allegro*, Jovial assembly of country folk, interrupted by 4. *Allegro*, thunderstorm; 5. *Allegretto*, pleasurable feelings after the storm, mixed with gratitude to God." (2) VAUGHAN WILLIAMS' 3rd symphony (1922/1955). (3) the name given to an orchestral movement in HANDEL's MESSIAH. (4) the name given to an instrumental section in BACH's CHRISTMAS ORATORIO.

"Pathetic" Sonata *see* **Sonate Pathétique**.

"Pathetic" Symphony *see* **Symphonie Pathétique**.

Patience a comic opera by GILBERT and SULLIVAN. It is a satire on contemporary aestheticism and pokes fun at the likes of Oscar Wilde (1856–1900). It was first performed in 1881.

patter song a kind of comic SONG that has a string of tongue-twisting syllables and is usually sung quickly to minimal ACCOMPANIMENT. It is often found in opera.

Patti, Adelina (1843–1919) Spanish soprano of Italian parentage, who made her debut in New York in 1859. A natural COLORATURA, she also sang lyric and dramatic roles, becoming the most successful singer of her age. Her sister, **Carlotta Patti** (1840–1889), was also a soprano but retired from operatic performances in 1863 because of lameness, and appeared with success in concert work and became a teacher in Paris. Her brother, **Carlo Patti** (1842–73) was a violinist and conductor.

Pauken (*German*) KETTLEDRUMS.

Paumann, Conrad (*c.*1410–1473) German organist and composer who was born blind. His *Fundamentum organisandi* (*Basics of Composition*) is among the earliest instrumental compositions.

Paul, Emil (1855–1932) Austrian conductor and composer, who worked in the USA for several years before working at COVENT GARDEN, London, and then in Berlin.

pausa (*Italian*) "REST."

pause a symbol over a NOTE or REST to indicate that this should be held for longer than its written value. (*See* Appendix for symbol.)

pavan, pavane a stately court dance, normally in slow DUPLE TIME, which was occasionally incorporated into instrumental music in the sixteenth century.

Pavane pour une Infante defunte (Pavane for a Dead Infanta) a piano piece by RAVEL (1899), who also wrote the orchestral version (1912). The name was chosen simply for its sonorous qualities.

Pavarotti, Luciano (1935-) Italian tenor, one of the most famous of the modern era. He has sung in all the world's major opera houses and has become a very popular concert performer. He reached a worldwide audience with his recording of "Nessun dorma" from PUCCINI's TURANDOT, which became a massive hit after being used as the theme for the 1990 World Cup soccer competition broadcasts.

pavillon (*French*) literally a "tent," so, with reference to the shape, the bell of a BRASS INSTRUMENT.

peal a set of church bells or, as a verb, to ring a set of church bells.

Pearl-Fishers, The *see* **Pêcheurs de Perles, Les**.

Pears, Sir Peter (1910-86) English tenor. He formed a lifelong personal and professional partnership with BRITTEN, who wrote parts with his voice in mind, for example in PETER GRIMES, and they were co-founders in 1948 of the ALDEBURGH FESTIVAL. He was also famed for singing pieces by Johann Sebastian BACH and SCHUBERT. He was knighted in 1978.

Pearsall, Robert Lucas de (1795-1856) English composer who revived the polyphonic style (*see* POLYPHONY) and who is most famous for his madrigals, part-songs and religious pieces.

Pearson, Henry Hugo *see* **Pierson, Henry Hugo**.

Pêcheurs de Perles, Les (The Pearl-Fishers) an opera by BIZET to a libretto by E. Cormon and M. Carré. It is set in ancient Ceylon and tells how Leïla, who has taken a vow of chastity, is loved by two men, Zurga and Nadir. It was first performed in Paris in 1863 and contains the celebrated BARITONE and TENOR duet "Au fond du temple saint."

ped abbreviation for PEDAL.

pedal the part of an instrument's mechanism that is operated by the feet, such as on a PIANO, ORGAN or HARP. The *forte*, or loud, pedal on a piano by raising the dampers enriches the TONE, permitting partials to sound from other strings. The *piano*, or soft, pedal enables the player to strike only one or two strings or to reduce the volume of tone. Harp pedals serve to sharpen, flatten or neutralize one NOTE throughout the COMPASS of the instrument. Organ pedals are of two kinds, producing notes of the lower REGISTER independently of those on the MANUAL, or combination pedals, by which the arrangement of the registers may be altered.

pedal point NOTES sustained in the PEDAL or other base while other parts move independently. The note or point sustained must be either the TONIC or DOMINANT of the KEY. When occurring elsewhere than in the base, the pedal point is called "inverted."

Pedrell, Felipe (1841–1922) Spanish composer and musicologist, who was mainly self-taught. His musical works include operas, cantatas, and songs, and his publications include a dictionary of music and books on folklore.

Peer Gynt (1) incidental piano music by GRIEG for the original production of the play by Henrik Ibsen (1828–1906) (1878). Grieg later arranged the work into two orchestral suites. (2) Incidental music for Ibsen's play by Harald Saeverud (1897–). (3) an opera by EGK, who also wrote the libretto (after Ibsen) (1938).

peg-box the part of a stringed instrument that houses the pegs that anchor and tune the strings.

Pelléas et Mélisande (1) an opera by DEBUSSY based on the play by Maurice Maeterlinck (1862–

1949). It tells the story of Golaud, grandson of King Arkel, who while wandering in a forest meets Mélisande, who wears the clothes of a princess, although they are tattered and torn. She is unable to tell him her name or her country. Golaud, a widower with a young son, Yniold, marries Mélisande and takes her to meet Arkel and his mother, Geneviève. His half-brother, Pelléas, arrives, and gradually Pelléas and Mélisande fall in love. Golaud becomes suspicious, and when he finally discovers the truth kills Pelléas. Mélisande dies giving birth to a baby daughter, but she has told Golaud that although she and Pelléas loved each other, they were not guilty. As the curtain falls, Golaud is weeping with grief. Influenced by WAGNER, Debussy eschewed the use of tunes, preferring recurrent themes to create an expressive mood of light and shade. The opera was first performed in 1902. (2) incidental music to Maeterlinck's play by FAURÉ (1898). (3) incidental music to Maeterlinck's play by SIBELIUS (1905). (4) a symphonic poem by SCHOENBERG (1903).

Penderecki, Krzysztof (1933-) Polish composer. He has experimented with all manner of unconventional sounds (for example, rustling paper, wood being sawn, clacking typewriters, etc) and has on occasion asked singers to whistle and hiss. Nevertheless, his music is easily accessible, and his works have proved popular. His compositions include the operas *The Devils of Loudon* and *Paradise Lost*, pieces for chorus and orchestra (such as *St Luke Passion*), and many orchestral works.

penillion (*Welsh*) IMPROVISATION of verses or music.

penny whistle *see* **tin whistle**.

pentatonic scale a SCALE composed of five notes in an octave. It is found in various types of folk music from Scottish to Chinese.

Pepusch, Johann Christoph (1667-1752) German-born composer, conductor, organist and teacher who settled in London in 1700. He became an expert in music theory and ancient music. His works include odes, motets, masques, cantatas and he wrote the overture to John GAY's BEGGAR'S OPERA.

per (*Italian*) "by" or "for."

perussion (1) the actual striking of a DISCORD after it has been prepared and before its RESOLUTION. (2) the mechanism by which the tongue of a REED is struck with a HAMMER as air is admitted from the wind chest, thus ensuring immediate "speaking."

percussion instrument an instrument that produces TONE when struck, such as the PIANO or XYLOPHONE, but more especially one of the family of instruments that produce SOUND when struck or shaken, for example, MARACAS, DRUMS, TRIANGLE.

perdendosi (*Italian*) "losing itself," i.e. dying away both in volume of TONE and in speed.

Perfect Fool, The a one-act comic opera to his own libretto by HOLST. The opera was first performed in London in 1923 and is a parody of WAGNER and VERDI, particularly PARSIFAL, although Holst never admitted this. The wicked Wizard prepares a potion that will make the Princess fall in love with him, but he is defeated by the Perfect Fool and his very wise Mother. The Princess falls in love with the Perfect Fool, but he rejects her, the only man to do so, and falls asleep. The work is now better known as an orchestral SUITE.

perfect interval *see* **interval**.

Pergolesi, Giovanni Battista (1710-36) an Italian composer, violinist and organist who became famous for his comic INTERMEZZOS, *La serva padrona* and *Livietta e Tracollo*. He also wrote church music and sonatas. Many pieces have been wrongly attributed to him.

Peri, Jacopo (1561-1633) an Italian composer and singer. He is credited with writing the music for *Dafne*, which is regarded as the first serious OPERA, and for *Eurydice* (1600), the first opera for which the complete music is extant. He wrote other operas as well as madrigals and ballets, but little of his work survives.

period a complete musical sentence (*see* PHRASE).

Perlman, Itzhak (1945-) an Israeli violinist who has been a soloist with many famous orchestras. He also plays chamber music.

Perosi, Lorenzo (1872–1956) an Italian priest and composer. He was choirmaster of the Sistine Chapel in Rome from 1898 until 1923 when he became mentally ill. After his recovery he began composing again. His works include hymns, madrigals, Masses, and oratorios.

Pérotin *or* **Perotinus Magnus** (*c*.1160-1220) a French composer, one of the first to be known by name. He wrote church music and motets.

perpetual canon a CANON so constructed that it may be repeated pertetually without break in time or rhythm.

perpetuum mobile (*Latin*) "perpetually in motion," i.e. a short piece of music with a repetitive note pattern that is played quickly without any pauses.

per recte et retro (*Latin* "straight and return") imitation in which at the UNISON the antecedent is repeated, reading the notes backwards.

pesante (*Italian*) "heavy," "ponderous" or "solid."

Pescetti, Giovanni Battista (1704-66) an Italian organist and composer who wrote church music, harpsichord sonatas and operas.

Peter and the Wolf a musical story for children told by a narrator with accompanying orchestral music by PROKOFIEV. It was first performed in 1936.

Peter Grimes an opera by BRITTEN to a libretto written by Montagu Slater (after George Crabbe's poem "The Borough"). Set in a Suffolk fishing village, the story concerns Peter Grimes, a fisherman, whose young apprentice has drowned. An introverted and difficult personality, he is told at the inquest not to take another apprentice, but with the help of the schoolmistress, Ellen Orford, his only friend, he finds another apprentice. The villagers determine to rescue the boy from Peter Grimes and pursue them. The new apprentice falls from a cliff to his death, and Peter Grimes sails his boat out to sea and sinks it as the village wakes to a new day. The opera was first performed in London in 1945 and has become a regular production in opera houses around the world.

Peterson, Oscar (1925–) a Canadian jazz pianist

and composer. A virtuoso pianist in the mode of his friend Art TATUM, his Oscar Peterson Trio became one of the best-known small jazz groups of the 1950s.

Petrassi, Goffredo (1904-) a progressive Italian composer whose works include the operas *The Tapestry* and *Death in the Air*, ballets, and orchestral and choral pieces.

Petrucci, Ottaviano dei (1466–1539) Italian music printer who invented the art of printing music from movable type although he used a double process, printing the lines of the stave and adding the notes in a second impression.

Petrushka a ballet with music by STRAVINSKY. The story concerns a puppet who comes to life. It was first performed in 1911.

petto (*Italian*) "chest," hence *voce di petto*, "chest voice."

peu à peu. (*French*) "little by little."

pezzi (*Italian*) "pieces," so *pezzi concertanti*, "concert pieces"; *pezzi di bravura*, "display pieces."

PF abbreviation for PIANOFORTE, PIANO, FORTE, and PIÙ *forte*.

Pfitzner, Hans (1869–1949) a Russian-born German composer and teacher. His works, in Romantic style, include the opera *Palestrina*, the only one of his works now regularly performed.

Phantasie (*German*) *see* **fantasia**.

Philémon et Baucis an opera by Gounod to a libretto by Barbier and Carré, which was first performed in 1860. It tells the story of an elderly couple who are transformed into youngsters by the activities of the gods.

philharmonic (*Greek*) literally "music loving"; an adjective used in the titles of many orchestras, societies, etc.

Philosopher, The the nickname given to HAYDN's symphony no. 22 in E flat (1764). It may be so called because of the slow, reflective opening movement.

Philtre an opera by AUBER to a libretto by SCRIBE, whose subject is identical to DONIZETTI's *L'ELISIR D'AMORE*. It was first performed in Paris in 1831.

phrase a short melodic section of a composition, of no fixed length, although it is often four bars long.

physharmonica a small reed organ invented in 1818, the forerunner of the HARMONIUM.

piacere (*Italian*) "pleasure," so *a piacere* means "at [the performer's] pleasure."

piacevole (*Italian*) "pleasantly."

Piaf, Edith [originally Edith Giovanna Gassion] (1915–63) French singer and songwriter. Nicknamed "Little Sparrow" for her small size and frail appearance, her songs, nostalgic and romantic, include the well-known "Non, je ne regrette rien," and "Mi'lord." She died of drug and alcohol abuse.

pianette a diminutive PIANO.

piangevole (*Italian*) "sadly."

pianissimo (*Italian*) "very quiet."

piano (1) (*Italian*) "soft". (2) the commom abbreviated form of PIANOFORTE.

piano accordion *see* accordion.

piano à queue. (*French*) a grand PIANO.

piano carré. (*French*) a square PIANO.

pianoforte (**piano**) a keyboard instrument that

pianola

was invented by Bartolomeo Cristofori in Florence in 1709, and for which important works were being written by the end of the eighteenth century. Most modern instruments usually have 88 KEYS and a COMPASS of $7^1/_3$ octaves, although it is possible to find larger versions. The keys operate HAMMERS that strike STRINGS at the back of the instrument. These strings can run vertically (upright piano) or horizontally (grand piano). Most pianos have one string for the very lowest notes, two parallel strings for the middle register notes and three strings for the highest notes. Normally, when a NOTE is played, a damper deadens the strings when the key returns to its normal position, but a sustaining (right) PEDAL suspends the action of the dampers and allows the note to coninue sounding. The soft (left) pedal mutes the sound produced, either by moving the hammers closer to the strings so that their action is diminished, or by moving the hammers sideways so that only one or two strings are struck. On some pianos, a third, sostenuto pedal, allows selected notes to continue sounding while others are dampened.

pianola *see* **player piano**.

piano score vocal or orchestral music arranged for the piano.

Piatti, Alfredo Carlo (1822–1901) an Italian cellist and composer who also wrote on the method for the cello. His compositions include three concertos for the cello.

pibroch (*Gaelic*) a type of Scottish BAGPIPE music with the form of THEME and variations.

Piccinni, Niccolò (1728-1800) an Italian composer who was also a notable opera producer. He had a famous competitive feud with GLUCK. He wrote some 120 operas including IPHIGENIE EN TAURIDE, for which settings were commissioned from both Piccinni and GLUCK, *Penelope* and *La buona figola* (The Good Girl), which had a libretto by the Venetian playwright Goldoni, based on Samuel Richardson's novel *Pamela*. His son, **Lodovico Piccinni** (1766–1827), was also a musician who became a choirmaster in Stockholm; and his grandson, **Louis Alexandre Piccinni** (1770–1850) was a composer of operas and other works for the stage.

piccolo a small FLUTE with a pitch an octave higher than a concert flute. It is used in orchestras and military bands.

picco pipe a small three-holed wooden WHISTLE capable of a range of three octaves.

pick a common expression for plucking the strings on a GUITAR.

Pictures at an Exhibition a piano SUITE by MUSSORGSKY (1874), which represents ten pictures at a memorial exhibition of the artist V. A. Hartmann. Several composers, including RAVEL, have arranged the work for orchestra.

piena, pieno (*Italian*) "full," as in *piena orchestra*, "grand orchestra," *organo pieno*, "full organ."

Pierné, Henri Constant Gabriel (1863–1937) French conductor, organist and composer who succeeded FRANCK (who became his teacher at the Paris Conservatoire) as organist of Ste Clotilde in Paris in 1890. His works include operas, sonatas, orchestral suites, and oratorios, but he is best known for his ballet *Cydalise and the Satyr*.

Pierrot Lunaire a MELODRAMA for voice and instruments by SCHOENBERG. It is a setting of twenty-one poems by Albert Giraud, translated from French into German by O. E Hartleben. It was first performed in 1912.

Pierson *or* **Pearson, Henry Hugo** (1815–73) English-born composer who settled in Germany. He composed songs, including the part-song "Ye Mariners of England," operas, overtures to *Macbeth*, *As You Like It* and *Romeo and Juliet*, and set the second part of Goethe's *Faust* to music.

pietosamente (*Italian*) "tenderly, with pity."

pietoso (*Italian*) "with pity."

Pijper, Willem (1894-1947) a Dutch composer, pianist and author. He is often considered to be the father of modern Dutch music, and his works include three symphonies, numerous pieces of chamber music, and the opera *Halewijn*.

Pilgrim's Progress, The an opera by Ralph VAUGHAN WILLIAMS, who also wrote the libretto (after Bunyan). It was first performed in 1951.

pipe a hollow cylinder in which vibrating air produces SOUND. On many instruments, the effective length of the pipe can be altered to produce a range of NOTES by means of holes that are opened or closed by the fingers.

pipe organ an American term for a real ORGAN, as opposed to a CABINET ORGAN.

Pirata, Il (The Pirate) an opera by BELLINI to a libretto by Romani, which was first performed in Milan in 1827. It tells the story of Imogene, who is forced into a loveless marriage to save her father's life. Her husband is killed by her lover, a pirate, who is then condemned to death, causing her to lose her reason.

Pirates of Penzance, The a comic opera by GILBERT and SULLIVAN, subtitled "The Slave of Duty." It tells of how Frederic, a novice pirate, is torn between loyalty to his band and his duty as citizen. It was first performed in 1879.

Piston, Walter (1894-1976) an American composer, teacher and author who became professor of music at Harvard University in 1944. His works, in traditional tonal style, include the ballet *The Incredible Flautist*, eight symphonies, and many pieces of chamber music.

pistons the VALVES on BRASS instruments that allow players to sound different NOTES.

pitch the height or depth of a SOUND, which determines its position on a SCALE.

pitch pipe a PIPE with a movable stopper for sounding PITCH.

più (*Italian*) "more," so *più allegro* means "faster," and *più forte* "more loudly."

pizz. an abbreviation of PIZZICATO.

Pizzetti, lldebrando (1880-1968) an Italian composer and an important academic. He is best known for his operas, for example *Deborah e Jaele, Vianna Lupa, Murder in the Cathedral*. His other works include orchestral pieces and compositions for piano.

pizzicato (*Italian*) "plucked" (with specific reference to using the fingers to pluck the STRINGS on a bowed instrument).

plainsong the collection of ancient MELODIES to which parts of Roman Catholic services have been sung for centuries. The best-known type is the GREGORIAN CHANT. Plainsong is usually unaccompanied and sung in unison. It is also in free rhythm, i.e. it does not have bars but follows the prose rhythm of the PSALM or prayer.

Planets, The a SUITE for orchestra, organ and female chorus by HOLST, consisting of seven movements describing the planets Mars, Venus, Mercury, Jupiter, Saturn, Uranus and Neptune. It was first performed in 1918.

planxty (*Welsh*) literally a "lament," although sometimes the name of a lively harp tune.

player piano *or* **pianola** a mechanical PIANO operated pneumatically by a perforated roll of paper.

plectrum a small piece of horn, plastic or wood that is used to pluck the STRINGS of a GUITAR, MANDOLIN, ZITHER, etc.

plein jeu (*French*) "with full power," used especially in ORGAN playing.

Pleyel, Ignaz Joseph (1757-1831) an Austrian pianist, violinist and composer who founded a piano-manufacturing company in Paris. His compositions, which include twenty-nine symphonies, piano sonatas and songs, were admired by HAYDN and MOZART.

pneumatic organ an ORGAN in which the wind pressure is maintained by bellows or fans, as opposed to water power.

pochette *or* **poche**. (*French*) a small FIDDLE used by dancing masters, so called from being carried in the pocket.

poco (*Italian*) "little" or "slightly," so *poco diminu-endo* means "getting slightly softer" and *poco a poco* means "little by little."

Pohl, Carl Ferdinand (1819–87) an Austrian musicologist whose works include *Mozart und Haydn im London* (Mozart and Haydn in London) and a history of the Vienna Gesellschaft der Musikfreunde and its conservatory, of which he became archivist and librarian in 1866.

Pohl, Richard (1826–96) a German music critic who also wrote biographies. He championed the music of WAGNER.

poi (*Italian*) "then," so *scherzo da capo, poi la coda* means "repeat the scherzo, then play the coda."

point the tip of a BOW; the opposite end to the part that is held (heel).

point d'orgue (*French*) "ORGAN point." It can indicate a harmonic pedal (a note sustained under changing harmonies); the sign for a PAUSE; or a CADENZA in a concerto.

pointillism a term borrowed from a style of late nineteenth-century painting used to describe a style of music in which notes seem to be isolated as "dots" rather than as sequential parts of a melody. It is applied to the works of certain twentieth-century composers, such as WEBERN.

polacca (*Italian*) *see* **polonaise**.

polka a round dance in quick 2/4 time from Czecho-slovakia. It became popular throughout Europe in the mid-nineteenth century.

Polly a sequel to his BEGGAR'S OPERA by John GAY, which, although published in 1729, was not per-formed during his lifetime as it was forbidden production by the Lord Chamberlain. It was first performed in London in 1777. The action takes place in the West Indies, where Macheath has been transported. Polly, in boy's clothing, comes in search of her husband, and encounters many adventures.

polo a Spanish gypsy dance from Andalusia, accompanied by singing.

polonaise (*French*), **polacca** (*Italian*) a stately ballroom dance of Polish origins in moderately fast 3/4 time. It was used by CHOPIN in sixteen strongly patriotic piano pieces.

polychord a ten-stringed instrument not unlike a DOUBLE BASS without its neck, invented by F. Hillmer in Leipzig in 1799.

polyphony (*Greek*) literally "many sounds," i.e. a type of music in which two or more parts have independent melodic lines, arranged in COUNTERPOINT. The blending of several distinct MELODIES is aimed at, rather than the construction of a single melody with harmonized accompaniment.

polytonality the use of two or more KEYS at the same time.

Pomp and Circumstance a set of five military MARCHES for orchestra by ELGAR. A. C. Benson's words, "Land of Hope and Glory," were later set to the finale of the first march for the *Coronation Ode*, sung at Edward VII's coronation in 1902.

pomposamente (*Italian*) "pompously."

Ponchielli, Amilcare (1834–86) an Italian composer of cantatas, ballets and operas. His most famous opera is *La* GIOCONDA, which includes the famous "Dance of the Hours."

Ponte, Lorenzo da [originally Emanuele Conegliano] (1749–1838) Italian poet and librettist. Of Jewish parentage, he trained as a priest but scandal prompted his move to Vienna, where he became secretary to Emperor Joseph II and poet to the court theatre. While in Vienna, he wrote his three famous libretti for MOZART: *Le* NOZZE DI FIGARO, DON GIOVANNI, and COSÌ FAN TUTTE. He moved to London after Joseph's death, and then to the United States to avoid his creditors. After unsuccessful attempts in business, he taught Italian literature in New York and wrote an account of his long and varied life.

ponticello (*Italian*) "BRIDGE" (of a stringed instrument).

pop music short for "popular" music, i.e. twentieth-century music specifically composed to have instant appeal to young people. There are many types of pop music, with influences ranging from JAZZ and FOLK to ROCK and REGGAE.

Popper, David (1846–1913) Czech-born cellist, composer and teacher. His compositions include a cello concerto, a string quartet, and many solos for the cello.

Porgy and Bess an opera by GERSHWIN to a libretto by D. Hayward and Ira Gershwin. It tells the story of a crippled man, Porgy, who longs for Bess but cannot have her because she belongs to a dock worker. It was first performed in 1935 with an all-black cast.

Porpora, Niccolò Antonio (1686–1767) an Italian composer and teacher of singing, the greatest of his day. He trained in Naples and worked in

Rome, Venice, Vienna (where one of his pupils was HAYDN), Dresden and London. His compositions include numerous operas, six oratorios, cantatas, Masses, and other church music.

Porta, Costanzo (1530–1601) an Italian Franciscan monk and composer. Practically his entire output was church music, and it included motets, introits, and madrigals.

portamento (*Italian*) literally "carrying"; an effect used in singing or on bowed instruments in which sound is smoothly "carried" or slid from one note to the next without a break.

Porter, Cole (1892-1965) an American composer of musical shows famous for the numerous popular songs—often with extremely witty lyrics—that they contained. His shows include *Kiss me Kate* and *Anything Goes*.

Posaune (*German*) the TROMBONE.

position a term used in the playing of stringed instruments for where the left hand should be placed so that the fingers can play different sets of notes; for example, first position has the hand near the end of the strings, second position is slightly further along the finger-board.

posthorn a simple (valveless) BRASS instrument similar to a BUGLE, but usually coiled in a circular form.

postlude the closing section of a composition.

pot-pourri (*French*) a medley of well-known tunes played at a concert.

Poulenc, Francis (1899-1963) a French composer and pianist who became a member of the group known as *Les* SIX. He was influenced by SATIE, and was friendly with the poets Cocteau and Apollinaire, some of whose works he set to music. His early works were witty and often satirical, while his later pieces were more serious. His works include the operas *Les Mamelles de Tiresias* and *Dialogues des Carmelites*, ballets (such as *Les Biches*), concertos, chamber music, choral works, and compositions for piano.

pp, PP an abbreviation for PIANISSIMO, very soft; *ppp* means even softer.

Praetorius, Hieronymus (1560–1629) a German organist and composer who wrote Masses, motets and other church music. His son, **Jacob Praetorius** (1586–1651), was also an organist and composer.

Praetorius, Michael (1571–1621) a German organist, composer and musical theorist. His monumental work, *Syntagma Musicum*, published in three volumes 1614–20, is a general survey of musical science and contains descriptions of the instruments of his time, the history of music, etc. His musical compositions include both sacred and secular works.

"Prague" Symphony the nickname for MOZART's symphony no. 38 in D. It is so called because it was first performed in Prague in 1787. It is unusual in that it has only three (not the more usual four) movements.

precentor the official in charge of music, or the leader of the singing, at a cathedral, monastery, etc.

Preciosa an overture and music by WEBER to a play by P. A. Wolf, which was first performed in

1821 in Berlin. The story concerns Preciosa, a girl stolen in her childhood by gypsies, her final restoration to her mother, and marriage to her noble and faithful lover, Alonzo.

precipitato, precipitoso (*Italian*) "precipitately," hence also impetuously.

prelude an introductory piece of music or a self-contained PIANO piece in one MOVEMENT.

Prélude à l'après-midi d'un faune (Prelude to the "Afternoon of a Faun") an orchestral piece by DEBUSSY to illustrate the poem by Mallarmé. It was first performed in 1894. Nijinsky later based a ballet on the piece.

Préludes, Les a SYMPHONIC POEM by LISZT, which was inspired by Lamartine's work *Nouvelles Meditations poetiques*. It was first performed in Weimar in 1894.

preparation a dissonant note introduced in a concordant combination as warning of a DISCORD.

Presley, Elvis (1935–77) American rock singer. He became one of the most popular (and controversial) singers in the world in the mid-1950s with his interpretation of songs such as "Blue Suede Shoes" and "Hound Dog." Condemned by some for the blatant sexual charge in his performances, he became universally recognized as a great popular singer and an outstanding interpreter of ballads. He died of drug and alcohol abuse.

pressante (*Italian*) "pressing" or "hurrying on."

presto (*Italian*) "lively"; *prestissimo* indicates the fastest speed of which a performer is capable.

Previn, Andre (1929-) a German-born conductor,

pianist and composer who has done much to make serious music more accessible to the public at large. He moved to the USA at the start of World War II and composed film music, for which he won four Oscars. He also became a highly respected JAZZ pianist. He has conducted many of the world's leading orchestras, and his compositions include concertos for violin, sitar and guitar, and many pieces for piano.

Price, Leontyne (1927–) an American soprano who excels in dramatic roles. She appeared as Bess in PORGY AND BESS, and is considered as one of the finest Aidas there have been.

Price, Margaret (1941–) Welsh soprano who made her debut in 1962 and who specializes in the music of MOZART.

prima donna (*Italian*) the "first lady," i.e. the most important female singer in an opera.

primo (*Italian*) "first," as the first or top part of a PIANO DUET (the lower part being termed *secondo*, second).

Prince Igor an unfinished opera by BORODIN, who also wrote the libretto (it was later finished by RIMSKY-KORSAKOV and GLAZUNOV). It tells the story of Prince Igor who gets captured by the Polovtsians but escapes. It was first performed in 1890.

Princess Ida a comic opera by GILBERT and SULLIVAN, which has the subtitle "Castle Adamant"). It tells the story of Princess Ida, who starts a women's university. It was first performed in 1884.

principal (1) the LEADER of a section of an orchestra (for example, principal horn). (2) a singer who regularly takes leading parts in an OPERA company, but not the main ones (for example, a principal tenor).

principal subject the first SUBJECT in a SONATA FORM or a RONDO.

Prix de Rome (*French*) an annual prize awarded by the French government to artists of various disciplines (including music) who were sent to study in Rome for four years. BERLIOZ, GOUNOD, BIZET and DEBUSSY were all winners, but RAVEL failed after many attempts. It was first awarded in 1803, and was discontinued in 1968.

programme music music that attempts to tell a story or evoke an image. The term was first used by LISZT to describe his symphonic poems. Parts of BEETHOVEN'S PASTORAL SYMPHONY can be described as programme music.

progression motion from NOTE to note, or from CHORD to chord.

Prokofiev, Sergey Sergeyvich (1891-1953) a Russian composer whose mother was a pianist. She encouraged her young son's obvious talents, and he composed his first opera when he was nine. He studied under RIMSKY-KORSAKOV and soon became known as a modernist composer. After the Revolution he left Russia and travelled all over the world, living in London, Paris, Japan and the USA at various times. He returned to the Soviet Union in 1934 and lived in Moscow until his death.

Prokofiev's early works were marked by violent rhythms and dissonant sounds, but when he returned to Moscow his compositions mellowed; his music was not much liked by the Soviet authorities. His principal compositions include: the operas *Magdalen*, *The Gambler*, LOVE OF THREE ORANGES, *Betrothal in a Monastery*, and *War and Peace*; the ballets *Romeo and Juliet* and *Cinderella*; seven symphonies; choral pieces; and the children's (instructional) entertainment, PETER AND THE WOLF, for narrator and orchestra.

Promenade Concerts an annual season of concerts given in London's ROYAL ALBERT HALL. The "Proms" were instituted in 1895 by Robert Newman and were conducted until 1944 by Sir Henry WOOD. Cheap tickets are available for standing-room; people do not, however, walk about. Several cities around the world (such as Boston, Mass.) have similar concert seasons.

Prometheus (1) a ballet with music by BEETHOVEN to a plot by Vigot, which was first performed in 1801. (2) a SYMPHONIC POEM by LISZT (1850). (3) a tone poem for orchestra by SKRYABIN (1819). (4) the title of song settings of Goethe's poem by SCHUBERT, WOLF and others.

Prophète, Le (The Prophet) an opera by MEYERBEER to a libretto by SCRIBE, which was based on an actual historical incident during the sixteenth-century Anabaptist uprising in Holland. It is the story of John of Leyden (in reality Jan Neuckelszoon) who becomes the leader of the Anabaptists and is corrupted by his power. The opera, which culminates in the blowing up of a palace, was first performed in Paris in 1849.

psalm a poem (song) in the Old Testament's Book of Psalms. Attributed to David, psalms were inherited by the Christian churches from the earlier service of the Jews. The word is from Greek, and means "to pluck a string," hence harp song.

psalmody the singing of PSALMS to music or the musical setting of a psalm.

psalter a book of PSALMS and psalm-tunes.

psaltery a medieval stringed instrument, similar to the DULCIMER except that the STRINGS are plucked and not struck. It is usually trapezium-shaped and is usually played horizontally.

Puccini, Giacomo Antonio Domenico Michele Secondo Maria (1858-1924) an Italian opera composer who came from a musical family. His works are often considered more superficial than his illustrious predecessor, VERDI, but his dramatic flair and talent for melody and orchestration have made many of his operas perennial favourites. His main works include: *La* BOHÈME, TOSCA, MADAMA BUTTERFLY, TURANDOT, MANON LESCAUT and *Edgar*.

pulse *see* **beat**.

Pult (*German*) "desk," i.e. the music stand that two orchestral players share.

punta (*Italian*) "POINT"; so *a punta d'arco* means "at the point of the BOW," indicating that only the tip of the bow should be used to play the strings.

Purcell, Henry (1659-95) an English composer and organist who started his musical career as a choirboy. In 1677 he was appointed "composer to the King's violins." He became the organist at Wesminster Abbey in 1679 and started to publish works that he wrote for pleasure rather than for a patron. He particularly excelled at writing music for stage plays; in all, he wrote incidental music to

some forty stage productions. By the time Purcell
died, he was recognized as being one of the most
important of all English composers, and his works
are still appreciated to this day for their brilliant
originality. His principal compositions include:
the opera DIDO AND AENEAS; music for plays: *King
Arthur*, *The Fairy Queen*, *The Indian Queen*, and
The Tempest; odes (four for St Cecilia's day, seventeen for the royal family); numerous songs and
cantatas; chamber music; and many keyboard
pieces. His brother, **Daniel Purcell** (*c*.1663–
1717), was also an able musician He, too, wrote
music for the theatre in addition to odes and
songs.

purfling an ornamental inlaid border on violins
and guitars.

Puritani, I (The Puritans) an opera by BELLINI to
a libretto by Count Pepoli, based on the novel *Old
Mortality* by Sir Walter Scott, which was first
performed in Paris in 1835. Set in England during
the Civil War, the story concerns Elvira, a Puri-
tan girl who is love with Arturo, a young Cavalier.
Believing, falsely, that Arturo has been unfaithful, Elvira becomes insane. Meanwhile, Arturo
has been condemned to die by Parliament, but he
is pardoned and the news of this restores Elvira to
sanity and both to happiness.

Q a symbol in cello scores that, when inverted, indicates that the thumb is to be used as a CAPOTASTO.

quadrille a French dance that was particularly fashionable in the early nineteenth century. It comprised five sections in alternating 6/8 and 2/4 time.

quadruple counterpoint four-part COUNTERPOINT so constructed that all the parts may be transposed.

quadruplet a group of four notes of equal value played in the time of three.

quadruple time *or* **common time** the time of four CROTCHETS (quarter notes) in a BAR; it is indicated by the time signature 4/4 or C.

quail an instrument that imitates the sound of the quail, a small game bird.

Quantz, Johann Joachim (1697-1773) a German composer and flautist. He was a virtuoso performer and after touring Europe he entered the service of FREDERICK THE GREAT, who recognized his talent. He composed some 300 flute concertos and many other works for the instrument. He also wrote an important treatise on flute playing.

quarter note (US) *see* **crotchet**

quarter tone half a SEMITONE, which is the smallest interval traditionally used in Western music.

quartet a group of four performers; a composition for four solo instruments or for four voices.

Quartet for the End of Time (*Quatuor pour la fin du temps*) a quartet by MESSIAEN for cello, clarinet, piano and violin, written while he was a prisoner of war. The instruments were determined by the players available to him among his fellow prisoners.

quartetto (*Italian*) a QUARTET.

quasi (*Italian*) literally "as if" or "nearly"; so *quasi niente* means "almost nothing," or as softly as possible.

quatuor (*French*) a QUARTET.

quaver a note that is half the length of a CROTCHET and the eighth of a SEMIBREVE (whole note).

Queen of France, The the nickname given to HAYDN's symphony no. 85 in B flat (1785). It is supposed to have been a favourite of Louis XVI's wife, Marie Antoinette.

Queen of Spades, The an opera by TCHAIKOVSKY to a libretto by his brother Modest, based on a novel by Pushkin. It is the story of Herman, a young army officer who, in the pursuit of the secret of the cards known only to her, inadvertently causes the death of the old Countess, known as the "Queen of Spades" because she was formerly a gambler, and the grandmother of Lisa, the girl Herman is in love with. Herman becomes obsessed with gambling, his obsession causing Lisa to drown herself. He stakes all he has, and loses when he draws the Queen of Spades. He becomes insane and kills himself. The opera was first performed in St Petersburg in 1890.

Queisser, Carl Traugott (1800–46) a German trombonist and the first notable soloist on that instrument. He also played the viola.

Querpfeife a six-hole Swiss FLUTE.

quick step a march in quick time, which also developed into the modern ballroom dance.

quieto (*Italian*) "calm," "quiet."

Quilter, Roger (1877-1953) an English composer who studied in Germany for a time. He is best known for his songs. His work also includes the light opera *Julia*, and the orchestral work *A Children's Overture*.

quintet a group of five performers; a composition for five solo instruments or for five voices.

quintole a group of five notes played in the time of four.

quintuple time five beats, usually crotchets, in a BAR, i.e. 5/4 time.

quodlibet (*Latin*) "what you will"; a term used to describe a collection of tunes that are cleverly woven together to create an amusing entertainment.

R

R an abbreviation for RIPIENO or right.

rabanna *or* **raban** a small Indian hand DRUM.

Rachmaninov, Sergei Vassilievich (1873-1943) a Russian composer and pianist. He established himself as a virtuoso pianist from an early age and after graduating from the Moscow conservatory, he embarked upon a series of concert tours. As well as playing the piano, he also conducted and composed; his early works were influenced by TCHAIKOVSKY. After the Revolution, he left Russia and emigrated to the USA. Rachmaninov was essentially a romantic, and many of his works express a powerful emotional energy. His principal compositions include: three operas (such as *The Miserly Knight*); three symphonies; pieces for piano and orchestra (such as *Rhapsody on a theme by Paganini*); choral pieces; numerous piano pieces; and songs.

racket *or* **rackett** *or* **ranket** a WOODWIND instrument with a double reed used between the late sixteenth and early eighteenth centuries. It came in four sizes (soprano, tenor, bass, double bass) and created a distinctive buzzing sound.

Raff, Joseph Joachim (1822–82) a Swiss romantic composer and teacher. Although the son of an organist, he was largely self-taught and was helped in his career by MENDELSSOHN, LISZT and von BÜLOW. His many compositions include eleven symphonies, a piano concerto, a suite for violin and orchestra, chamber music, songs, and the operas *König Alfred* (King Alfred), *Dame Kobold* and *Samson*.

rag a piece of RAGTIME music, notably as developed by Scott JOPLIN.

raga a type of Indian scale or a type of melody based on such a scale. Each raga is associated with a mood and with particular times of the day and year.

ragtime a style of syncopated popular dance music, dating from the late nineteenth century, which was adopted by many composers, for example DEBUSSY with *Cakewalk*, and STRAVINSKY with *Ragtime*. The combination of ragtime and BLUES led to the development of JAZZ. Scott JOPLIN was a famous ragtime piano player.

"Raindrop" Prelude the nickname for CHOPIN's piano prelude in D flat. It is so called because the repeated note A flat resembles the sound of raindrops.

Rainier, Priaulx (1903-1986) a South African composer and violinist who won a scholarship to study in England and remained there for the rest of her life. Her works include orchestral pieces (for example *Sinfonia da Camera*), chamber music, compositions for piano, and many songs.

Rake's Progress, The an opera by STRAVINSKY to a libretto by W. H. Auden (1907–73) and Chester

Kallman (1921–75). The story is derived from a series of Hogarth paintings depicting the road to ruin of a dissolute gambler. It was first performed in 1951.

Rakhmaninov *see* **Rachmaninov, Sergei**.

Rákóczi March the Hungarian national air, named for Prince Rákóczi, who led the rebellion against Austria 1703–11. Its authorship is uncertain, but it has been used by many composers, notably LISZT in *Hungarian Rhapsody* and BERLIOZ in *Damnation of Faust*.

rallentando (*Italian*) "slowing down."

Rameau, Jean Philippe (1683-1764) a French composer, organist and harpsichordist. He spent the greater part of his early life as an organist in various major cities in France. However, during this period, he published an several influential textbook, *Traite de l'harmonie* (Treatise on Harmony), and composed motets and cantatas. When he was fifty, he started to write operas, with Voltaire contributing several libretti. His major compositions include the operas *Hippolyte et Aricie*, *Castor et Pollux* and *Dardanus*; the opera-ballets *Les Indes galantes* and *Les Fêtes d'Hébé*; pieces of chamber music; church music and trio sonatas; and works for harpsichprd.

ranket *see* **racket**.

rank (of pipes) a row of organ pipes belonging to one STOP. From one to five ranks are controlled by one REGISTER.

Ranz des Vaches (*French*) *or* **Kuhreigen** (*German*) a flourish or tune played on the ALPHORN by Alpine herdsmen to call their cattle.

rap a term for an influential type of POP MUSIC of the late twentieth century, which has a pulsating rhythm and in which lyrics for songs are usually spoken to the BEAT and not sung.

Rape of Lucretia, The a chamber opera by BRITTEN to a libretto by R. Duncan (after Obey's play *Le Viol de Lucrèce*). The story is set in ancient Rome and tells the tragic tale of Lucretia, who killed herself after being raped by Tarquin. It was first performed in 1946.

rasgado (*Spanish*) the striking of an ARPEGGIO on the GUITAR with a sweep of the thumb.

rataplan in opera, music in march time.

rattle a type of PERCUSSION INSTRUMENT that traditionally consists of a hollowed-out gourd filled with seeds that rattle when shaken. An alternative type of rattle is a contraption in which a strip of wood, held in a frame, strikes against a cogwheel as the frame is twirled round. It is occasionally required as a percussion instrument in orchestras.

Rattle, Simon (1955-) an English conductor of international standing and principal conductor of the City of Birmingham Symphony Orchestra. He is especially noted for his interpretation of twentieth-century music.

Ravel, Maurice (1875-1937) a French composer and pianist. He was born in the Basque region of the South of France but was brought up in Paris. By the time he was twenty, he had evolved his own style of composition, but his unconventional harmonies were not well liked by traditional academicians, and he failed four times to win the coveted PRIX DE ROME. Ravel was labelled an "impressionist" early in his career, but later he drew on many different sources (such as JAZZ, FOLK MUSIC, Eastern music) while at the same time being influenced by the works of LISZT and RIMSKY-KORSAKOV. As well as being a versatile and talented composer for the piano, he was also a master of orchestration. His principal works include: the ballets DAPHNIS ET CHLOÉ and *Ma Mère l'oye*; the operas *L'Heure espagnole, L'Enfant et les sortilèges*; pieces for orchestra (such as *Bolero*); chamber music; many pieces for piano; and numerous songs.

Ravenscroft, Thomas (*c*.1590–*c*.1633) an English composer and publisher of many collections of rounds, catches, canons and popular songs of the time. He also composed instrumental works.

Ravi Shankar *see* **Shankar, Ravi**.

Rawsthorne, Alan (1905-71) an English composer and pianist who was trained as a dentist before turning to music. His works include three symphonies, two piano concertos, three string quartets, pieces of chamber music, and many songs.

ray *see* **re**.

Razor Quartet the name given to HAYDN's string quartet in F minor and major (published 1789). The story goes that when Haydn was visited by the English music publisher, John Bland, he said he would give his "best quartet for a good razor." When Bland obliged, Haydn repaid him with a quartet.

re *or* **ray** in the TONIC SOL-FA, the second note of the major scale.

rebec *or* **rebeck** a small instrument with a pear-shaped body and, usually, three strings that were played with a bow. It developed from the Arabian *rebab* and was used in Europe from the sixteenth century.

rebop *see* **bebop**.

recapitulation *see* **sonata form**.

recit. an abbreviation of RECITANDO or RECITATIVE.

recital a public concert given by just one or two people, for example a singer with piano accompaniment.

recitando (*Italian*) "reciting," i.e. speaking rather than singing.

recitative a way of singing (usually on a fixed note) in which the rhythm and lilt are taken from the words, and there is no tune as such. It is commonly used in opera and oratorio.

reciting note in PLAINSONG, the note on which the first few words of each verse of a PSALM are sung.

recorder a straight, end-blown FLUTE, as opposed to a side-blown (concert) flute. Notes can be played by opening or closing eight holes in the instrument with the fingers. Recorders come in consorts (families): descant, treble, tenor and bass.

redowak *or* **redowazka** *or* **redowa** a Czechoslovakian dance that resembles the POLKA.

reed the small part found in many blown instruments that vibrates when air is blown across it and actually creates the sound. It is usually made of cane or metal. In single-reed instruments (for example, CLARINET, SAXOPHONE), the reed vibrates against the instrument itself; in double-reed instruments (for example, COR ANGLAIS, BASSOON), two reeds vibrate against each other; in free-reed instruments (for example, HARMONIUM, CONCERTINA), a metal reed vibrates freely within a slot.

reed-organ the generic term for a number of instruments that have no pipes and use FREE REEDS to produce their notes. Examples are the ACCORDION and the HARMONIUM.

reed-pipe an ORGAN pipe with a metal reed in the mouthpiece, which vibrates when air is passed over it.

reel a Celtic dance, usually in quick 4/4 time and in regular four-bar phrases.

"Reformation" Symphony the title given by MENDELSSOHN to his symphony no. 5 in D (1830). It was composed for the tercentenary of the Augsburg Confession of Faith, Martin Luther's founding of the German Reformed Church. However, it was not performed in Augsburg because of opposition from the Roman Catholic Church.

refrain the CHORUS of a BALLAD.

regal a portable REED-ORGAN of the sixteenth and seventeenth centuries.

Reger, Max (1873-1916) a German composer, pianist, organist, conductor and teacher. He was opposed to PROGRAMME MUSIC and claimed to be a progressive composer, while in fact he was musically a conservative. He was an undoubted master at developing COUNTERPOINT and complex harmonies. He made a name for himself as an organist while touring Europe and Russia. His works include many pieces for organ and piano, several orchestral pieces, and compositions for chamber orchestra.

reggae a type of Jamaican POP MUSIC with a heavy and pronounced rhythm and strongly accented upbeat. Its best-known exponent was Bob MARLEY.

register (1) a set of ORGAN pipes that are controlled by a single stop. (2) a part of a singer's vocal COMPASS, for example chest register, head register, etc. The term is also applied to certain instruments, for example, the Chalumeau register of the clarinet.

rehearsal practice of a work to be performed. A *full rehearsal* is attended by the soloists, chorus, and complete orchestra. In *dress rehearsal* members of the cast appear in costume, and, like the *public rehearsal*, it is really a complete preliminary performance.

Reich, Steve (1936-) an American composer, a pupil of MILHAUD, whose work is marked by the use of repetition progressing through gradual change, and shows the influence of non-European music. His compositions include *Music for Eighteen Musicians* and *Music for Large Ensemble*.

Reichardt, Johann Friedrich (1752–1814) German composer and writer on music. He became court composer and Kapellmeister to FREDERICK THE GREAT at the age of twenty-four (1776–93). He is noted for his songs.

Reid, General John (1721–1807) a Scottish army officer and amateur musician who bequeathed his substantial estate to the University of Edinburgh for the foundation of the Reid chair of music.

Reiner, Fritz (1888–1963) Hungarian conductor and composer who worked in Budapest and Dresden before settling in the USA, where he conducted the Cincinatti, Pittsburgh and Chicago Symphony Orchestras, and opera in San Francisco. His own compositions include songs and chamber music.

Reinhardt, Jean-Baptiste ("Django") (1910-53) a Belgian jazz guitarist of gypsy origin who, with Stephane GRAPELLI, led the quintet the Hot Club de France (1934-39). He lost the use of two fingers in a fire when aged eighteen, which caused him to develop his highly individual technique and style.

Reinicke *or* **Reinken, Johann Adam** (1623–1722) Dutch-born organist and composer who was organist at the Catherine Church in Hamburg for sixty-eight years from 1654. He was greatly admired by the youthful Johann Sebastian BACH. His compositions include an organ chorale, four other organ pieces, and *Hortus Musicus* for two violins, viola and bass.

related keys *see* **modulation**.

relative major, relative minor terms used to describe the connection between a major key and a minor key that share the same key signature, for example A minor is the relative key of C major.

religioso (*Italian*) "religiously."

repeat two or four dots in the spaces of the stave that indicate that the passage so marked is to be played through twice.

répétiteur (*French*) a person hired to teach musicians or singers their parts, particularly in opera.

replica (*Italian*) "repeat," so *senza replica* means "without repetition."

reprise a musical repetition; it is often found in musical comedies when songs heard in one act are repeated in another.

Requiem a MASS for the dead in the Roman Catholic Church, so called because of the opening words at the beginning of the INTROIT, *Requiem aeternam dona eis, Domine* ("Grant them eternal rest, O Lord"). It is sung annually in commemoration of the dead on All Souls' Day and may also be sung at the funeral and on the anniversary of the death of an individual. Besides the Introit, the other chief divisions are the KYRIE; the Gradual, *Requiem aeternam* and tract, *Absolve Domine*; the *Sequence*, DIES IRAE; the *Offertorium, Domine Jesu Christi* ("Lord Jesus"); the SANCTUS; the BENEDICTUS; the AGNUS DEI, the *Communion, Lux aeterna* ("Light eternal"); and sometimes the *Responsorium, Libera me* ("Deliver me"); and the *Lectio, Taedet animam meam.*

Notable settings of the Requiem have been composed by PALESTRINA, MOZART, BERLIOZ, BRAHMS, BEETHOVEN, VERDI and FAURÉ.

resolution a term for a process in harmony by which a piece moves from DISCORD to CONCORD.

resonance the intensification and prolongation of a sound or a musical note produced by sympathetic vibration.

resonance box *or* **resonance body** the hollow body of a violin or other string instrument that reinforces the tones produced by the vibration of the strings.

Respighi, Ottorino (1879-1936) an Italian composer, violinist, conductor, pianist and teacher.

He studied composition with RIMSKY-KORSAKOV, who influenced him greatly, and then taught composition himself in Rome. His works include operas (such as *Belfagor*); a ballet (*La Boutique fantastique*, which was adapted from music by ROSSINI); orchestral compositions, notably *The Fountains of Rome* and *The Pines of Rome*; and pieces for voice and orchestra.

responses the PLAINSONG replies of a choir or congregation to solo chants sung by a priest.

rest a sign employed in notation indicating silence.

resultant tone *see* **combination tone**.

"Resurrection" Symphony the nickname for MAHLER's symphony no. 2 (1894). It is so called because it ends with a choral setting of Klopstock's poem *"Auferstehen"* which means "resurrection."

Reszke, Jean de (1850–1925) Polish tenor who made his debut as a baritone. His robust tenor voice and a good stage presence made him the foremost interpreter of his time of roles by WAGNER, although his repertoire also included Italian and French operas. His brother, **Edouard de Reszke** (1855–1917), was also an eminent singer who sang baritone and bass roles, particularly in the operas of VERDI and Wagner. His sister, **Josephine de Reszke** (1855–91), was a soprano who also had great success until retiring on marriage.

retardation a SUSPENSION in which a discordant note is resolved upwards by one step rather than downwards.

retrograde motion a term for music that is played backwards.

Reubke, Julius (1834-58) a German pianist and composer who studied under LISZT. He is best known for his organ sonata *The Ninety-fourth Psalm*.

reveille (pronounced "revally") a bugle call used by the British Army to awaken soldiers.

"Revolutionary" Étude the nickname for CHOPIN's étude in C minor. He wrote the piece when he heard that Warsaw had been invaded by the Russians.

Reznicek, Emil Nikolaus von (1860-1945) an Austrian composer and conductor who worked in Germany. His works include operas (for example, *Donna Diana*, *Till Eulenspiegel*), four symphonies, choral pieces, and many songs.

rf, rfz abbreviations for RINFORZANDO.

RG abbreviation for "responsorium graduale."

RH abbreviation for "right hand."

rhapsody the title commonly given by nineteenth- and twentieth-century composers to an instrumental composition in one continuous movement. Rhapsodies are often based on folk tunes, and are nationalistic or heroic in tone.

Rhapsody in Blue a work for piano and orchestra by GERSHWIN. It was the first "serious" work to include jazz idioms and was first performed in 1924.

Rheingold, Das *see* **Ring des Nibelungen, Der**.

"Rhenish" Symphony (*Rheinische Sinfonie*) the name given to SCHUMANN's symphony no. 3 in E (1850) because it was composed after he visited Cologne on the River Rhine.

rhythm the aspect of music that is concerned with

time. In notation, rhythm is determined by the way in which notes are grouped together into bars, the number and type of beats in a bar (as governed by the time signature), and the type of emphasis (accent) that is given to the beats. Along with melody and harmony, it is one of the essential characteristics of music.

rhythm and blues a type of popular music that combines elements of BLUES and JAZZ. It developed in the USA and was widely accepted by white audiences and pop musicians. ROCK'N' ROLL evolved from rhythm and blues.

rhythm-names *see* **time-names**.

rhythm section the name given to the PERCUSSION and DOUBLE BASS section of a JAZZ band; it provides the all-important beat.

ribs the sides uniting the back and belly of an instrument of the VIOLIN family.

Richard, Cliff [originally Harry Roger Webb] (1940–) an Indian-born English pop singer. His first hit record, with his backing group, the Drifters (renamed the Shadows), was "Move It" in 1958, since when he has become an institution in British popular music.

Richard, Keith *see* **Jagger, Mick**.

Richter, Hans (1843–1916) an Austro-Hungarian conductor who became the foremost conductor of WAGNER's music and was music director at Bayreuth from its inception until 1912. He was also music director at the Vienna Opera House (1893–1900) and worked with Wagner on the scores of MEISTERSINGER and the RING, the the first performance of which he conducted in 1876.

Ricordi

Ricordi an Italian music-publishing house, established by **Giovanni Ricordi** (1785–1853), a conductor and violinist who became VERDI's publisher. His son **Tito Ricordi** (1811–88) continued and enlarged the business, as did his son, **Giulio Ricordi** (1840–1912), who also composed under the pseudonym Jules Burgmein, brought PUCCINI to the company, a relationship that was weakened by his son **Tito Ricordi** (1865–1933), who resigned from the company in 1919.

Rienzi *or* **Cola Rienzi, der letzte der Tribunen** (Cola Rienzi, the Last of the Tribunes) an opera by WAGNER to his own libretto based on a novel by Bulwer-Lytton. Set in Rome in the middle of the fourteenth century, it concerns a feud between the patrician Orsini and Colonna families also involving Rienzi, who leads a revolt of the people against the patricians. It was first performed in Dresden in 1842.

rigaudon *or* **rigadoon** a jaunty dance from the South of France that has two or four beats to the bar. It was used in French ballets and operas, and it became popular in England in the late seventeenth century.

Rigoletto an opera by VERDI to a libretto by F.M. Piave (based on Victor Hugo's play *Le Roi s'amuse*), which was first performed in Venice in 1851. It tells the story of Rigoletto, a hunchbacked jester at the court of the Duke of Mantua, who unwittingly has his daughter, Gilda, killed instead of her lover, the Duke. It contains possibly the most famous of all operatic tenor arias, sung by the Duke, "La donna è mobile" (Woman is fickle).

rigoroso (*Italian*) "rigorously," i.e. in exact time.

rikk an Egyptian TAMBOURINE.

Riley, Terry (1935-) an American composer and saxophonist. He is best known for his unconventional compositions, which only take on a comprehensible form during rehearsals. He usually performs his own works and uses assorted electronic equipment. His works include *Poppy Nogood and the Phantom Band* and *Rainbow in Curved Air*.

Rimsky-Korsakov, Nikolay Andreyevich (1844–1908) an influential Russian composer. He was born into a wealthy family who gave him a conventional education. He joined the Russian Navy for a time but became increasingly interested in music. He was encouraged by BALAKIREV to write a symphony, which was first performed in 1865. Thereafter, he took composing seriously and became a leading member of the group known as "The FIVE". He was also made a professor of music at the St Petersburg Conservatory, a post that he held until his death, apart from a short period when he supported the 1905 revolution.

Rimsky-Korsakov's music is typically Russian, and he freely used local history, folk tunes, legends and myths as sources of inspiration. His principal compositions include: sixteen operas (for example, *The* SNOW MAIDEN, *The Tsar's Bride, The Golden Cockerel*); three symphonies; numerous orchestral pieces (such as SHEHERAZADE); many pieces for chamber orchestra; and many songs. He also wrote an autobiography, *My Musical Life*.

rinforzando (*Italian*) literally "reinforcing," i.e. a sudden strong accent on a note or chord.

Ring des Nibelungen, Der (The Ring of the Nibelungs) a cycle of four operas by WAGNER, who also wrote the libretti. The operas are: *Das Rheingold* (The Rhine Gold), *Die Walkure* (The Valkyrie), *Siegfried* and *Götterdämmerung* (The Twilight of the Gods). The story told in the operas is based upon a convoluted Norse myth concerning the conflict between power and love and involving gods, dragons, dwarfs and humans. The entire cycle was first performed in 1876.

ripieno (*Italian*) literally "full"; a term used to describe passages that are to be played by the whole BAROQUE orchestra, rather than only a soloist.

Rise and Fall of the City of Mahagonny, The an opera by Kurt WEILL to a libretto by Bertolt Brecht. It is a biting satire on capitalism and was first performed in 1930.

risentito (*Italian*) "with expressive energy."

risoluto (*Italian*) "resolute" or "in a resolute manner."

rit. an abbreviation of RITARDANDO.

ritardando (*Italian*) "becoming gradually slower."

ritenuto (*Italian*) "held back" (in tempo), i.e. slower.

Rite of Spring, The (*Le Sacre du printemps*) a ballet with music by STRAVINSKY. It concerns the sacrifice of a virgin. When it was first performed in 1913, it caused an uproar, as much for the strident music as for the story line.

ritmo, ritmico (*Italian*) "rhythm," "rhythmic."

ritornello (*Italian*) literally a "small repetition." (1) a short passage for the whole orchestra in a BAROQUE aria or concerto, during which the soloist is silent. (2) a short instrumental piece, played between scenes in early opera.

Robeson, Paul (1898–1976) an American bass singer and actor. He qualified as a lawyer before becoming a highly popular stage actor in the 1920s. Notable performances include *Showboat*, in which he made his rendition of "Ol' Man River" entirely his own. His warm, sensitive recordings of spirituals and folk songs were also very popular. A noted advocate of civil rights, he came under strident attack in the USA for Communist sympathies and spent much of his life from the early 1960s in seclusion.

rock a type of POP MUSIC that evolved from ROCK'N'ROLL in the USA during the 1960s. It mixes COUNTRY AND WESTERN with RHYTHM AND BLUES and is usually played loudly on electric instruments. Revered exponents include bands such as the Rolling Stones and the Who.

rock'n'roll a type of POP MUSIC, with a strong, catchy rhythm, that evolved in the USA during the 1950s and is often associated with "jiving" (fast dancing that requires nimble footwork). Chuck Berry, Little Richard and Elvis PRESLEY were some of its greatest early exponents.

rococo the highly decorative, florid style of architecture and painting typical of the eighteenth century. Music from the same period is sometimes similarly termed.

Rodgers, Richard (1902-80) an American composer of musicals. With Lorenz HART as his librettist, he created such shows as *The Boys from Syracuse* and *Pal Joey*. After Hart's death, Rodgers collaborated with Oscar HAMMERSTEIN on several more successful musicals, for example *Oklahoma*, *South Pacific* and *The Sound of Music*, all of which were turned into memorable films.

Rodrigo, Joaquin (1902-) a Spanish composer who was blind from the age of three but composed many outstanding works, such as *Concierto de Aranjuez* (for guitar and orchestra) and *Concierto heroico* (for piano and orchestra).

roll a TRILL on PERCUSSION INSTRUMENTS produced by sounding notes so rapidly that they overlap and appear to produce a continuous sound.

Roman, Johan Helmich (1694- 1758) a Swedish composer. He initially made a name for himself as an oboe player and violinist but, after studying in England, turned to composition. He is often referred to as the "father of Swedish music," and he wrote some twenty symphonies and many violin and piano sonatas.

romance a love song or composition of a romantic character.

romantic music music dating from the so-called Romantic Era, i.e. *c*.1820–*c*.1920. During this phase music tended to be more poetic, subjective and individualistic than in the previous "Classical Era." Lyricism, drama and often nationalistic feeling were characteristic of romantic music.

romanza (*Italian*), **Romanze** (*German*) a ROMANCE.

Romberg, Andreas Jakob (1767-1821) a German violinist and composer. His works include operas, choral works and symphonies. His cousin, **Bernhard Romberg** (1767–1841), was a cellist who greatly increased the capability of the cello by careful study of its technique. He also became a notable composer, writing many works for the solo cello, a cello concerto, chamber music, and operas.

Romberg, Sigmund (1887–1951) a Hungarian composer of operettas who settled in the USA in 1901. He wrote more than seventy works, the most famous of which are *The Student Prince* and *The Desert Song*.

Rome, Prix de *see* **Prix de Rome**.

Romeo and Juliet (*French: Roméo et Juliette*) Shakespeare's tragedy has been used by many composers as a basis for works. These include (1) an opera by BELLINI, to a libretto by Romani, entitled *I Capuleti e I Montecchi* (The Capulets and the Montagues), in which the story was freely adapted and given a happy ending; (2) BERLIOZ's 5th symphony, described as a "*symphonie drama-tique avec choeurs, solos de chant, et prologue en recittafic choral, Op. 17*" which was dedicated to PAGANINI and was first performed in Paris in 1839; (3) an opera by GOUNOD to a libretto by Barbier and Carré, which was first performed in in 1867. The characters are identical with those in Shakespeare's play, with the addition of Stephano, a page to Romeo, and Gregorio, a watchman; (4) a symphonic poem by TCHAIKOVSKY, which was first performed in Moscow in 1870; (4) a ballet by PROKOFIEV, which was first performed in Moscow in 1935, and the music for which he also arranged as two orchestral suites.

ronde (*French*) literally "round," as a noun a SEMIBREVE.

Rondine, La (The Swallow) a comic opera by PUCCINI to a libretto by G. Adami translated from a German libretto. The plot is reminiscent of *La* TRAVIATA and concerns a courtesan, Magda, and her love for and renunciation of Ruggero. It was first performed in 1917.

rondo a form of instrumental music that incorporates a recurring theme, either in an independent piece or (more usually) as part of a movement. It usually starts with a lively tune (the "subject"), which is repeated at intervals throughout the movement. Intervening sections are called EPISODES, and these may or may not be in different keys from the subject. Rondo forms often occur in the final movements of symphonies, sonatas and concertos.

root the lowest ("fundamental" or "generating") note of a CHORD. Hence, for example, the chord C-E-G has a root of C

Rore, Cipriano de (*c*.1516–65) Flemish organist and composer who studied with WILLAERT and succeeded him as organist at St Mark's, Venice. His compositions include secular and church music, including madrigals, motets and Masses.

Rosa, Carl [originally Karl August Nicolaus Rose] (1842–89) a German violinist and conductor who, with his wife, the soprano **Euphrosyne Parepa** (1836–74), founded the Carl Rosa Opera Company, which gave the first British performances of many operas and toured until 1958.

rose an ornamental border around the sound hole of guitars and other stringed instruments.

Rosenkavalier, Der (The Knight of the Rose) an

opera by Richard STRAUSS to a libretto by Hugo von Hofmannsthal. Set in Vienna during the reign of Maria Theresa, the story concerns Octavian (the *Rosenkavalier*), a young nobleman who, as a favour to his mistress, the *Marschallin* (the Field Marshal's wife), is the bearer of the traditional silver rose from Baron von Ochs, a boorish relative of the Marschallin, to Sophie Faninal, the girl to whom Ochs has become betrothed. When Octavian and Sophie meet, they fall in love and conspire to involve Ochs in a scandal that will preclude his marriage to Sophie. The scandal succeeds, and the Marschallin acknowledges that Octavian must be free to marry a younger woman. The opera was first performed in 1911 and has retained its popularity ever since.

rosin a hard resin that is applied to the hair of bows used to play violins, etc. It causes increased friction between the hairs of the bow and the strings.

Rossini, Gioacchino Antonio (1792-1868) an Italian composer both of whose parents were musical. He wrote his first opera, *La Cambiale di matrimono* (The Marriage Contract) in 1810. In 1815 he went to Naples, where he composed some of his greatest operas, including OTELLO and *La Cenerentola*. In 1823 he elected to live in Paris, where he became director of the Theatre Italien. He went back to Italy in 1830, but returned to Paris before his death. His major works were operas (thirty-eight in all), which include *The Italian Girl in Algiers*, *The* BARBER OF SEVILLE, WILLIAM TELL, and *The* THIEVING MAGPIE. However, he also wrote songs, piano pieces and instrumental quartets.

Rostropovich, Mstislav Leopoldovich (1927-) a Russian cellist and pianist. He was possibly the greatest cellist of the twentieth century, and many composers, notably PROKOFIEV, BRITTEN and SHOSTAKOVICH, wrote pieces for him. He has also given many recitals as a pianist, often accompanying his wife, the singer **Galina Vishnevskaya** (1926–). He is also a conductor of international repute.

Rouget de Lisle, Claude Joseph (1760-1836) a French royalist soldier and composer who is best remembered for writing the words and music for the MARSEILLAISE.

round a short CANON in which each part enters at equal intervals and in unison.

round dance a dance in which partners start opposite each other and subsequently form a ring.

roundelay a poem with certain lines repeated at intervals, or the tune to which such a poem was sung.

Rousseau, Jean-Jacques (1712-78) French philosopher, composer and writer on music. He earned his living for a time as a music copyist, learning sufficient skills to support his creative talent, as in his short pastoral opera, *Le Devin du Village* (The Village Soothsayer), one of the most influential and successful works of its time. He also wrote 100 songs, which he published as *Les consolations des miséres de ma vie* (Consolations for the Miseries of My Life), and wrote articles for Diderot's *Encyclopédie*, which lead to confronta-

tion with RAMEAU. He published a dictionary of
music that was published in 1767.

Roussel, Albert (1869-1937) a French composer
who was influenced by Chinese and Indian music.
His highly individualistic works include four symphonies, the opera-ballet *Padmavati*, ballets (such
as *Bacchus and Ariadne*), chamber music, and
many songs.

Royal Albert Hall a purpose-built, domed concert
hall in central London at the southern edge of
Hyde Park, renowned for its good acoustics. Con-
ceived by Prince Albert (1819–61), it was built in
his memory following his death, and was opened
in 1871.

Royal Festival Hall a concert hall in London
which was opened in 1951 as part of the Festival
of Britain.

ruana an East Indian instrument of the VIOL
family.

rubato (*Italian*) literally "robbed," i.e. the taking
of time from one note or passage and passing it on
to another note or passage.

Rubbra, [Charles] Edmund (1901-86) English
composer who studied under VAUGHAN WILLIAMS
and HOLST. A traditionalist composer, he found
much of his inspiration in English lyric poetry,
and in his religious beliefs (originally an Anglican, he converted to Roman Catholicism in 1948).
His works include ten symphonies, concertos,
Masses, motets, and modern-day madrigals.

Rubinstein, Anton Gregoryevich (1821-94) a
Russian virtuoso pianist and composer who flew
against the wind by composing Western as op-

posed to Russian (nationalistic) music. Most of his works have not survived the test of time, but his songs and piano pieces are still occasionally performed. His brother, **Nicholas Rubinstein** (1835–81) was also a pianist, a conductor and composer, and founded the Moscow conservatory of Music in 1864.

Rubinstein, Artur (1887-1982) a Polish-born pianist who became an American citizen in 1946. He was one of greatest interpreters of piano music of the twentieth century and was especially noted for his performance of works by BRAHMS, CHOPIN, BEETHOVEN, SCHUBERT and SCHUMANN.

Ruddigore a comic opera by GILBERT and SULLIVAN, subtitled "The Witch's Curse." It parodies Victorian melodrama, and was first performed in London in 1887.

Ruggles, Carl (1876-1971) an American composer and painter who experimented with various forms of music and helped to establish an "American" style of "modern" composition. His works include *Angels* (for muted trumpets and trombones), and various pieces for assorted instruments. *Sun-Treader is* his most notable work.

Ruins of Athens (*Die Ruinen von Athen*) incidental music by BEETHOVEN for the play by Kotzebue, which was composed for the opening of a new theatre in Pest in 1812. It consists of an overture and eight numbers for orchestra and chorus.

Rule Britannia a patriotic English song with words (possibly) by James Thomson and music by ARNE, first performed in a MASQUE called *Alfred* in 1740.

rullante (*Italian*) "rolling," as in *tamburo rullante*, drum roll.

rumba a sexually suggestive and fast Afro-Cuban dance in syncopated 2/4 time.

run a scale or succession of notes rapidly played, or, if vocal, sung to one syllable.

Russell, Henry (1812–1900) an English singer and composer who lived for a while in Canada. He is best known for his popular songs, such as "A life on the ocean wave," and "Woodman, spare that tree." His son, **Henry Russell** (1871–1937), was a singing teacher and impresario.

Russian Quartets the title given to a set of six string quartets by HAYDN (1781), who dedicated them to Grand Duke Paul of Russia.

S

s abbreviation for SEGNO, SENZA, SINISTRA, SOLO, SORDINO, SUBITO.

Sabata, Victor de (1892–1967) Italian conductor and composer, who concentrated on opera, working in Monte Carlo, at La Scala in Milan and in Bayreuth. He was particularly noted for his masterly and exciting performances of works by VERDI and WAGNER. His own works included operas, for example *Il Macigno*, orchestral and chamber works.

Sachs, Hans (1494–1576) a German cobbler, poet and composer, who was the chief MEISTERSINGER of his time. He wrote poems, stories and dramatic pieces and composed songs. WAGNER used him as his cobbler-poet hero in his MEISTERSINGER VON NÜRNBERG.

sackbut an instrument of the fifteenth century, probably originating in Spain. It is similar to the TROMBONE, but smaller.

Sackpfeife (*German*) a BAGPIPE.

Sacre du Printemps, Le *see* **Rite of Spring, The**.

Sadler's Wells a theatre in London, dating originally from the seventeenth century, which was famed for its opera, ballet and dance companies. The opera company became the English National Opera in 1974.

"St Anthony" Variations a work by BRAHMS (in two forms, for orchestra and for two pianos), first performed in 1873. It is also known as *Variations on a Theme by Haydn* (the "St Anthony" Chorale).

St Cecilia *see* **Cecilia, St**.

St John Passion the accepted name for Johann Sebastian BACH's *Passion according to St John,* a setting of the PASSION for solo voices, chorus and orchestra. It was first performed in 1723.

St Matthew Passion the accepted name for Johann Sebastian BACH's *Passion according to St Matthew,* a large-scale setting of the PASSION for solo voices, chorus and orchestra. It was first performed in 1729.

Saint-Saëns, Charles Camille (1835-1921) a French composer and pianist who gave his first recital when aged ten. He was a prolific composer, but his works have often been written off as superficial, despite their popularity. His output includes operas (for example SAMSON AND DELILAH), several symphonies, pieces for piano duet and orchestra (such as CARNIVAL OF ANIMALS), and many works for individual piano.

Saite (*German*) a STRING.

Saiteninstrumente (*German*) STRING instruments.

salamanie an oriental FLUTE.

Salieri, Antonio (1750-1825) an Italian composer, conductor and teacher. He taught BEETHOVEN, LISZT and SCHUBERT at various times but is, rightly or wrongly, more often remembered for his jeal-

ousy of MOZART. His works include some forty
operas, and many pieces of church and piano
music.

salmo (*Italian*) a PSALM.

Salome an opera by Richard STRAUSS with a libretto taken from a translation of Oscar Wilde's
drama based on the biblical story of St John the
Baptist and Salomé. It was first performed in
Dresden in 1910.

Salomon, Johann Peter (1745-1815) a German-
born violinist and composer who settled in England. He became an influential advocate of HAYDN
and MOZART. He organized Haydn's visits to England and commissioned several works from the
great composer, whose LONDON Symphonies are
sometimes called the "Salomon" Symphonies. He
was a notable concert promoter.

saltando (*Italian*) literally "leaping," i.e. an instruction to the string player to bounce the bow
lightly off the string.

saltarello a festive Italian folk dance in 3/4 or 6/8;
time.

Salvatore, Carlo *see* **Cherubini, [Maria] Luigi**.

Salve Regina (*Latin*) "Hail, Queen," a hymn to
the Virgin Mary. The words and music are as-
cribed to Hermann Contractus (1013–54), a monk
of St Gallen in Switzerland. PALESTRINA composed
a famous setting of it.

Salzburg Festival an annual festival of music
and drama, established in 1920 to celebrate the
works of MOZART (who was born in Salzburg).
Today many other composers' works are also
performed.

samba a Brazilian carnival dance, in 2/4 time but with syncopated rhythms.

samisen *see* **shamisen**.

Sammartini *or* **San Martini, Giovanni Battista** (*c*.1698-1775) an important Italian composer and organist who may have instructed GLUCK. He composed a large body of work, including operas, symphonies, violin concertos, and over 200 chamber works. His brother, **Giuseppe Sammartini** (1693–1750), was also a famous composer of the time, who became director of chamber music for the Prince of Wales. His works included concertos and sonatas for flute and violin, overtures, and concerti grossi.

Samson an oratorio by HANDEL to a libretto by Hamilton based on Milton's *Samson Agonistes* and other poems. It was first performed in London in 1743.

Samson and Delilah (*Samson et Dalila*) an opera by SAINT-SAËNS to a libretto by F. Lemaire. It retells the biblical story and was first performed in 1877.

samtlich (*German*) "complete," as in *samtliche Werke,* the "complete works."

San Carlo, Teatro di one of Italy's leading opera houses, in Naples. It was built in 1737 but was destroyed by fire in 1816. It was replaced and that building was remodelled in 1844.

Sanctus (*Latin*) "Holy, holy, holy"; a part of the ordinary of MASS in the Roman Catholic Church. It has been set to music by many composers.

Sandor, György (1912-) a Hungarian-born pianist who has lived in the USA since 1939. He specializes in performing works by BARTOK and PROKOFIEV.

sanft (*German*) "soft."

Sankey, Ira David (1840–1908) an American singer and writer of hymns. He composed "The Ninety and Nine" and other hymns, which were very popular at the revival meetings at which the preacher **Dwight Lyman Moody** (1837–99) preached and Sankey sang. The Sankey and Moody hymnals were bestsellers.

San Martini *see* **Sammartini**.

Sappho the Greek poet of ancient times who has been the subject of several operas including ones by: (1) PACINI to a libretto by Cammarano, which was first performed in Naples in 1840; (2) GOUNOD to a libretto by Emile Augier, first performed in Paris in 1851 and later expanded; (3) MASSENET to a libretto by Cain and Bernède, first performed in Paris in 1897.

sarabande (*French*) a slow dance in 3/2 or 3/4 time, which came to Italy from Spain.

Sarasate [y Navascues], Pablo Martin Meliton (1844–1908) a Spanish violinist and composer who trained in Paris and quickly became an international soloist. LALO wrote his first violin concerto for him, and BRUCH his second violin concerto and *Scotch Fantasia*.

Sargent, Sir [Harold] Malcolm [Watts] (1895-1967) an immensely popular English conductor who began as a pianist and composer. He will be remembered for his performances as conductor-in-chief of the London PROMENADE CONCERTS for sixteen years. He was knighted in 1947.

Sarti, Giuseppe (1729–1802) an Italian composer and conductor who worked in Italy and Denmark before becoming director of music to Empress Catherine II of Russia from 1784 to 1802, with one period of imperial disfavour when she banished him to the Ukraine where he founded a music school. His works include operas (for example *Fra due litiganti*, an aria from which MOZART used in *Don Giovanni*), an oratorio. and a Requiem for Louis XVI of France.

Satie, Erik Alfred Leslie (1866-1925) a French composer and pianist whose mother was a Scottish composer. For a time he worked as a café pianist. He became an accepted member of Parisian "Left Bank" society, and met DEBUSSY, Picasso, Cocteau and Diaghilev. He was regarded with some suspicion by contemporary critics, being at once witty and serious—characteristics reflected in his compositions, which include three ballets (for example *Parade*), operettas, and many piano pieces, often with ironic titles, for example "Three Pieces in the form of a pear," written for two pianos.

Satz (*German*) a "movement" or "piece of music".

Saul an oratorio by HANDEL to a libretto by Jennens based on the biblical story. It was first performed and London in 1739. It contains the famous "Dead March."

sautille (*French*) a SALTANDO.

Savoy Operas a name for the light operas written by GILBERT and SULLIVAN, which were first performed at the Savoy Theatre in London by the D'Oyly Carte company.

Sax, Charles Joseph (1791–1865) a Belgian instrument maker. He trained as a cabinet maker but as a keen amateur player of the SERPENT turned to improving woodwind and brass instruments. his son, **Adolphe Sax** [originally Antoine Joseph Sax] (1814-94), continued his father's work and invented the SAXAPHONE and SAXHORN.

saxhorn a family of bugle-like brass instruments patented by Adolphe SAX in 1845. They were innovative in that they had VALVES, as opposed to the keys normally associated with the bugle family.

saxophone a family of instruments patented by Adolphe SAX in 1846 which, although made of brass, actually belong to the WOODWIND group because they are REED instruments. Saxophones come in many different sizes (for example soprano, tenor) and are commonly used in JAZZ bands as well as orchestras.

scala (*Italian*) "staircase," from which the Teatro alla SCALA gets its name, but in music a run or scale.

Scala di Seta, *La* see Silken Ladder, The.

Scala, La *or* **Teatro alla Scala** Milan's, and Italy's, premier opera house, which was opened in 1778.

scale an ordered sequence of notes that ascend or descend in pitch. The most frequently used scales in European music are the "major" and "minor" scales, which use TONES (whole notes) and SEMITONES (halfnotes) as steps of progression.

Scaria, Emil (1838–86) an Austrian bass singer who created the roles of Wotan in the RING and Gurnemanz in PARSIFAL for WAGNER in Bayreuth in 1876 and 1882 respectively. He died insane.

Scarlatti, Alessandro (1660-1725) an Italian composer who was instrumental in developing opera when it was in its formative years. In all he composed some 115 operas (for example *Mitridate Eupatore*) of which only seventy or so survive. He also wrote 150 oratorios and hundreds of cantatas. Although few of his pieces are performed today, virtually all operas owe something to his inspiring inventiveness. His son, **[Guiseppe] Domenico Scarlatti** (1685-1757), was also a composer and a harpsichordist. He devised new techniques of playing keyboard instruments and was as influential as his father. He wrote some 550 pieces (*essercizi*) for the harpsichord.

scat singing a type of singing used in JAZZ in which nonsense sounds rather than words are sung.

scena (Italian) "scene," a division of an act marked by a change of scenery. In opera, a solo movement of dramatic purpose, generally an extended aria.

Schack, Benedict (1758–1826) a Bohemian tenor who created the role of Tamino in the MAGIC FLUTE and sang in the unfinished Requiem at MOZART's deathbed. He also composed five operas.

Schauspieldirektor, Der (The Manager) a comedy with music by MOZART and words by Gottlieb Stephanie, which was first performed at the Schönbrunn Palace in Vienna in 1786. The plot concerns the efforts of two rival prima donnas to obtain the same part.

Schelling, Ernest Henry (1876–1939) an American pianist and composer who studied in Basle and Paris and with PADEREWSKI. His works include a violin concerto (performed by KREISLER), a symphony, and *Impressions*, a set of variations for piano and orchestra.

scherzando, scherzoso (*Italian*) "playful," or "lively," as of a phrase or movement.

scherzetto (*Italian*) a short SCHERZO.

scherzo (*Italian*) literally a "joke," i.e. a cheerful, quick piece of music, either vocal or instrumental. The third movement (of four) in many symphonies, sonatas, etc, often takes the form of a scherzo.

Schicksalslied *see* **Song of Destiny**.

Schikaneder, Emmanuel (1751–1812) a German singer, theatre manager and librettist. He settled in Vienna, where he wrote the libretto for the MAGIC FLUTE and also created the role of Papageno in it. With his profits he built the Theater an der Wien, which he managed until 1806. He also wrote a libretto for SCHACK.

Schlag (*German*) a beat of time.

Schleifer (*German*) a slurred note or grace.

Schluss (*German*) end, finale.

Schlüssel (*German*) CLEF.

Schmerz (*German*) grief, sorrow.

Schmidt, Franz (1874-1939) an Austrian composer, cellist, organist and pianist. His works include two operas, the oratorio *The Book of the Seven Seals,* four symphonies, and chamber music.

Schnabel, Artur (1882–1951) an Austrian pianist and composer. Noted in particular for his interpretations of BEETHOVEN, SCHUBERT and MOZART, he settled in the USA from 1939, after the Nazi seizure of Austria.

schnell (*German*) "quick."

Schnorr von Carolsfeld, Ludwig (1836–65) a German tenor who created the role of Tristan at WAGNER'S request in Munich in 1865, when he caught a chill that led to his death. His wife, **Malvina Schnorr von Carolsfeld** [originally Malvina Garrigues] (1832–1904), a Danish soprano, created the part of Isolde to her husband's Tristan.

Schoenberg *or* **Schönberg, Arnold** (1874-1951) an Austrian composer who was one of the most influential of the twentieth century. Although he learned the violin as a child, he was largely self-taught as a composer. His early works were influenced by BRAHMS and WAGNER. His *Gurrelieder*, for example, first performed in 1900, is a lush chromatic composition in the late romantic tradition. Between the turn of the century and 1920 he taught music in both Berlin and Vienna but continued to compose in an increasingly experimental and "expressionistic" style. By 1910 he had (temporarily) abandoned the use of key signatures and was interested in exploring the most fundamental basics of music. In the mid 1920s he perfected the concept of TWELVE-NOTE MUSIC, which gave him more freedom to manoeuvre when composing. In 1933 he fled from the Nazi regime (he was Jewish) and emigrated to the USA, where he continued to teach. During this phase of his life he returned to more traditional forms of music but continued to pour out compositions as fruitfully as ever.

Schoenberg's lyrical yet complex music was not

always popular (it still is not universally appreciated), but few would deny his influence; he explored the boundaries of serious music and created a wake in which others (for example WEBERN)
followed. His principal compositions include: the
monodrama *Erwartung,* for soprano and orchestra; the operas *Die gluckliche Hand, Von Heute
auf Morgen* and *Moses und Aron* (unfinished);
orchestral works (such as *Pelléas und Mélisande*);
piano and violin concertos; chamber music; and
many vocal works, including PIERROT LUNAIRE for
SPRECHGESANG.

Scholes, Percy Alfred (1877–1958) an English
music critic and writer on music. He wrote for *The
Observer* and the London *Evening Standard*, and
published many books. He also lectured on music
and was an examiner for London University.

Schönberg, Arnold *see* **Schoenberg, Arnold**.

school a system of teaching; in music, the characteristics of certain composers, whose style made a
school.

Schottische (*German*) literally "Scottish"; a round
dance, similar to the POLKA, that was popular in
the nineteenth century. It is not in fact Scottish,
but is so called because it is what those on the
Continent thought a Scottish dance should be
like.

Schrammel quartet a Viennese ensemble usually comprising two violins, a guitar and an accordion, or the music composed for such an ensemble. It takes its name from **Joseph Schrammel**
(1858-93), who wrote waltzes for such a group.

Schreker, Franz (1878-1934) an Austrian avant-garde composer and conductor whose works include operas (for example *Der ferne Klang*), orchestral pieces, and songs.

Schubert, Franz (1808–78) a German violinist and composer whose works include *L'Abeille* (The Bee) for solo violin, a duo for violin and piano, and for violin and cello.

Schubert, Franz Peter (1797-1828) an Austrian composer who was the son of a musically minded school teacher. He learned the piano, organ and violin and became a chorister at the Imperial Chapel in Vienna. He composed his first songs when he was fourteen and received composition lessons from SALIERI after leaving school at the age of sixteen. After teaching for four years in his father's school, he devoted his life to music. He lived a Bohemian lifestyle in Vienna, living largely off the generosity of friends. In 1822 he caught syphilis. He died of typhoid at the age of thirty-one.

Schubert is famous for his songs, some 600 in all, but he also composed operas (for example *Alfonso and Estrella*), nine symphonies (including the GREAT C MAJOR SYMPHONY and the "UNFINISHED" SYMPHONY), chamber music (including the TROUT QUINTET), piano music, and Masses.

Schuman, William Howard (1910-) an American composer of distinctively American music. His works include nine symphonies, concertos for piano and violin, ballets, and the opera *The Mighty Casey,* which is about a baseball player.

Schumann, Clara Josephine (née Wieck) (1819-96) a German pianist and composer who married

375

Robert SCHUMANN in 1840. She became famous for playing work by her husband after he died, but she was also a talented composer of piano music herself.

Schumann, Elisabeth (1888–1952) a German soprano whose pure silvery voice enabled her to shine in operatic roles by MOZART and Richard STRAUSS, and later in lieder. She left Austria after the Nazi invasion and settled in the USA.

Schumann, Robert (Alexander) (1810-56) a German composer who was the son of bookseller and publisher. He learned to play the piano when he was young, but was sent to law school in Leipzig by his mother after his father's death. He gave up law in favour of music in 1830 but was devastated two years later when damage to his right hand prevented him from becoming a concert pianist. Instead, he concentrated on composing. In 1840 he married Clara Wieck, the daughter of his former teacher, despite the opposition of her father, and during this happy stage of his life he composed many of his greatest works. In 1844 he had a mental breakdown, and he and his wife moved to Dresden. He later became a conductor in Dusseldorf, but in 1854 he attempted to commit suicide. He spent the last years of his life in a mental asylum. His principal works include: the opera *Genoveva;* choral pieces (such as *Paradise and the Peri*); four symphonies; concertos for piano and cello; chamber music; piano pieces (such as PAPILLONS); and more than 250 songs.

Schütz, Heinrich (1585-1672) a German composer and organist who was possibly the greatest

German composer of his era. His works include many religious pieces, which married Lutheran philosophy to contemporary Italian musical styles, for example *Twelve Sacred Songs, Christmas Oratorio,* as well as three impressive PASSIONS.

schwach (*German*) "soft."

Schwarz, Rudolf (1905–) an Austrian conductor who was imprisoned in Belsen by the Nazis during World War II and settled in Britain in 1947. He has held various posts as conductor in, for example, Birmingham (1951–57) and Newcastle, as conductor of the Northern Sinfonia Orchestra (1964–73).

Schwarzkopf, Elisabeth (1915-) a German soprano who is recognized as being one of the great singers of the twentieth century. She had a very wide repertoire, which included in particular MOZART, Richard STRAUSS and WOLF.

Schweitzer, Albert (1875–1965) Alsatian theologian, organist, philosopher and doctor. He trained as an organist in Paris under WIDOR before studying philosophy and theology and deciding that when he reached the age of thirty he would devote his life to helping humanity. He published two important works on music: a study of Johann Sebastian BACH in 1905 and on ORGAN design in 1906 while continuing to tour as an organist and becoming principal of a theological college. Keeping to his vow, he trained as a doctor and founded a medical mission in Gabon in 1913.

scioltamente, scioltezza (*Italian*) "with ease or freedom."

sciolto (*Italian*) "freely," "with ease."

scordatura (*Italian*) "mistuning," i.e. the tuning of stringed instruments to abnormal notes, so as to produce special effects.

score music written down in such a way that it indicates all the parts for all the performers, i.e. the whole composition. A *full* or *orchestral score* is one with separate staves for each part. A *piano score* is one in which all the instrumental parts are represented on two staves. A *vocal score* is a piano score with two additional staves for the vocal parts. A *short close* or *compressed score* has more than one part to the stave.

scoring the writing of a SCORE.

Scotch snap the name for a rhythm that leaps from a short note to a longer note. It is found in many Scottish folk tunes.

"Scotch" *or* **"Scottish" Symphony** the name given by MENDELSSOHN to his symphony in A minor (Op 56), which was intended to convey his impressions of Scotland, gained on his tour in 1829. Dedicated to Queen Victoria, it was first performed in 1842.

Scott, Cyril Meir (1879-1970) an English composer and poet who was nicknamed "the English Debussy." His works include the opera *The Alchemist,* many pieces for piano, and several orchestral compositions.

Scott, Lady John Douglas [originally Alicia Ann Spottiswoode] (1836–1900) an English composer of Scottish songs, including "Annie Laurie," and possibly "The Banks of Loch Lomond."

"Scottish" Symphony *see* **"Scotch" Symphony**.

scraper a PERCUSSION INSTRUMENT in which sound is

produced by scraping a stick over a series of notches cut into a piece of wood or bone.

Scriabin *see* **Skryabin**.

Scribe, Eugène (1791–1861) A French librettist whose output was enormous. In all, he wrote more than 250 opera libretti, comedies and ballets. He wrote libretti for, among others, AUBER, GOUNOD, MEYERBEER, OFFENBACH, ROSSINI, and VERDI.

scroll the decorative end of the PEG-BOX of a violin (or other stringed instrument), which may be carved into a curl resembling a scroll, or an animal head.

Seasons, The (*Die Jahreszeiten*) an oratorio by HAYDN to a libretto by Van Swieten, which was based on a poem of the same name by James Thomson and which was first performed in Vienna in 1801. It was Haydn's last important work.

sea trumpet *see* **tromba marina**.

sec (*French*), **secco** (*Italian*) "unornamented," "plain."

segno (*Italian*) "sign," used in notation to mark a repeat, usually as *al segno*.

Segovia, Andrés (1893-1987) a Spanish guitarist of lasting fame. He was responsible for reviving interest in the guitar as a serious "classical" instrument and was honoured by many composers (such as VILLA-LOBOS) writing pieces especially for him. He also composed works for the guitar himself.

segue (*Italian*) "follows," i.e. a direction to start playing the following movement without a break.

seguidilla a Spanish dance in 3/8 or 3/4 time in the style of the BOLERO, but much faster.

sehr (*German*) "extremely," as in *sehr lebhaft*, "extremely slow."

semibreve a "half of a BREVE"; the note with the longest time-value normally used in modern Western notation. In US notation, this is called a whole note.

semichorus a passage marked to be sung by only a section of the chorus.

semidemisemiquaver a name for a HEMIDEMI-SEMIQUAVER or sixty-fourth note.

semiquaver a note with half the time-value of a QUAVER, and a sixteenth the time-value of a SEMI-BREVE. In US notation, it is called a sixteenth-note.

Semiramide an opera by ROSSINI to a libretto by Rossi, based on Voltaire's play *Semiramis*, which was first perfomed in Venice in 1823. The story concerns Semiramide, the Queen of Babylon, who has murdered her husband with the help of her lover, Assur. She meets and becomes infatuated with Arsace, who, unknown to her, is her own son and who is in love with Azema, a princess. The king's ghost appears, to declare that Arsace shall succeed him. Assur attempts to stab Arsace but kills Semiramide instead. Arsace kills Assur and ascends the throne. Other composers among the many who have written operas of the story include GLUCK and MEYERBEER.

semitone "half a TONE"; the smallest INTERVAL regularly used in modern Western music.

semplice (*Italian*) "inornamented," "in a simple manner."

sempre (*Italian*) "throughout," "continually"; as *sempre forte*, "loud throughout"; *sempre più forte*, "continually increasing in loudness."

sensibile (*Italian*) "expressive," or "sensitive."

sentence *see* **phrase**.

senza (*Italian*) "without," so *senza sordino* means "without mute" (in music for strings).

septet a group of seven performers or a piece of music written for such a group.

septuplet a group of seven notes of equal time-value to be played in the time of four or six.

sequence (1) the repetition of a short passage of music in a different pitch. (2) a form of hymn in Latin used in the Roman Catholic Mass, such as DIES IRAE and STABAT MATER.

Serafin, Tullio (1878–1968) an Italian opera conductor who worked in Rome, London, Chicago and Milan. He worked frequently with CALLAS and coached SUTHERLAND.

Seraglio, Il (*Italian*) "harem," an alternative title of *Die* ENTFÜHRUNG AUS DEM SERAIL.

serenade (1) a love song, traditionally sung in the evening and usually accompanied by a guitar or mandolin. (2) a DIVERTIMENTO performed during an evening entertainment.

serenata (*Italian*) an eighteenth-century form of secular CANTATA or a short opera composed for a patron.

seria, serio (*Italian*) "tragic" or "serious."

serialism a method of composition developed by SCHOENBERG in which all semitones are treated as equal, i.e. tonal values are eliminated. *See also* TWELVE-NOTE MUSIC.

serpent an obsolete bass woodwind instrument with several curves in it (hence its name). It was used during the sixteenth century in church orchestras and military bands.

service a part of a religious service that is sung by the choir, for example CANTICLE, SANCTUS.

Sessions, Roger (1896-1985) an American composer whose talent was recognized early—he wrote his first opera when he was thirteen and went to Harvard University a year later. He absorbed all types of music into his own compositions and was a champion of "modern" music. His works include operas (for example *The Trial of Lucullus*), symphonies, chamber music and pieces for piano.

seventh an INTERVAL in which two notes are seven steps apart (including the first and last), for example F to E.

sevillana a Spanish folk dance originally from the city of Seville. It is similar to the SEGUIDILLA.

sextet a group of six performers or a piece of music written for such a group.

sextolet *or* **sextuplet** a group of six notes to be performed in the time of four notes.

sf *or* **sfz** abbreviation for SFORZANDO.

sforzando (*Italian*) "forcing," i.e. a strong accent placed on a note or chord.

shake an alternative term for TRILL.

shamisen *or* **samisen** a Japanese long-necked lute with three strings. It has no frets and is plucked with a plectrum.

shanai a double reed instrument from India, similar to a SHAWM.

Shankar, Ravi (1920-) an Indian sitar player and

composer. Regarded as one of India's greatest modern musicians, he became world-famous after teaching George HARRISON to play the sitar in the 1970s, and made several very popular international tours, doing more than anyone else to popularize the instrument (and Indian music) in the West. Another pupil was Philip GLASS. He wrote and performed the music scores for Satyajit Ray's *Apu* trilogy of films.

shanty a song, with a pronounced rhythm, that was sung by sailors to help them coordinate their actions in the days of sailing ships. Shanties usually follow a format in which solo verses are followed by a chorus.

sharp the sign that raises the pitch of the line or space on which it stands on a stave by a semitone.

Sharp, Cecil James (1859-1924) a pioneer collector of English and American folk music who founded the English Folk Dance Society. His endeavours spurred a revival of interest in folk song and dance.

Shaw, George Bernard (1856–1950) Irish dramatist who was also a music critic, writing as "Corno di Bassetto" ("basset horn") in *The Star* newspaper. He also wrote music criticism for *The World* (1890–94).

shawm *or* **shawn** a double-reed woodwind instrument that dates from the thirteenth century. It was developed from Middle Eastern instruments and produced a coarse, shrill sound. It was a forerunner of the OBOE.

Shéhérazade (*French*) a set of three songs with orchestra by RAVEL (1903).

Sheherazade a symphonic suite by RIMSKY-KORSAKOV (1888), based on stories from the *Arabian Nights*.

sheng a sophisticated Chinese mouth organ, dating back some 3000 years.

She Stoops to Conquer an opera by MACFARREN to a libretto based on Goldsmith's comedy. It was first performed in London in 1864.

Shield, William (1748-1829) an English composer whose works include some fifty operas (for example *Rosina*), songs, and trio sonatas.

shift a change of position of the hands when playing on a string instrument.

shofar *or* **shophar** an ancient Jewish wind instrument made from a ram's horn, which is still used in synagogues.

shop ballad *see* **ballad**.

Shostakovich, Dmitri (1906-75) a Russian composer who wrote his first symphony for his graduation from the St Petersburg (Leningrad) Conservatory. This work established him as an important composer. Many of his subsequent works were reviled by the Soviet authorities. He responded by writing his ironic 5th symphony, "a Soviet artist's reply to just criticism," which was duly officially praised as a masterpiece. He was in Leningrad as the city was besieged by the Germans in 1941 and during this time wrote the LENINGRAD SYMPHONY, which became an anthem for liberty. After the demise of Stalin in 1953, Shostakovich was more able to explore an individual style of composition, (including some TWELVE-NOTE MUSIC) although the bulk of his work adopts classical idioms. His works include operas (for example, *The Nose, Lady Macbeth of Mtsensk*), ballets (such as *The Age of Gold*), fifteen symphonies, chamber music and theatre scores. His son, **Maxim Shostakovich** (1938–) is a pianist conductor, who settle in the USA in 1981.

Sibelius, Jean (1865-1957) a Finnish composer and undoubtedly the most famous of all Finnish musicians. He started to compose when he was ten. He began to study law but reverted to music. Always interested in folklore, he based many of his compositions around Finnish epics and legends. After the turn of the century his pieces became more abstract, but in 1929 he gave up composing altogether, either because he was ill or because he was not satisfied with his output. Sibelius's works have always had popular appeal, mainly because they are comparatively accessible. His works include fifteen symphonies, symphonic poems (for example, FINLANDIA, *En Saga*), a violin concerto, theatre music (such as *The Tempest*), choral works, chamber music, and many pieces for piano.

siciliano a slow dance from Sicily in 6/8 or 12/8 time, with a characteristic lilting rhythm.

Sicilian Vespers, The (*I Vespri Siciliani*) an opera by VERDI to a libretto by SCRIBE and Duveyrier, which was first performed in Paris in 1855 and is an account of the thirteenth-century occupation of Sicily by the French.

side drum *or* **snare drum** a cylindrically shaped drum that is the smallest usually used in an orchestra. Snares, made of gut or sprung metal, are stretched across the bottom parchment and vibrate against it when the upper membrane of parchment is struck; this gives the drum its characteristic rattling sound. The snares can be released so that a more hollow sound is produced.

Siegfried *see* **Ring des Nibelungen**.

Siegfried Idyll a work for orchestra by WAGNER, which incorporates themes from the opera *Siegfried*.

signature *see* **key signature; time signature**.

signature tune a few bars of catchy music that are associated with a performer or broadcast show.

Signor Bruschino, ll a comic opera by ROSSINI to a libretto by Foppa. It is famous largely because of its overture in which the violinists are instructed to tap their music stands. It was first performed in 1813.

Silken Ladder, The (*La Scala di Seta*) an opera by ROSSINI to a libretto by G. Rossi. The ladder in question leads a lover to his beloved. It was first performed in 1812.

similar motion the simultaneous progression of two or more parts in the same direction.

simile (*Italian*) "like" or "similar," i.e. a direction to continue in the same vein that has already been indicated.

Simone Boccanegra an opera by VERDI to a libretto by Piave, which was first performed in Venice in 1857, where it failed. The text was revised by Boito, and the opera was put on in Milan in 1881, when it was a success. It is the story of a Doge of Venice.

simple interval any INTERVAL that is an octave or less. *Compare* COMPOUND INTERVAL.

simple time *see* **compound time**.

Sinatra, Frank (1915–) an American singer and film actor. He became a highly popular crooner of romantic songs in the 1940s. He is regarded as one of the finest modern popular singers, with a finely tuned jazz-like sense of phrasing.

Sinding, Christian (1856-1941) a Norwegian composer and pianist who studied in Leipzig. His works include operas, four symphonies, and many songs. However, he is best remembered for his piano piece *The Rustle of Spring*.

sine tone an electronically produced note that is entirely "pure."

sinfonia (*Italian*) literally "symphony," i.e. an instrumental piece. It is also a term used for a small orchestra.

sinfonietta a short symphony or a symphony for a small orchestra.

singing the act of producing musical tone by means of the voice. Unlike mechanical instruments, singing can produce a complete scale, ranging from the highest to the lowest musical sounds that the human ear can distinguish, with all the intermediate tones, every shade and inflection of expression together. Instruments as those of the violin family that approximate the perfection of the voice are sometimes said to sing.

single chant *see* **Anglican chant**.

Singspiel (*German*) literally "sing-play," i.e. a comic opera in German with spoken dialogue replacing the sung RECITATIVE.

sinistra, sinistro (*Italian*) "left," as in *mano sinistra,* meaning "left hand."

sistrum an ancient type of RATTLE in which loose wooden or metal discs are suspended on metal bars strung across a frame.

sitar a type of Indian LUTE, which is believed to have originated in Persia. It has moveable metal frets and three to seven "melody" strings; below these strings lie twelve or so SYMPATHETIC STRINGS, which create a droning sound. The sitar is plucked with a long wire plectrum. It has a distinctive "twangy" sound and is usually played in consort with the TABLA. Ravi SHANKAR is perhaps the world's best player of the sitar.

Six, Les (*French*) "The Six," the name given in 1920 to six young French composers by the poet and music critic H. Collet who, with another of their champions, Jean Cocteau, was passionately anti-WAGNER. The six were AURIC, Louis Edmond Durey (1888–1979), HONEGGER, MILHAUD, POULENC, and Germaine Tailleferre (1892–1983). Subsequently a number of other composers became members of the group, but it ceased to have an effective function after 1925.

sixteenth-note (US) *see* **semiquaver**.

Skalkottas, Nikos (1904-49) Greek composer and violinist who was a disciple of SCHOENBERG but who later incorporated Greek folk music into his compositions. His works include *Greek Dances* for orchestra, much chamber music, and pieces for piano.

sketch a short piano or instrumental piece.

skiffle a type of pop music played in England

during the 1950s. Skiffle bands relied on American idioms (for example BLUES) and attempted to become "authentic" by incorporating home-made instruments (such as tea-chest basses) into their outfits.

Skilton, Charles Sanford (1868–1941) an American composer who studied in the USA and Germany. His compositions, influenced by American Indian music, include a sonata for violin and piano, the symphonic poem *Mount Oread*, songs, and the orchestral suites, *Primeval* and *East and West*.

Skryabin *or* **Scriabin, Alexander Nikolaievich** (1872-1915) a Russian composer and pianist. He was hailed as a talented pianist at an early age and played his own works on European concert tours. His work was initially influenced by CHOPIN and LISZT, but from 1905 it became increasingly mystical. His compositions often involved extra-musical effects, for example *Prometheus*, a piece for piano first performed in 1902, was accompanied by coloured light projected on a screen. His other works include symphonies and orchestral pieces (for example *The Divine Poem, Poem of Ecstasy*), and many piano sonatas.

slancio, con (*Italian*) "with impetus."

Slavonic Dances two sets of dances by DVORAK, inspired by folk music. They were originally composed as piano duets but were later orchestrated.

Slavonic Rhapsodies three orchestral compositions by DVORAK.

Sleeping Beauty, The a ballet by TCHAIKOVSKY, originally choreographed by Petipa. It was first performed in 1890.

sleigh bells small metal bells with steel balls inside which are mounted together in groups to produce a richly textured jingling sound. They are traditionally hung on sleighs, but are occasionally used in orchestras to create special effects.

slide (1) a passing from one to note to another without an INTERVAL. (2) a mechanism on the TRUMPET and TROMBONE that lengthens the tube to allow a new series of harmonics.

slide trombone *see* **trombone**.

slide trumpet an early form of TRUMPET that had a slide similar to that used in the TROMBONE. It became obsolete when the VALVE trumpet was invented.

slur a curved line that is placed over or under a group of notes to indicate that they are to be played, or sung, smoothly, that is, with one stroke of the bow (violin music) or in one breath (singing).

Smetana, Bedrich (1824-84) a Czech composer who studied in Prague, the city where he later taught until 1856. He worked for a time as a composer and teacher in Sweden, but in 1863 he returned to Prague where he wrote his most famous work, the opera *The* BARTERED BRIDE, and also composed MA VLAST (My Country), his greatest instrumental piece. In the later 1870s Smetana became stone deaf, but he continued to write music. Smetana's work was strongly nationalistic, and he is considered the father of Czech music. His works include nine operas (the last, *Viola,* was unfinished), piano pieces, chamber music, and symphonic poems (such as *Richard III*).

Smith, Bessie (1895-1937) an American jazz singer who earned the title "Empress of the Blues" for the emotional intensity of her singing. She became very popular with jazz audiences in the 1920s, and made several classic recordings with Louis ARMSTRONG. She died in a car crash.

Smith, John Stafford (1750-1836) an English composer and organist. One of his major achievements was to collect and publish old English music dating back to the twelfth century. He also wrote church music and songs, including *Anacreon in Heaven,* the tune of which was adapted for the American national anthem, *The* STAR-SPANGLED BANNER.

smorzando (*Italian*) "fading" or "dying away", i.e. the music is to become softer and slower.

Smyth, Dame Ethel Mary (1858-1944) an English composer and writer who studied music in Germany. She was an active supporter of the women's suffrage movement and was jailed in England in 1911. Her works include operas (such as *The Wreckers, The Boatswain's Mate*), chamber music, and choral works. She also wrote an acclaimed autobiography, and was made a DBE in 1922.

snare drum *see* **side drum**.

Snow Maiden, The an opera by RIMSKY-KORSAKOV, who also wrote the libretto. The story tells of the Snow Maiden who falls in love but melts in the spring sunshine. It was first performed in 1882.

soave (*Italian*) "soft" or "gentle."

soca music a type of powerful, rhythmic dance music from the English-speaking islands of the Caribbean. It evolved from soul (hence *so*) and calypso (*ca*).

soft pedal *see* **piano**.

soh in the TONIC SOL-FA, the fifth note (or DOMINANT) of the major scale.

solemnis (*Latin*) "solemn," as in *Missa Solemnis,* "Solemn Mass."

solenne (*Italian*) "solemn."

solennelle (*French*) "solemn."

sol-fa *see* **tonic sol-fa**.

solfeggio (*Italian*) a type of singing exercise in which the names of the notes are sung. *See* **tonic sol-fa**.

solo (*Italian*) "alone," i.e. a piece to be performed by one person, with or without accompaniment.

solo organ a manual on an ORGAN with strong, distinctive stops, used for individual effect.

solo pitch the tuning of an instrument higher than the regular pitch, to obtain a more brilliant tone.

Solti, Sir Georg (1912-) a Hungarian-born British conductor. A student under both BARTOK and KODALY, he left Hungary for Switzerland in 1939 as anti-Semitic repression intensified. He has worked with many of the world's leading orchestras, including the London Philharmonic Orchestra and, since 1969, the Chicago Symphony Orchestra. He is especially famous for conducting works by WAGNER, MAHLER and ELGAR, and his recording of Wagner's RING cycle is particularly renowned. He was knighted in 1972.

sonata originally a term for any instrumental piece to distinguish it from a sung piece or CAN-TATA. However, during the seventeenth century two distinct forms of sonata arose: the *sonata da camera* (chamber sonata), in which dance movements were played by two or three stringed instruments with a keyboard accompaniment, and the *sonata da chiesa* (church sonata), which was similar but more serious. In the eighteenth century the sonata came to be a piece in several contrasting movements for keyboard only or for keyboard and one solo instrument.

sonata form a method of arranging and constructing music that is commonly used (since *c*.1750) for symphonies, sonatas, concertos, etc. There are three sections to sonata form: the "exposition" (in which the subject or subjects are introduced), the "development" (in which the subject(s) are expanded and developed), and the "recapitulation" (in which the exposition, usually modified in some way, is repeated).

sonata-rondo form a type of RONDO, popular with such composers as BEETHOVEN, which is a combination of rondo and SONATA FORM.

Sonate Pathétique BEETHOVEN's piano sonata in C minor. The title *pathétique* means "with emotion."

sonatina a short SONATA.

Sondheim, Stephen (1930-) an American composer and lyric-writer. He studied with HAMMERSTEIN wrote the lyrics for BERNSTEIN's musical *West Side Story,* before writing the music and lyrics for several of his own compositions including *A Funny Thing Happened on the Way to the Forum, Company, Sweeney Todd* and *A Little Night Music* and *Into the Woods*.

song (1) a musical setting of poetry or prose. (2) a poem that can be sung. (3) a name used to designate the second subject of a SONATA.

song cycle a set of songs that have a common theme or have words by a single poet. SCHUBERT, SCHUMANN and MAHLER wrote notable song cycles.

song form *see* **ternary form**.

Song of Destiny (*Schicksalslied*) a ode by BRAHMS to words by the German poet Hölderlein, which was first performed in Germany in 1871.

Song of the Earth, The (*Das Lied von der Erde*) a song cycle by MAHLER, for mezzo-soprano, tenor and orchestra, first performed in 1908. The words are a translation of ancient Chinese poems.

Songs of a Wayfarer (*Lieder eines Fahrenden Gesellen*) a set of four songs for contralto or baritone and orchestra by MAHLER, composed 1883-85. Mahler also wrote the words, which concern the feelings of a man rejected in love.

Songs without Words (*Lieder ohne Worte*) a collection of forty-eight piano pieces in eight books by MENDELSSOHN, composed 1832-45.

Sonnambula, La (The Sleepwalker) an opera by BELLINI to a libretto by Romani, which was first performed in Milan in 1831. Amina is a sleepwalker. This leads to her being found asleep in a handsome stranger's bedroom by Elvino, her lover, who becomes jealous and decides to forsake her for Lisa. When Amina, again in her sleep, crosses a slender bridge that threatens to break at any moment, Elvino discovers that she is his true love, having also found out that Lisa is a flirt.

sonore (*French*), **sonoro** (*Italian*) sonorous, resonant, harmonious.

sons étouffés (*French*) "dampened sounds," muffled tones produced on string instruments by the use of the MUTE.

sopra (*Italian*) "above," so *come sopra* means "as above."

soprano the highest pitch of human voice, with a range of about two octaves above approximately middle C. The term is also applied to some instruments, such as soprano saxophone (the highest pitched saxophone).

Sorcerer, The a comic opera by GILBERT and SULLIVAN . It was first performed in 1877.

Sorcerer's Apprentice, The (*L'Apprenti sorcier*) a tone poem by DUKAS (1897), based on a ballad by Goethe. The story is about a sorcerer's apprentice who casts a spell in his master's absence, then discovers that he does not know how to reverse it. Conducted by STOKOWSKI, it makes a particularly entertaining sequence in the film *Fantasia*, with Mickey Mouse as the apprentice.

sordino (*Italian*) "mute."

sospirando (*Italian*) "sighing."

sospiro (*Italian*) literally "sigh," in music meaning a CROTCHET rest

sostenuto (*Italian*) "sustained."

sotto (*Italian*) "below," as in *sotto voce,* which literally means "under the voice" or whispered.

soubrette (from Old French) "cunning," hence in opera a term for a cunning female servant.

soul music a type of emotionally charged music developed by black musicians in America. "Soul," as it is usually called, derives from BLUES and GOSPEL music with the addition of ROCK rhythms.

soum a Burmese HARP.

sound hole the opening in the BELLY of a stringed instrument, for example, the f-shaped holes in a violin or the round hole in a guitar.

soundpost a piece of wood connecting the BELLY of a stringed instrument (such as a violin) to the back. It helps to distribute vibrations through the body of the instrument.

soupir (*French*) literally "sigh," in music meaning a rest of a specified length.

Sousa, John Philip (1854-1932) an American bandmaster and composer who formed a successful military-style band that toured the world giving concerts. He composed many marches (such as *The Stars and Stripes Forever*). The giant tuba, the "sousaphone," that encircles the player's body, was especially designed for his band.

sousaphone *see* **Sousa, John Philip**.

Sowerby, Leo (1895–1968) an American composer, pianist and organist who was a pupil of GRAINGER. His compositions include symphonic works, for example, a violin concerto and a piano concerto; and chamber music, for example, a violin sonata, a string quartet and a woodwind quintet.

Spanish guitar the classic GUITAR with a narrow waist, six strings and a central SOUND HOLE.

spassapensieri (*Italian*) the Jew's harp.

special effects a non-specific term used of any extraordinary noises or sounds that may be required of an orchestra, or part of an orchestra, to satisfy the demands of a composer, such as cow bells, etc.

species a discipline used in teaching strict COUNTERPOINT, developed by FUX, who listed five rhythmic patterns, or "species," in which one voice part could be combined with another.

spianato (*Italian*) "even," "smooth."

spiccato (*Italian*) "detached," "distinct," marked in notation by dots over the notes.

spinet a type of small harpsichord.

spirito (*Italian*) "spirit", so *con spirito* means "with spirit."

spiritual a type of religious folk song or hymn that was developed by black (and white) Americans in the eighteenth and nineteenth centuries. Spirituals are characterized by strong syncopated rhythms and simple melodies. They were superseded by GOSPEL music.

Spohr, Ludwig *or* **Louis** (1784-1859) a German violinist, composer, conductor and teacher. He toured Europe giving concerts and was among the first conductors to use a BATON. His works include nine symphonies, ten operas (for example *Faust*), and numerous miscellaneous pieces for violin, piano and harp.

Spontini, Gasparo Luigi Pacifico (1774-1851) an Italian composer whose best-known works include the spectacular operas *La Vestale* and *Fernand Cortez*.

Sprechgesang (*German*) literally "speech-song," i.e. a type of singing that is half speech. It was used by SCHOENBERG in his song cycle PIERROT LUNAIRE.

Spring Sonata the title given to BEETHOVEN's sonata in F for violin (1801).

Spring Symphony (1) the title of SCHUMANN's symphony no. 1 in B flat (1841). (2) a song-symphony for three solo singers, mixed chorus, boys' choir and orchestra by BRITTEN (1949).

square piano a PIANO in a square case, with horizontal strings.

Stabat Mater (*Latin*) "His Mother stood," the initial words of a verse from the Gospel account of the Crucifixion. It was set to music by, for example, PALESTRINA. Later settings include those by HAYDN, SCHUBERT and ROSSINI, amongst others.

staccato (*Italian*) "detached," i.e. notes should be shortened and played with brief intervals between them.

staff *see* **stave**.

Stainer, Sir John (1840–1902) an English organist, composer and teacher. He was organist to Oxford University and of St Paul's Cathedral in London, and became professor of music at Oxford. He was knighted in 1888. His compositions include many choral works, for example the oratorios *Gideon* and *The Crucifixion*.

Stamitz, Karl (1745-1801) a German-born violinist and composer of Czech descent. His works include seventy symphonies, a symphony for two orchestras, and two operas. His father, **Johann Stamitz** (1717–57), and brother, **Anton Stamitz** (1721–68), were also noted musicians.

Ständchen (*German*) a SERENADE.

Stanford, Sir Charles Villiers (1852-1924) an Irish-born composer, and also an influential teacher (VAUGHAN WILLIAMS and BLISS were among his pupils). Little of his music is now performed, but he is remembered for his opera *Shamus O'Brien,* and his 3rd (*Irish*) symphony. His church music is still heard. He was knighted in 1901.

Stanley, John (1713-86) an English composer and famous organist, who was blind from early childhood. His works include concertos for strings, pieces for flute, and compositions for organ.

stark (*German*) "loud."

Star-Spangled Banner, The the song officially adopted as the US national anthem in 1931. The words were written by an American lawyer, Francis Scott Key (1779–1843), in 1814 to a tune by John Stafford SMITH.

Starr, Ringo (1940–) an English rock drummer, who was the Beatles' drummer (*see* LENNON and MCCARTNEY) and occasionally sang on their records, for example "Yellow Submarine."

stave *or* **staff** a set of horizontal lines (usually five) on which music is written. Each line, and the gaps between them, represent a different PITCH.

steel drum a PERCUSSION INSTRUMENT ("pan") made by West Indian musicians (particularly from Trinidad) out of discarded oil drums. Each drum can be tuned to play a range of notes by beating and heat-treating different sections of the "head," i.e. the top of the drum.

Steg (*German*) the BRIDGE of a violin, etc.

Steinway & Sons a firm of piano manufacturers founded by Henry Steinway [originally Heinrich Steinweg] (1797–1871) in New York in 1853. A London branch opened in 1875.

stem the line, or "tail," attached to the head of all notes smaller than a semibreve.

stentando (*Italian*) "retarding," a holding back of a note.

Stern, Isaac (1920–) a Russian-born violinist who has lived in the USA since childhood. He made his first public appearance (in the USA) at the age of fifteen and has remained a premier solo performer ever since.

stesso (*Italian*) "same," so *lo stesso tempo* means "the same speed."

Stockhausen, Karlheinz (1928–) a German composer who was a pupil of MESSIAEN and MILHAUD. He became interested in electronic music and has influenced many composers. Such music is now a recognized art form. Stockhausen has challenged the concepts of established formulae (for example with *Gruppen,* a piece for three orchestras and three conductors) and has frequently been considered outrageous by traditionalists. The element of chance is incorporated into his compositions, and luck, as much as anything else, makes a performance succeed or fail. His works include pieces for piano (usually electrically amplified), pieces that are largely allowed to flow with the performers' own whims (such as *Mantra*), and hundreds of experimental compositions (such as *Carré* for four orchestras and choruses).

Stokowski, Leopold (1882–1977) a British-born American conductor of Polish-Irish descent. A popularizer of classical music, he is best known for his collaboration with Walt Disney in conducting the music for the film *Fantasia* (1940).

stomp a BLUES composition in which the beat is literally stamped on the floor.

stop a handle or knob on an ORGAN that admits or prevents air from reaching certain pipes and that can therefore be used to modify the potential output of the MANUALS and PEDALS.

stopping on stringed instruments, the placing of fingers on a string to shorten its effective length and raise its PITCH.

Storace, Stephen (1763-96) an English composer who travelled Europe (meeting MOZART in the process). His works include romantic operas and opeettas (such as *No Song, No Supper*), chamber music, and songs.

Stradella, Alessandro (1642-82) an Italian composer, singer and violinist who was eventually murdered (at the second attempt) for eloping with a nobleman's mistress. His works include six oratorios, and assorted sonatas and concertos, and his sensational life was the basis for an opera by FLOTOW.

Stradivari *or* **Stradivarius, Antonio** (1644-1737) an Italian violin-maker whose instruments are unsurpassed for the quality of their sound. He was taught the craft by AMATI and founded his own business in Cremona.

strathspey *see* **reel**.

Strauss, Johann, "the elder" (1804-49) an Austrian conductor and composer whose works include various waltzes and other pieces. His son, **Johann Strauss, "the younger"** (1825-99), was a violinist, conductor and composer of light music, especially Viennese waltzes. He formed his own orchestra, which performed successfully throughout Europe. He composed sixteen operettas (for example *Die Fledermaus*), and hundreds of dances including the famous BLUE DANUBE waltz, gaining him the title "Waltz King." Another son, **Joseph Strauss** (1827-70) was also a composer of well over 200 waltzes, while his youngest son, **Eduard Strauss** (1835–1916) became conductor of court balls in Russia and toured with his own orchestra, borrowing his brother's title of "Waltz King." He composed more than 200 pieces of dance music.

Strauss, Richard (1867–1949) a German composer who was the son of a distinguished horn player. He started composing when he was six and wrote his first symphony when he was sixteen. He combined composition with an international career as a conductor. His compositions essentially comprise three types: symphonic poems, operas, and songs. His work was initially influenced by LISZT and WAGNER, and he was seen by many as Wagner's successor. His first opera, SALOMÉ, caused controversy, and his second, ELEKTRA, was equally sensational. Later, influenced perhaps by his main librettist, the Austrian poet Hugo von Hofmannsthal (1874–1929), he concentrated on more joyous music. This resulted in *Der* ROSENKAVALIER and *Arabella*. A later opera, *The Silent Woman*, on which he collaborated with the Austrian writer Stefan Zweig (1881–1942), was first performed in 1935 but was banned by the Nazis after four performances. He wrote particularly notably for the female voice, and also for the horn. His works include: operas (for example *Daphne, Capriccio, Die Liebe der Danae,* orchestral poems (for example ALSO SPRACH ZARATHUSTRA, DON QUIXOTE), songs (for example FOUR LAST SONGS), and two horn concertos.

Stravinsky, Igor Feodorovich (1882–1971) a Russian composer whose father was a bass singer. For a time he studied under RIMSKY-KORSAKOV and was influenced by Russian music and also by that of DEBUSSY. The Russian impresario Sergei Diaghilev (1872–1929) commissioned his first masterpiece, the ballet The FIREBIRD, and he later wrote PETRUSHKA and *The* RITE OF SPRING for Diaghilev's ballet company. In 1914 he left Russia and, after spending time in France, emigrated to the USA (becoming a US citizen in 1945). On leaving his native land, he left behind his innate nationalism and started to experiment with traditional forms of music that he had not been entirely familiar with, such as neoclassical music. While living in the USA he adopted SERIALISM, evolving it to his own technique. Stravinsky greatly furthered the cause, and acceptability, of "modern" music, and his place in history is assured. His principal compositions include the ballets *Petrushka, The Rite of Spring* and *Agon*; the orchestral pieces *Fireworks* and DUMBARTON OAKS; choral works; and assorted pieces for miscellaneous instruments.

Streichinstrument (*German*) a string instrument.

Streichquartett (*German*) a STRING QUARTET.

strepitoso (*Italian*) "boisterously."

stretto "close together," i.e. a quickening of tempo.

stride (piano) a JAZZ piano technique character-ized by the use of single bass notes on the first and third beats and chords on the second and fourth.

string a vibrating cord for the production of tone, in the piano of drawn cast steel wire, in instru-ments of the violin family of catgut or spun silk, and in the guitar of catgut or wire.

stringendo (*Italian*) "tightening," i.e. increasing tension, often with accelerated tempo.

string quartet a group of four performers who use stringed instruments (two violins, viola and cello); or a piece of music written for such a group.

strings a general term for the stringed instru-ments of the violin family.

Stroh violin a violin made of metal (invented by Charles Stroh in 1901) that incorporates a trum-pet bell and does not have a normal violin body.

Stück (*German*) "piece."

study music written to demonstrate technique in playing a musical instrument or using the voice.

subdominant the fourth note of the major or minor scale.

subito (*Italian*) "suddenly," as in *piano subito,* meaning "suddenly soft."

subject a musical theme (a substantial group of notes) on which a composition (or part of a compo-sition) is constructed, for example, the first and second subjects in the exposition in SONATA FORM; the subject in a FUGUE; also the leading voice (first part) of a fugue.

submediant the sixth note of the major or minor scale.

subsidiary theme any THEME that is less important than the main theme(s) of a composition.

succentor the deputy of a PRECENTOR in a cathedral, etc.

suite a collection of short pieces that combine to form an effective overall composition; the BAROQUE suite was a set of (stylized) dances.

suivez (*French*) "follow." (1) a direction to begin the next section without pausing. (2) a direction to an accompanist to accommodate the accompaniment to the soloist.

Suk, Josef (1874-1935) a Czech composer, violinist and viola player who was the son-in-law of DVORAK. He composed two symphonies and, amongst other works, symphonic poems.

sul, sull' (*Italian*) "on" or "over," so *sul ponticello* means "over the bridge" (in violin bowing).

Sullivan, Sir Arthur Seymour (1842-1900) an English composer, organist and conductor who wrote many successful light operas to libretti by W. S. GILBERT. This partnership produced some of the most popular comic operas of all time, including HMS PINAFORE, *The* PIRATES OF PENZANCE, *The* MIKADO, RUDDIGORE, *The* YEOMEN OF THE GUARD, and *The* GONDOLIERS. However, Sullivan also wrote serious operatic music (for example *Ivanhoe*), ballet music, oratorios and church music. He was knighted in 1883.

Suor Angelica (Sister Angelica) a one-act opera by PUCCINI, the second of the TRITTICO. It is the story of a woman who has become a nun after a love affair and the birth of an illegitimate child. When she hears of the child's death, she commits suicide, but as she dies she is forgiven her sins by the Virgin and Child appearing to her in a vision.

Suppé, Franz von (1819-95) a Dalmatian-born composer and conductor of Belgian descent. He is best remembered for his satirical songs, his operettas and his overture *Poet and the Peasant*.

Surprise Symphony the name given to HAYDN's symphony no. 94 in G (1791). It is so called because the slow, opening movement is rudely interrupted by a sudden, very hard drumbeat.

suspension a device used in harmony, in which a note sounded in one chord is sustained while a subsequent chord is played (or sung), producing a DISSONANCE that is then resolved.

Süssmayer, Franz Xaver (1766–1803) an Austrian composer who was a pupil of MOZART and SALIERI. His compositions include Masses, cantatas and music for the theatre. He became a friend of Mozart and completed his *Requiem*, obtaining final instructions at Mozart's deathbed.

sustaining pedal *see* **piano**.

Sutherland, Dame Joan (1926-) an Australian soprano who became one of the world's leading BEL CANTO operatic sopranos in the 1950s and 1960s. She was made a DBE in 1979 and retired in 1990.

Svendsen, Johan Severin (1842-1911) a Norwegian composer, violinist and conductor. Having been a virtuoso violin player, he turned to composing while studying in Leipzig, where he was influenced by WAGNER. He wrote orchestral works, including two symphonies.

Swan Lake a ballet by TCHAIKOVSKY, which was

originally choreographed by Petipa and Ivanov. It was first performed in 1877 and has subsequently become the best known of all ballets.

Sweelinck, Jan Pieterszoon (1562–1621) a Dutch composer, organist and harpsichordist. His important keyboard music was influenced by English composers. He himself became an influential teacher of Dutch and German composers.

swell organ a manual on an ORGAN. The notes played on this manual can become louder and softer by the opening and closing of the shutters on the swell box, which encloses the pipes.

swing a type of American popular music of the 1935-45 era; it was played by big bands and had an insistent rhythm. Glenn MILLER and his ensemble were influential in its development.

Sylphides, Les a ballet with music taken from piano pieces by CHOPIN. It was first performed (as a ballet) in 1909.

sympathetic strings strings on certain instruments, such as the SITAR, which are not actually plucked or bowed, but which are set in sympathetic vibration and produce a note without being touched, when the same note is played on a "melody" string.

symphonic poem an orchestral composition, a form of PROGRAMME MUSIC, usually in one movement, which attempts to interpret or describe an emotion, idea, or story. The term was coined by LISZT.

Symphonie fantastique (Fantastic Symphony) an orchestral work in five movements by BERLIOZ (1830). It was inspired by the composer's love for the actress Harriet Smithson.

Symphonie Pathétique

Symphonie Pathétique (Pathetic Symphony) the name, authorized by the composer, of TCHAIKOVSKY's 6th symphony in B minor

symphony in essence, a prolonged or extended SONATA for an orchestra. Most symphonies have four movements (sections) that, although interrelated, tend to have recognized forms, for example, a quick first movement, a slow second movement, a MINUET third movement, and a vibrant fourth movement (FINALE).

syncopation an alteration to the normal arrangement of accented beats in a bar. This is usually done by placing accents on beats or parts of a beat that do not normally carry an accent.

synthesizer an electronic instrument, operated by a keyboard and switches, that can generate and modify an extensive range of sound.

Szymanowski, Karol (1882-1937) a Polish composer who is considered the father of modern Polish music. After being influenced first by the German Romantic composers and then by DEBUSSY and STRAVINSKY, he turned to Polish folk music, and his later works were in a nationalistic style. His works include operas (such as *King Roger*), the ballet *Harnasie,* four symphonies, and many pieces of chamber music.

Tabarro, Il (The Cloak) a one-act opera by PUCCINI, the first part of the TRITTICO. It is the story of Michele, a bargee on the Seine, who murders the lover of his wife, Giorgetta, and covers the body with the cloak under which Michele and Giorgetta would shelter when they had been in love.

tabla a pair of Indian DRUMS, beaten by the hands, which are often used to accompany the SITAR in classical Indian music.

table an alternative name for the upper surface, or BELLY, of members of the violin family.

tabor an early type of SNARE DRUM.

tace (*Italian*) "silent."

Tafelmusik (*German*) "table music," i.e. music sung during a banquet as an entertainment.

tail the STEM attached to the head of a minim (half note) or a smaller note.

tail piece the piece of wood at the base of a VIOLIN to which the strings are attached.

tail pin the metal rod at the bottom of a CELLO or DOUBLE BASS, which can be pulled out to adjust the height of the instrument above the floor.

Takt (*German*) "time," so *im Takt* means "in time."

Tales of Hoffmann, The (*Les Contes d'Hoffmann*)

an opera by OFFENBACH to a libretto by J. Barbier and M. Carré. It is based on three stories by E. T. A. Hoffmann, which each recount love affairs. Unfinished at the time of Offenbach's death, it was completed by Ernest Guiraud (1837–92).

Tallis, Thomas (*c.*1505-85) an English composer and organist who is considered to be one of the most important and influential musicians of his era. His works include many religious pieces (for example motets, Masses, Magnificats), secular choral works, and compositions for keyboard.

talon (*French*) the "nut" or heel of a BOW.

tambourin (1) a lively eighteenth-century piece in the style of a folk dance from Provence, usually in 2/4 time. (2) a narrow DRUM, played along with a pipe, as the accompaniment to dancing.

tambourine a small, shallow DRUM with a single skin fastened over a circular frame. Small metal cymbals (jingles) are slotted into the frame and rattle when the instrument is shaken or beaten with the hand.

tam-tam a large bronze GONG of Chinese origin.

tampon a drumstick that has a head at each end, held in the middle to produce a drum roll.

tango a Latin-American dance in moderately slow 2/4 time, originating from Argentina. It makes use of syncopated rhythms and became popular in Europe in the 1920s.

Tannhäuser (*Tannhauser, und der Sangerkrieg auf Wartburg*, Tannhauser and the Singing Contest at the Wartburg) an opera by WAGNER, who also wrote the libretto. The story concerns the two conflicting loves of Tannhäuser, a minstrel knight, for the goddess Venus and the mortal Elisabeth. It was first performed in 1845.

tanto (*Italian*) "so much," as in *allegro non tanto*, meaning "quick, but not too quick."

Tanz (*German*) "dance."

tap dance a dance in which the feet are used to tap out a rhythm. Tap dancing was made popular by Fred Astaire's performances in films during the 1930s. Special shoes with steel plates at the toe and heel are usually worn.

tarantella a very fast, wild folk dance from Southern Italy in 6/8 time, and gradually increasing in speed. CHOPIN used the form in a concert piece.

Tartini, Guiseppe (1692-1770) an Italian violinist, composer and teacher. He founded a famous violin school in Padua and wrote several treatises on violin playing and on acoustics in harmony. His works include many violin concertos, sonatas (such as *The Devil's Trill*), symphonies, and church music.

tasto (*Italian*) the keyboard of a piano or the finger-board of a stringed instrument.

tattoo originally a night drum beat calling soldiers to their quarters, now a military display.

Tatum, Art (1910–56) an American JAZZ pianist. Blind in one eye and partially sighted in the other, he was largely self-taught and became an acclaimed virtuoso of piano music in SWING mode.

Tavener, John Kenneth (1944–) an English composer who studied under Lennox BERKELEY and became noted particularly for his religious compositions, for example the cantata *Cain and Abel* and the opera *Therese*.

Taverner, John (*c.*1490-1545) an important English composer who taught at Oxford University and is best known for his religious works (chiefly Masses and Magnificats).

Tchaikovsky, Piotr Ilyich (1840-93) a Russian composer. His mother's death when he was fourteen may have stimulated him to compose. After four years as a civil servant he enrolled at the St Petersburg Conservatory. He then moved to Moscow to teach and met members of "The FIVE." In 1877, after the success of his first piano concerto, he started a correspondence with Nadezhda von Meck that lasted for fifteen years. She offered to sponsor him, and this gave him the financial freedom to compose. In 1877 Tchaikovsky, in an apparent attempt to "cure" his homosexuality, married Antonia Milyukova, but the marriage was such a disaster that he tried to kill himself after just eleven weeks. However despite his problems, he continued to write music, and the last years of his life were fruitful. He toured Europe and the USA as a conductor and won international praise. He died of cholera in St Petersburg after drinking unboiled water.

Tchaikovsky was the outstanding Russian composer of the nineteenth century. Among his greatest works are his ballets, in which his theatrical flair is expressed most completely. Although he admired many Russian contemporaries and their works, the musicians that influenced him most were European, for example BIZET, SAINT-SAENS, and MOZART. His principal works include the operas *Vakula the Smith*, EUGENE ONEGIN, *The*

Maid of Orleans, *Yolanta* and *The* QUEEN OF SPADES;
the ballets SWAN LAKE, *The* SLEEPING BEAUTY and
The NUTCRACKER; six symphonies, including the
MANFRED symphony and the SYMPHONIE PATHÉ-
TIQUE; concertos for piano and violin; miscellane-
ous orchestral pieces; and many songs.

Te Deum laudamus (*Latin*) "We Praise Thee, O
God"; a Christian hymn sung at Matins. Numerous composers (e.g PURCELL, HANDEL, VERDI) have
set it to music.

Te Kanawa, Kiri (1944-) New Zealand soprano.
She is one of the world's leading operatic sopranos
and is especially famous for roles in operas by
VERDI, MOZART and Richard STRAUSS.

Telemann, Georg Philipp (1681-1767) German
composer. He taught himself music while studying law at Leipzig University. He became friendly
with Johann Sebastian BACH and was hugely
prolific. His works include forty-four Passions,
forty operas, 600 French overtures and numerous
pieces of chamber music.

temperament the way in which INTERVALS between notes have been "tempered," or slightly
altered, in Western music so that the slight dis-
crepancy in seven octaves is distributed evenly
over the range. In "equal temperament" an octave
is divided into twelve semitones, which means
that, for example, D sharp is also E flat: this is a
compromise, for strictly there is a marginal difference between D sharp and E flat.

tempestoso (*Italian*) "agitated, tempestuous."

tempo (*Italian*) "time." The time taken by a composition, therefore the speed at which it is per-

formed, hence the pace of the beat. *A tempo* means "in time." Tempo can also mean a movement of a sonata or symphony, as in *il secondo tempo*, "the second movement".

ten. (*Italian*) an abbreviation for TENUTO.

Tennstedt, Klaus (1926-) German conductor and violinist. He has worked with many noted orchestras and is known for his interpretations of the works of MAHLER.

tenor (1) the highest adult male voice with a range an octave to either side of middle C. (2) as a prefix to the name of an instrument, it indicates the size between an ALTO member of the family and a BASS, for example tenor SAXOPHONE. (3) the RECITING NOTE in psalm singing. (4) an obsolete term for a viola (tenor violin).

tenor drum a drum, frequently used in military bands, between a SIDE DRUM and BASS DRUM in size and pitch, and without snares.

tenor violin a viola.

tenuto (*Italian*) "held"; a term that indicates that a note should be held for its full value, or in some cases, even longer.

ternary form a term applied to a piece of music that is divided into three self-contained parts, with the first and third sections bearing strong similarities.

ternary time *see* **triple time**.

terzett, terzetto (*Italian*) *see* **trio**.

tessitura (*Italian*) "texture"; a term that indicates whether the majority of notes in a piece are high up or low down in the range of a voice (or instrument).

414

tetrachord a group of four notes.

theme the melody, or other musical material, that forms the basis of a work or a movement and which may be varied or developed. It may return in one form or another throughout a composition.

theory of music rules made from a knowledge of the principles of sound for composition and arrangement of music for both voices and instruments.

Thieving Magpie, The (*La Gazza ladra*) an opera by ROSSINI to a libretto by G. Gherardini. The story tells of a maid, Ninetta, who is sentenced to death for a theft; she is saved when a magpie is discovered to be the guilty party. It was first performed in 1817.

third stave the stave upon which the pedal music for the ORGAN is written.

thirty-second note (US) a DEMISEMIQUAVER.

Thomas, Theodore (1835–1905) German-born American violinist and conductor, who formed his own orchestras, pioneering the large orchestra in the USA. He organized the formation of the Chicago Symphony Orchestra and championed new works.

Thomson, Virgil (1896-) an American composer and music critic of great originality. He lived in Paris for fifteen years, where he was influenced by the music of *Les* SIX and STRAVINSKY. His works include operas (for example *Four Saints in Three Acts*), ballets (for example *The Filling Station*), film music, chamber music, and many songs.

thorough bass *see* **figured bass**.

Threepenny Opera, The (*Die Dreigroschenoper*)

415

thunder stick

an opera by Kurt WEILL to a text by Bertolt Brecht (plus some lyrics from Kipling and Villon). It is a reworking of *The* BEGGARS' OPERA and was first performed in 1928.

thunder stick *or* **bull roarer** *or* **whizzer** an instrument consisting of a flat piece of wood fastened to a piece of string. When the piece of wood is whirled around the head, it creates a roaring sound.

Thus spoke Zoroaster *see* **Also sprach Zarathustra**.

tie a curved line that joins two NOTES of the same pitch together, indicating that they should be played as one long note.

Till Eulenspiegel (full title: *Till Eulenspiegels lustige Streiche*, Till Eulenspiegel's Merry Pranks) a symphonic poem by Richard STRAUSS. It is based on a German folk tale of a famous rogue and was first performed in 1895.

timbre (*French*) the quality of a tone, or the characteristic sound of an instrument.

time the rhythmic pattern (number of BEATS in a bar) of a piece of music, as indicated by the TIME SIGNATURE. Duple time has two beats in a bar, triple time has three beats in a bar, and so on.

time-names *or* **rhythm-names** a French method of teaching time and rhythm, in which beats are given names, such as "ta," "ta-te," etc.

time signature a sign placed at the beginning of a piece of music that indicates the number and value of BEATS in a bar. A time signature usually consists of two numbers, one placed above the other. The lower number defines the unit of measurement in relation to the SEMIBREVE (whole note); the top figure indicates the number of those units in a bar, for example, 3/4 indicates that there are three CROTCHETS (quarter notes) in a bar.

timpani *or* **kettledrums** the main orchestral PERCUSSION INSTRUMENTS, consisting of bowl-shaped shells over which the membrane is stretched. The shell is supported on a frame at the base of which, in "pedal timpani," is the foot pedal that can alter the pitch of the drum as it is played. The drum can also be tuned by means of screws, which alter the tension of the membrane.

Tin Pan Alley the nickname given to West 28th Street in New York, where the popular-song publishing business used to be situated. It consequently became a slang expression for the popular music industry.

tin whistle *or* **penny whistle** a metal whistle-flute, similar to a RECORDER but with six finger holes. It produces high-pitched sounds and is commonly used to play folk music.

Tippett, Sir Michael Kemp (1905-) English composer, who started to play the piano when he was five and later went to the Royal College of Music. He was influenced by MADRIGALS, BLUES and JAZZ. During World War II, he was imprisoned for three months for his pacifist beliefs. He has written several important and impressive pieces, such as his oratorio *A Child of Our Time*. His output has not been huge, but his pieces are invariably well crafted. They include operas (for example *King Priam*, *The Knot Garden*, *The Midsummer Marriage*), four symphonies, many choral works, and chamber music. He was knighted in 1966

tirade the filling up of an interval between two notes with a run in either vocal or instrumental music.

toccata (*Italian*) "touched"; a type of music for a keyboard instrument that is intended to show off a player's "touch" or ability.

Tod und das Mädchen, Der *see* **Death and the Maiden**.

Tod und Verklärung, Der *see* **Death and Transfiguration**.

tom-tom an Indian DRUM.

tonality the use of a KEY in a composition.

tone (1) an INTERVAL comprising two semitones, for example the interval between C and D. (2) (US) a musical note. (3) the quality of sound, for example good tone, sharp tone, etc. (4) In PLAINSONG, a melody.

tone poem *see* **symphonic poem**.

tonguing in the playing of a wind instrument, this means interrupting the flow of breath with the tongue so that detached notes are played, or the first note of a phrase is distinguished.

tonic the first note of a major or minor SCALE.

tonic sol-fa a system of notation and sight-singing used in training, in which notes are sung to syllables. The notes of the major scale are: doh, re, me, fah, soh, la, te, doh (doh is always the TONIC, whatever the key). The system was pioneered in England by John Curwen (1816–80) in the mid-nineteenth century.

Tortelier, Paul (1914-90) a French cellist, conductor and composer. He performed with BEECHAM in 1947 and afterwards played with many of the world's leading orchestras. A renowned teacher of the cello, his pupils iclude Jacqueline DU PRÉ. His son, **Jan Pascal Tortelier** (1947-) is a noted violinist and conductor.

Tosca an opera by PUCCINI to a libretto by G. Giacosa and L. Illica (based on Sardou's play *La Tosca*). The story tells how Tosca, a famous singer, agrees to succumb to Scarpia, the chief of police, if he spares the life of Cavaradossi, her lover. Amid much treachery, all three come to grief. It was first performed in 1900.

Toscanini, Arturo (1867-1957) an extremely famous Italian conductor who worked in both Europe and the USA. He had a reputation for being something of a disciplinarian, but he was also renowned for his devotion to authenticity, his disdain for showy interpretation for the score and for his remarkable musical memory, and his performances were noted for their clarity and dynamism. His forte was Italian and German opera.

tosto (*Italian*) "rapid," as in *piu tosto*, "quicker."

Toy Symphony (*Kindersymphonie* Children's Symphony) a symphony by HAYDN, scored for two violins, doublebass, and seven "toys," for example QUAIL, whistle, triangle, trumpet, and drum.

trachea *or* **windpipe** the tube that connects the lungs and the LARYNX.

trad jazz literally "traditional jazz"; a term referring to the type of comparatively simple JAZZ with a strong melody, as played in New Orleans, which preceded the development of BEBOP.

Tragic Overture (*Tragische Ouvertüre*) a concert

overture by BRAHMS. It was first performed in 1881.

"Tragic" Symphony SCHUBERT's symphony no. 4 in C minor (1818). The composer named the work himself, and it is, indeed, very serious in mood.

tranquillo (*Italian*) "calm."

transcription *see* **arrangement**.

transition (1) the changing from one KEY to another during the course of a composition. (2) a passage linking two sections of a piece, which often involves a change of key.

transposing instruments instruments that sound NOTES different from those actually written down, for example, a piece of music in E flat for the B flat clarinet would actually be written in F.

transposition the changing of the PITCH of a composition. Singers sometimes ask accompanists to transpose a song higher or lower so that it is better suited to their voice range.

Traviata, La (The woman who has been led astray) an opera by VERDI to a libretto by F.M. Piave, based on the play *La Dame aux camélias* by Alexandre Dumas *fils* (1824–95). The story concerns Violetta, a courtesan who is sick with consumption (tuberculosis). She falls in love with Alfredo and abandons her former way of life to live with him in the country, but she is persuaded to give Alfredo up by his father and returns to Paris. Alfredo insults her but is forgiven, and she dies in his arms.

treble the highest boy's voice.

treble clef G CLEF on the second line of the stave, used for treble voices and instruments of medium or high pitch, such as violins, flutes, oboes, clarinets, horns, and trumpets.

tremolando (*Italian*) "trembling."

tremolo (*Italian*) the rapid repetition of a single NOTE, or the rapid alternation between two or more notes.

triad a CHORD of three notes that includes a third and a fifth.

Trial by Jury a comic opera by GILBERT and SULLIVAN. It is the only one of their operettas that is sung throughout. It was first performed in London in 1875.

triangle a PERCUSSION INSTRUMENT comprising a thin steel bar bent into a triangle but with one corner left unjoined. It is normally struck with a thin metal bar.

trill *or* **shake** an ORNAMENT in which a note is rapidly alternated with the note above. It is used in both vocal and instrumental pieces.

trio (1) a group of three performers, or a piece of music written for such a group. (2) the middle section of a minuet, as found in sonatas, symphonies, etc. It was originally a section scored for three parts.

triplet a group of three NOTES played in the time of two notes.

Tristan und Isolde (Tristan and Isolde) an opera by WAGNER, who also wrote the libretto, based on the tragic Celtic legend of Tristan and Iseult. Tristran is escorting Isolde to Cornwall, to the castle of his uncle, King Mark, to whom Isolde is betrothed. The two drink a love potion, thinking it to be poison, and while duty requires Isolde to become Mark's queen, their love grows so strong that they cannot hide it. Mark surprises them, and Tristan is mortally wounded. His servant takes him home to his castle in Brittany, and there he is joined by Isolde. The joy of seeing her saps his remaining strength, and he dies in her arms. Isolde sings in the LIEBESTOD that they can only love in death and dies by his side. The opera was first performed in Munich in 1865.

tritone an INTERVAL consisting of three whole tones.

Trittico, Il (Triptych) three quite unrelated one-act operas by PUCCINI that are usually performed together. They are *Il* TABARRO, SUOR ANGELICA, and the comic opera GIANNI SCHICCHI. They were first performed in 1918.

Triumphes of Oriana, The a collection of twenty-five madrigals, edited by Thomas MORLEY and published in 1601. It is believed that they were written as a tribute to Queen Elizabeth I.

Trojans, The (*Les Troyens*) an opera in two parts (*The Taking of Troy* and *The Trojans at Carthage*) by BERLIOZ, who also wrote the libretto, based on Virgil's account in the *Aeneid* of the Trojan War and its aftermath. The complete opera was first performed in 1890.

tromba marina a long, stringed instrument of the fifteenth century, also known as a "sea-trumpet." It consisted of a long, tapered box with one string, mounted on top, which was played with a bow; inside the box were some twenty SYMPATHETIC STRINGS.

trombone a brass instrument that has changed little for 500 years. The body of the instrument has a cylindrical bore with a bell at one end and a mouthpiece at the other. A U-shaped SLIDE is used for lengthening or shortening the tubing and therefore for sounding different notes. TENOR and BASS trombones are often used in orchestras.

trope (*Latin*) an addition of music or words to traditional PLAINSONG liturgy.

troppo (*Italian*) "too much," as in *allegro non troppo*, meaning "fast but not too fast."

troubadours poet-musicians of the early Middle Ages who originally came from the South of France and sang in the Provençal language.

Trout Quintet the popular name of SCHUBERT's quintet in A major for violin, viola, cello, double bass and piano (1819). The piece is so called because the fourth movement is a set of variations of his song *Die Forelle*(The Trout)

Trovatore, ll (The Troubadour) an opera by VERDI to a libretto by S. Cammarano. The story tells of how Manrico, the son of a count, is kidnapped by gypsies when a child and becomes a TROUBADOUR. Later he falls in love with Leonora, who is also wooed by the Count di Luna. The count has Manrico put to death and then realizes that he has killed his own brother..

Troyens, Les *see* **Trojans, The**.

Trumpet Voluntary a popular name for a piece that used to be wrongly attributed to PURCELL. It was composed by Jeremiah CLARKE and originally entitled *The Prince of Denmark's March*.

trumpet a brass instrument that has a cylindrical bore with a funnel-shaped mouthpiece at one end and a bell (flared opening) at the other. The modern trumpet has three valves (operated by pistons) which bring into play extra lengths of tubing and are therefore used to change the pitch of the instrument. Trumpets are used in orchestras, jazz bands and military bands. Trumpet is also a generic term used to describe any number of very different wind instruments that are found all over the world.

tuba a large brass instrument with a wide conical bore, a large cup-shaped mouthpiece, and a large bell that faces upwards. It can have between three and five valves and comes in three common sizes: tenor (EUPHONIUM), bass, and double bass. Tubas are found in orchestras and military bands.

tubular bells *see* **bell**.

Tuckwell, Barry (1931-) an Australian hornplayer who has lived in Britain since 1951. He has played as a soloist with many leading chamber orchestras and has formed his own quintet, known as the Tuckwell Wind Quintet.

tune a MELODY or AIR.

tuning the adjusting of the PITCH of an instrument so that it corresponds to an agreed note, for example, an orchestra will usually have all its instruments tuned to the note of A.

tuning fork a two-pronged steel device that, when tapped, will sound a single, "pure" note. It was invented by John Shore in 1711 and is used to tune instruments, etc.

Turandot an opera by PUCCINI (completed after his death by Alfano) to a libretto by G. Adami and R. Simone (based on a play by Gozzi). Turandot is a beautiful Chinese princess who, averse to marriage, says she will marry any man who can answer three riddles, the penalty for failure being death. Several have gone to their death when Calaf, son of the deposed King Timur, solves the riddles and wins the princess. The opera, which contains the famous tenor aria "Nessun dorma," was first performed in Milan in 1926.

tutti (*Italian*) "all"; in orchestral music, a *tutti* passage is one to be played by the whole orchestra.

twelve-note music *or* **twelve-tone system** a method of composition formulated and advanced by SCHOENBERG. In the system, the twelve CHROMATIC notes of an octave can only be used in specific orders, called "note rows"; no note can be repeated twice within a note row, and the rows must be used complete. In all, there are forty-eight ways in which a note row can be arranged (using INVERSION, RETROGRADE MOTION and inverted retrograde motion), and it is with note rows that compositions are constructed.

Twilight of the Gods *see* **Ring des Nibelungen, Der**.

tympani *see* **kettledrums**.

Tyrolienne a country dance in the style of the Ländler, which has been used by various composers, for example by ROSSINI in WILLIAM TELL, and which may have originated in the folksongs of the Tyrol.

tzetze an Ethiopian instrument similar to the GUITAR, consisting of a long carved neck attached to a gourd. It has frets and one string.

U

ukelele a small, four-stringed GUITAR that was developed in Hawaii during the nineteenth century. It was a popular music-hall instrument during the 1920s.

Un Ballo in Maschera *see* **Masked Ball, A**.

undersong a CHORUS of a song.

unequal voices voices of mixed qualities such as those of men and women in chorus.

"Unfinished" Symphony, The title given to SCHUBERT's symphony no. 8 in B minor, written in 1822. He completed only two movements. Its first performance was in 1865, long after the composer's death.

unison the sounding of the same note or its octave by two or more voices or instruments.

up beat the upward movement of a conductor's baton or hand, indicating the unstressed (usually the last) beat in a bar.

upright *see* **piano**.

Urtext (*German*) "original text."

V

V an abbreviation for VIOLINO, VOCE, VOLTA.

VA an abbreviation for viola.

Va (*Italian*) "go on," as *Va cresendo*, "go on increasing the power," *Va rallentando* "go on dragging the time."

Vaet, Jacques (1529–67) Flemish composer who became KAPELLMEISTER at the Austrian court in Vienna. His works include a *Te Deum*, twenty-five motets, and much other church music.

vago (*Italian*) "with a vague, indefinite expression."

valeur (*French*), valore (*Italian*) "value," "worth," i.e. the length of a note.

Valkyrie, The *see* **Ring des Nibelungen, Der**.

valore *see* **valeur**.

valse (*French*) *see* **waltz**.

valve a device attached to horns, trumpets and other brass instruments to lengthen or reduce the extend of tubing, hence lowering or raising the pitch respectively, to complete the scale.

vamp to improvise an accompaniment.

Varèse, Edgard (1885-1965) a French-born experimental composer who was encouraged by DEBUSSY. He emigrated to the USA in 1916, where

427

he was a champion of "modern" music. He described his own music as "organized sound," and he ignored the traditional conventions of melody and harmony. Towards the end of his life he experimented with electronic and taped music. His compositions include works for solo flute, percussionists, and *Deserts,* for orchestra and taped sounds.

variation the modification or development of a theme.

vaudeville (*French*) originally a type of popular, satirical song sung by Parisian street musicians. In the eighteenth century these songs (with new words) were incorporated into plays, and the word came to mean the last song in an opera in which each character sang a verse. In the nineteenth century stage performances with songs and dances were called "vaudevilles," and the Americans used the term to describe music-hall shows.

Vaughan Williams, Ralph (1872-1958) English composer who studied music in Germany, France and England. He became passionately interested in folk music and was for a time president of the English Folk Song and Dance Society. He also studied sixteenth-century polyphonic music, which was the other great influence on his work. His music can be violent, jolly and mysterious, and he remains one of the most important English composers of the twentieth century. His works include nine symphonies (for example A *London Symphony, Sea Symphony, Pastoral Symphony*), operas, (for example *Sir John in Love, The Poi-*

soned Kiss), ballets, (for example *Job*), choral works, piano music, and chamber music.

veloce (*Italian*) "fast."

Venite (*Latin*) the first word of Psalm 95, *"Venite, exultemus Domino"* ("O come let us sing unto the Lord"), which is sung as a prelude to psalms at Anglican Matins.

Verdi, Giuseppe (1813-1901) Italian composer of opera who started his musical career as an organist. A wealthy grocer, Antonio Barezi, spotted his talent and paid for his private education in Milan (he later became Verdi's father-in-law). He became a musical director at Busseto, but returned to Milan in 1836 to write his first opera, *Oberto,* which was given its first performance at La Scala in 1839. The success of this work led to commissions. However, when his wife and two children died within a couple of years of each other, he vowed never to write music again. In 1841, however, he wrote *Nabucco,* which was performed in 1842 and was sufficiently successful to establish his reputation. He married again and continued to write a string of operas that guarantee his place in history as one of the greatest of opera composers. After his second wife, Giuseppina, died in 1897, his own health began to deteriorate and he eventually died of a stroke.

Verdi transformed Italian opera, which had traditionally favoured singers in preference to orchestras, by developing the importance of the orchestral element. His works include: twenty-seven operas (for example MACBETH, RIGOLETTO, *Il* TROVATORE, *La* TRAVIATA *Un Ballo in Maschera (A*

MASKED BALL), DON CARLOS, AIDA, OTELLO and
FALSTAFF); choral works (for example *Messa da
Requiem, Te Deum*); chamber music; and many
songs.

verismo (*Italian*) "realism"; the term is used to
describe a type of opera that was concerned with
representing contemporary life of ordinary people in an honest and realistic way, for example
CAVALLERIA RUSTICANA by MASCAGNI.

Vespers the seventh of the Canonical Hours (services of the day) in the Roman Catholic Church.
Many composers (such as MOZART) have written
musical settings for the service.

Vestri Siciliani, I *see* **Sicilian Vespers, The**.

Viadana, Lodovico (*c*.1565–1627) an Italian monk
and composer. He invented the FIGURED BASS, and
was the first to apply this to church music, of
which he was a prolific composer.

Viardot-Garcia, Pauline *see* **Garcia, Manuel**.

vibraphone *or* **vibes** an American instrument,
similar to the GLOCKENSPIEL, which consists of a
series of metal bars that are struck with mallets.
Underneath the bars hang tubular resonators,
which contain small discs that can be made to
spin by means of an electric motor. When the
notes are sustained the spinning discs give the
sound a pulsating quality.

vibrato (*Italian*) literally "shaking," i.e. a small
but rapid variation in the pitch of a note.

Vickers, Jon (1926-) a Canadian tenor who is
especially famous for his roles in WAGNER and
VERDI operas.

Victoria, Tomas Luis de (*c*.1548-1611) an outstanding Spanish composer of POLYPHONIC music, who was also a priest. He held various church positions in Rome before returning to Madrid. His works include motets, Masses, Magnificats and hymns.

Vienna State Opera one of the world's leading opera companies. Its famous conductors have included GLUCK, DONIZETTI, MAHLER, KARAJAN.

vierhandig (*German*) "four-handed," i.e. a piano duet.

Villa-Lobos, Heitor (1887-1959) a Brazilian pianist and composer who was largely self-taught. When he was eighteen, he joined an expedition up the Amazon to collect Indian folk music, and his own music was much influenced by this and by Brazilian folk songs. He settled in Paris from 1923 to 1930, where his work, combining elements of traditional Brazilian music with the European classical tradition, became highly popular. His works include twelve symphonies, operas (for example *Yerma, Amazonas*), piano concertos, chamber music, and pieces for the guitar.

Village Romeo and Juliet, A an opera by DELIUS, who also wrote the libretto. The story tells of two young lovers, the children of quarrelling landowners, who fulfil a suicide pact. It was first performed in 1907.

villanella (*Italian*) literally a "rustic song," a popular part-song of the seventeenth century.

vina an Indian GUITAR or BINA.

viol a family of stringed instruments played with a bow, which were widely used in the sixteenth and seventeenth centuries. The instruments came in several sizes and designs, but they all usually had six strings and frets. Although they were similar in appearance to members of the VIOLIN family, they were constructed differently and gave a much softer sound.

viola originally a general term for any bowed stringed instrument. However, it is now the name of the ALTO member of the VIOLIN family. It has four strings.

viola d'amore (*Italian*) literally a "love viol," i.e. a tenor VIOL with seven strings (instead of six) and seven or fourteen SYMPATHETIC STRINGS. It is so called because it had a particularly sweet tone.

viola da braccio (*Italian*) literally an "arm viol"; a generic term for any stringed instrument played on the arm. It came to mean a violin or viola.

viola da gamba (*Italian*) literally a "leg viol," a term originally used of those members of the VIOL family played vertically between the legs or on the lap, but it came to be used exclusively for the bass viol.

violetta a small VIOL.

violin a stringed instrument, played with a bow, which was introduced in the sixteenth century. It was developed independently of the VIOL from the medieval fiddle. It has no frets and just four strings. The violin family includes the violin itself (treble), VIOLA (alto) and VIOLONCELLO or "cello" (tenor). The DOUBLE BASS developed from the double bass VIOL, but it is now included in the violin family.

violoncello the tenor of the VIOLIN family, normally abbreviated to cello, dating from the sixteenth century. It is held vertically between the legs of the seated player, and the TAIL PIN rests on the ground. It has four strings, which are played with a bow.

violino (*Italian*) the VIOLIN, hence *violino primo* first violin, *violino principale* solo violin or LEADER, *violino secondo* second violin.

violino ripieno (*Italian*) literally "full violin," a violin part required only to fill in.

virginal a keyboard instrument dating from the sixteenth century in which the strings are plucked by quills. It was similar to the HARPSICHORD, except that it had an oblong body with strings running parallel to the keyboard. The word has also been used to describe any member of the harpsichord family.

virtuoso (*Italian*) a skilled performer on the violin or some other instrument. The word was formerly synonymous with "amateur."

Vishnevskaya, Galina *see* **Rostropovich, Mstislav**.

vivace (*Italian*) "lively."

Vivaldi, Antonio (1675-1741) an Italian composer and violinist who was ordained as a priest in 1703. He taught music at a school for orphan girls in Venice and managed to travel extensively as well as write copious amounts of music. In 1740 he moved to Vienna and died in relative poverty. His music had an impact on Johann Sebastian BACH and was revived during the nineteenth century, his four concertos for violin, which are collectively known as *The* FOUR SEASONS, becoming especially popular. His works include some

450 concertos (200 of them for violin), seventy sonatas, fifty operas, and oratorios (such as *Judith*). He also wrote many religious pieces.

vivamente (*Italian*) "in a lively way."

vivo (*Italian*) "lively."

vocalization control of the voice and vocal sounds, and the method of producing and phrasing notes with the voice.

vocal score *see* **score**.

voce (*Italian*) "voice," as in *voce di petto*, "chest voice."

voice (1) the sound produced by human beings by the rush of air over the vocal chords, which are made to vibrate. There are three categories of adult male voice (BASS, BARITONE and TENOR); three female categories (CONTRALTO, MEZZO-SOPRANO and SOPRANO); and two boy categories (TREBLE and ALTO). (2) Parts in contrapuntal compositions are traditionally termed "voices."

volta (*Italian*) "time," hence *una volta* "once," *prima volta* "first time."

volti subito (*Italian*) "turn over quickly" (of a page).

voluntary (1) an improvised piece of instrumental music (sixteenth century) (2) an organ solo (sometimes improvised) played before and after an Anglican service.

W

Wagenseil, Georg Christoph (1715-77) Austrian composer and keyboard player, who was a pupil of Fux. He became a court composer in Vienna, and his works include symphonies, concertos, oratorios, and operas.

Wagner, [Wilhelm] Richard (1813-83) a German composer and conductor who was born in Leipzig but moved to Dresden in 1815 with his mother and stepfather. He became interested in opera while he was still young and after leaving Leipzig University became a conductor at various opera houses. He married Minna Planer in 1836 and lived in poverty in Paris for a time while he worked on his first two operas, Rienzi and *The Flying Dutchman*. They were accepted by the Dresden opera house, and he was appointed an assistant conductor there in 1842. Six years later, he was obliged to flee Dresden because of his liberal sympathies for a minor uprising. He went to Zurich, where he started to work on his epic cycle of operas, *Der* Ring des Nibelungen. The *Ring* took some twenty-five years to complete, and in the meantime, he wrote Lohengrin (produced at Weimar in 1850) and Tristan und Isolde, completed in 1859, which may have been inspired by an illicit relationship with Mathilde Wesendonck. By 1864 Wagner was deeply in debt but was saved from imprisonment by an offer from Ludwig II of Bavaria (the "mad king") to stay in Munich as his "adviser." *Tristan* finally had its first performance in Munich in 1865. Marital problems arose again when he had an affair with Cosima, the wife of his friend and conductor Hans von Bülow and the daughter of Liszt. After his wife died and Cosima had obtained a divorce, they were married in 1870.

The city of Bayreuth offered Wagner a site for an opera house in 1872, and the theatre, built with the help of Ludwig II, was opened four years later with the first complete performance of the *Ring*. In 1876 he began to work on Parsifal, which was produced at Bayreuth in 1882. The following year Wagner died of a heart attack while spending the winter in Venice.

Wagner's operas were designed as "total art works," a synthesis of music, movement, poetry and the visual arts. In the *Ring* cycle, each character has a signature tune (Leitmotif), which unifies the huge work and also helps to inform the audience of the visible action and the thoughts of the characters, as conveyed by the music. Wagner's intense, romantic pieces are some of the greatest of all operas, and he is one of the giants in the history of music.

His operas include *Rienzi, The Flying Dutchman,* Tannhauser, *Lohengrin, Tristan and Isolde, The* Mastersingers of Nuremberg, *The Ring of the*

Nibelungen (*The Rhine Gold, The Valkyrie, Siegfried, The Twilight of the Gods*), and *Parsifal*. In addition, he also wrote the SIEGFRIED IDYLL for orchestra, and some choral works.

Waldteufel, Emil (1837-1915) a French composer and pianist. He wrote many dances, mainly waltzes, which include *The Skater's Waltz* and *España*.

Waller, Fats (1904–43) an American jazz pianist and composer. Renowned for his sense of humour, he became one of America's favourite entertainers and a much admired exponent of the "STRIDE" school of jazz piano. His many compositions include "Honeysuckle Rose" and "Ain't Misbehavin'."

Walter, Bruno [originally Bruno Walter Schlesinger] (1876–1962) German-born American conductor. Noted for his concerts and recordings of the great German ROMANTIC composers, he is particularly associated with the works of his friend MAHLER. He held various important posts in German and Austrian music, for example with the SALZBURG FESTIVAL, but, being Jewish, was forced to leave Germany in 1933 and Austria in 1938. In the US he conducted both the METROPOLITAN OPERA and the New York Philharmonic Orchestras. He was also an accomplished pianist and often accompanied Kathleen Ferrier. He once said that the two most important musical encounters of his life were with Ferrier and Mahler—in that order.

Walton, Sir William [Turner] (1902-1983) an English composer who learned the basics of music as a chorister but taught himself composition. He made his reputation with FAÇADE, a sequence of instrumental pieces to accompany poems by Edith Sitwell (1887–1964). He was initially influenced by *Les* Six and JAZZ, but the majority of his later works were traditionally English. His works include two symphonies, operas (such as *Troilus and Cressida* and *The Bear*), oratorios (for example BELSHAZZAR'S FEAST), assorted concertos, chamber music, and music for films (for example *Hamlet* and *Henry V*).

waltz a dance in triple time. Waltzes evolved in Germany and Austria during the late 18th century and became particularly popular in Vienna.

Warlock, Peter [pseudonym of Philip Heseltine] (1894-1930) an English composer and writer who was influenced by DELIUS (on whom he wrote a book) and Elizabethan music. He had an unstable personality that veered between aggressiveness and shyness. He eventually took his own life. His works include many songs and choral compositions (such as *The Curlew*), and orchestral pieces, including the *Capriol Suite*.

War Requiem, A an ambitious choral work by BRITTEN for choirs, organ, solo voices and chamber orchestra. The piece consists of alternating settings of poems by Wilfred Owen (1893–1918) and the REQUIEM Mass. It was first performed in 1962.

Water Music an orchestral suite by HANDEL. It is known that Handel composed music for a royal occasion on the Thames in 1717, and this is presumed to be the music.

Watts, Charlie *see* **Jagger, Mick**.

Weber, Carl Maria Ernst von (1786-1826) German composer, conductor and pianist who studied under Michael HAYDN. He had various jobs as a conductor, and in 1813 he went to Prague, where he was appointed conductor of the opera. In 1817 he was made conductor of the Dresden opera, and he started work on *Der* FREISCHÜTZ, his best-known opera, which was performed in Berlin in 1821. He visited England in 1826 to conduct the first performance of OBERON but died shortly afterwards, of tuberculosis.

Weber is considered by many to be the creator of German romantic opera; using French opera as a framework, he introduced German themes. He had a colossal influence on subsequent composers up to, and including, WAGNER. His works include the operas *Abu Hassan, Freischütz, Euryanthe* and *Oberon*, two symphonies, concertos, four piano sonatas, and many songs.

Webern, Anton von (1883-1945) Austrian composer, who studied with SCHOENBERG. With Schoenberg and Alban BERG, he formed a group known as the Second Viennese School, which was concerned with developing new forms of music. He adopted the TWELVE-NOTE SYSTEM and produced several, extremely short pieces that stripped music to its essentials, for instance, his *Six Bagatelles* for string quartet lasts precisely 3 minutes 37 seconds. Webern's influence on a new generation of composers was immense after he died, and he was one of the most important developers of SERIALISM. His works include orchestral pieces (for example *Variation*), choral compositions, and pieces for voice and piano.

wedding march a tune played at the start or end

of a wedding service. The two most famous wedding marches are MENDELSSOHN's "Wedding March," from his incidental music to *A* MIDSUMMER NIGHT'S DREAM, and WAGNER's "Bridal Chorus" (familiar to most by its common title "Here Comes the Bride") from the opera LOHENGRIN .

Wedding of Camacho (*Die Hochzeit des Camacho*) the first of three attempts at opera by MENDELSSOHN to a libretto by Klingemann, based on Cervantes' *Don Quixote*. It was performed for the first and only time in Berlin in 1827.

Weill, Kurt (1900-50) a German-born composer who was initially influenced by SCHOENBERG. His first success was *The* THREEPENNY OPERA (based on *The* BEGGARS' OPERA), which he wrote in collaboration with Bertolt Brecht, and which was first performed in 1928. He began to adopt JAZZ idioms and this, coupled to the facts that his works were social satires and that he was a Jew, made him unwlecome in Nazi Germany. First he fled to Paris and then, in 1935, to the USA. While living in the USA, his music mellowed somewhat, and he wrote several Broadway musicals. His works include the operas *The Threepenny Opera*, *Rise and Fall of the City of Mahagonny* and *Down in the Valley*; the musicals *Knickerbocker Holiday* and *Lost in the Stars*; orchestral pieces, and many songs.

Welsh harp a HARP played in Wales, originally single action.

Werther an opera by MASSENET to a libretto by Blau, Millet and Hartmann, based on the novel *The Sorrows of Young Werther* by Goethe (1749–

1832). It is the story of a romantic young man and his requited but tragic love for the wife of his friend. It was first performed in Vienna in 1892.

Wesley, Samuel (1766-1837) an English organist and composer who was the son of the famous hymn writer, Charles Wesley. He is known for his many anthems (such as *The Wilderness*), church music, symphonies, and organ pieces, and also as a noted promoter of the music of BACH.

whistle (1) a toy FLUTE. (2) the making of a musical sound with the lips and breath without using the vocal cords, the hollow of the mouth forming a resonance box. Whistling pitch is an octave higher than is generally supposed.

whizzer *see* **thunder stick**.

whole note (US) a SEMIBREVE.

whole-tone scale a scale in which all the INTERVALS are whole-tones, i.e. two semitones.

Widor, Charles Marie Jean Albert (1845-1937) a French composer and organist who taught at the Paris Conservatoire. He is famous for his organ music. His works include operas, ten organ "symphonies" (his famous toccata comes from the fifth), piano concertos, and chamber music.

Wigmore Hall a concert hall in Wigmore Street, London, famous for its chamber concerts and recitals. It was built in 1910.

Willaert, Adrian (*c*.1485-1562) an influential Flemish composer who went to live and work in Venice. His works include Masses, motets, and various instrumental pieces.

Williamson, Malcolm (1931–) an Australian composer who has lived and taught in Britain since 1950. Master of the Queen's Music since 1975, his works include several operas (for example *Our Man in Havana*, *The Happy Prince* and *Julius Caesar Jones*), ballets, orchestral pieces, and songs. He has written pieces especially for children, and music for film and television.

William Tell (*Guillaume Tell*) an opera by ROSSINI to a libretto by V. J. E. de Jouy and H. L. F. Bis, based on the play by Schiller (1759–1805). It tells the story of the Swiss, William Tell, who resists the invading Austrians. It was first performed in Paris in 1829.

wind instrument a musical INSTRUMENT whose SOUND is produced by the breath of the player or by means of a pair of bellows.

windpipe *see* **trachea**.

Winterreise, Die (The Winter Journey) a cycle of twenty-four songs by SCHUBERT, to words by W. Miller. The songs tell the story of a lovelorn young man.

Wolf, Hugo (1860-1903) an Austrian composer who had a fanatical respect for WAGNER. He worked fitfully, but had an extraordinary talent for writing songs. He ultimately went mad and died in an asylum. His works include many song cycles, two operas (for example *Der Corregidor*), and chamber music.

Wood, Sir Henry Joseph (1869-1944) an English conductor who is famed for conducting the London PROMENADE CONCERTS from 1895 until 1940. He was responsible for introducing new music to British audiences and was internationally respected. He was knighted in 1911.

woodwind a term for a group of blown instruments that were traditionally made of wood (some of which are now made of metal, for example, flutes, oboes, clarinets and bassoons, etc.

Wyman, Bill *see* **Jagger, Mick**.

Wranitzky, Paul (1756–1808) Austrian violinist, composer and conductor. His compositions include much forgotten dramatic music, twelve symphonies, chamber music and the opera OBERON. His brother, **Anton Wranitzky** (1761–1819), was also a violinist and conductor.

XYZ

Xenakis, Iannis (1922-) a Romanian-born Greek composer who trained to be an architect in Paris. His interest in mathematics has greatly influenced his work, and he uses computers while composing (although his works are usually scored in a traditional manner). His compositions include a ballet, *Kraanerg* (for orchestra and taped music), orchestral pieces (such as *Atrées* for ten instruments), and choral works.

xylophone a PERCUSSION INSTRUMENT made up of hardwood bars arranged like a keyboard on a frame. It is played by striking the bars with mallets. Xylophones used in orchestras have steel resonators suspended beneath each bar.

yang kin a Chinese instrument like a DULCIMER with brass strings that are struck with two little hammers.

Yeomen of the Guard, The a comic opera by GILBERT and SULLIVAN. The story is an escape saga set in the Tower of London. It was first performed in 1888.

Youmans, Vincent (1898-1946) an American composer who is best known for his musicals, for example *No! No! Nanette* and *Hit the Deck*.

yu kin a Chinese instrument similar to a GUITAR, sometimes called "moon guitar."

Zadok the Priest the first of four anthems composed by HANDEL for the coronation of George II (1727). It is still performed at British coronations.

Zaïde an opera by MOZART to a libretto by Schachtner, with a plot along the lines of that of ENTFÜHRUNG. Mozart composed it about 1780 but left it unfinished. The text was rewritten and an overture and finale added before its first performance in Frankfurt in 1866.

Zandonai, Riccardo (1883-1944) an Italian composer who composed operas in a VERISMO style. His operas include *Il grillo del Focolare* and *Francesca da Rimini*.

Zappa, Frank (1940–) an American rock musician. founder of the rock band Mothers of Invention. His songs include "Weasels Ripped My Flesh" and "Hot Rats."

zarzuela a type of Spanish comic opera that has a satirical theme and includes dialogue. It usually comprises just one act.

Zauberflote, Die *see* **Magic Flute, The**.

Zeichy, Count Geza 1849–1919) a Hungarian pianist and composer who was a pupil of LISZT. Despite the loss of his right arm when he was seventeen, he was a skilful pianist and composed piano studies for the left hand. He became director of the Pest Opera and also composed operas and a cantata.

zelo (*Italian*) "zeal."

zelosamente (*Italian*) "zealously, ardently."

zeloso (*Italian*) "zealous or energetic."

zimbalom *see* **dulcimer**.

Zingarelli, Niccolò Antonio (1752–1837) Italian composer of thirty-one operas, for example *Berenice*, his last and most popular, and church music. He was choirmaster of the Sistine Chapel in Rome when he was ordered to compose a Te Deum for the King of Rome, Napoleo's brother. When he refused, he was imprisoned and sent to Paris, where Napoleon released and gave him a pension in return for a Mass.

zither the generic term for a range of stringed instruments. The European zither consists of a flat box that is strung with a variety of different kinds of string (up to forty). The player uses a plectrum to play melodies on one set of strings while the fingers on the other hand pluck a series of open strings to form a drone accompaniment.

zurna a Turkish wind instrument similar to the OBOE.

Time values

o	semibreve (or whole note)
♩	minim (or half note)
♩	crotchet (or quarter note)
♪	quaver (or eight note)
♪	semiquaver (or sixteenth note)
♪	demisemiquaver (or thirty-second note)
♪	hemidemisemiquaver (or sixty-fourth note)

A dot following a note increases its value by a half.

Clefs

𝄞	treble clef
𝄢	bass clef
	soprano clef
𝄡	alto clef
𝄡	tenor clef

Accidentals

♯	sharp (raises note one semitone)
×	double sharp (raises note one tone)
♭	flat (lowers note one semitone)
♭♭	double flat (lowers note one tone)
♮	natural (restores the normal pitch after a sharp or flat)

The most commonly used time signatures

Simple duple:

or ¢	two minim beats
$\frac{2}{4}$	two crotchet beats
$\frac{2}{8}$	two quaver beats

Compound duple:

$\frac{6}{4}$	two dotted minim beats
$\frac{6}{8}$	two dotted crotchet beats
$\frac{6}{16}$	two dotted quaver beats

Simple triple:

$\frac{3}{2}$	three minim beats

Music Symbols

$\frac{3}{4}$ three crotchet beats

$\frac{3}{8}$ three quaver beats

Compound triple:

$\frac{9}{4}$ three dotted minim beats

$\frac{9}{8}$ three dotted crotchet beats

$\frac{9}{16}$ three dotted quaver beats

Simple quadruple:

$\frac{4}{2}$ four minim beats

$\frac{4}{4}$ or **c**   four crotchet beats

$\frac{4}{8}$ four quaver beats

Compound quadruple:

$\frac{12}{4}$ four dotted minim beats

$\frac{12}{8}$ four dotted crotchet beats

$\frac{12}{16}$ four dotted quaver beats

Dynamics

$<$ *crescendo*

$>$ *diminuendo*

Curved lines

tie or bind; the two notes are played as one

slur or legato; play smoothly (on a stringed instrument, in one bow)

Staccato marks and signs of accentuation

mezzo-staccato (shortens note by about 1/4)

staccato (shortens note by about 1/2)

staccatissimo (shortens note by about 3/4)

detached: accented

attack

Miscellaneous

$\|$: repeat preceding section

$\|$ end of section or piece

⌒ pause

𝄋 al segno, dal segno